O9-AIF-110

THE TEX-MEX COOKBOOK

Casa Rio's Gondola

Robb Walsh

THE TEX-MEX COOKBOOK

MEX

A HISTORY
IN RECIPES AND
PHOTOS

BROADWAY BOOKS
NEW YORK

THE TEX-MEX COOKBOOK. Copyright © 2004 by Robb Walsh. All rights reserved.
No part of this book may be reproduced or transmitted in any form or by any means,
electronic or mechanical, including photocopying, recording, or by any information
storage and retrieval system, without written permission from the publisher.
For information, address Broadway Books, a division of Random House, Inc.

PRINTED IN THE UNITED STATES OF AMERICA

BROADWAY BOOKS and its logo, a letter B bisected on the diagonal, are trademarks of
Random House, Inc.

Visit our website at www.broadwaybooks.com

First edition published 2004

Book design by Erin Mayes and DJ Stout, Pentagram, Austin

Library of Congress Cataloging-in-Publication Data
Walsh, Robb, 1952–
    The Tex-Mex cookbook : a history in recipes and photos / Robb Walsh.—1st. ed.
        p.   cm.
    1. Mexican American cookery. 2. Mexican American cookery—History. 3. Cookery,
American—Southwestern style. I. Title.

TX715.2.S69W36 2004
641.59'268720764—dc22

2003063673

ISBN 0-7679-1488-0

10   9   8   7   6   5   4   3

DEDICATED WITH LOVE TO MY MOTHER,
MARY ANN WALSH

MEXICANS IN SAN ANTONIO, TEXAS, 1887

The back of this souvenir card reads, in part:

A larger percentage of our citizens are Mexicans. They are found in all parts of the city, in all occupations, holding official positions and making good citizens generally. They are good horseman, good traders, and some of them are very handsome . . . Their chief diet is tamales, torties, chilli con carne and enchilades, washed down with black coffee . . . In cooking Mexican dishes, and serving them up hot in the open air, loading a half a cord of wood onto a wagon causing it to seem like a cord and a half, in selling Mexican candy, birds, and fruit on the street, in begging from house to house on Saturday and attending church on Sunday they have few equals and no superiors.

PREVIOUS BOOKS BY ROBB WALSH

Are You Really Going to Eat That?

Legends of Texas Barbecue Cookbook

A Cowboy in the Kitchen *(with Grady Spears)*

Nuevo Tex-Mex *(with David Garrido)*

ACKNOWLEDGMENTS

THANKS, FIRST AND FOREMOST, TO THE pioneers of Tex-Mex and their descendants who shared the stories, family photographs, and recipes that appear in this book.

Thanks to Rebecca Staffel of the Doe Coover Agency and Jennifer Josephy of Broadway Books for making it all possible. Thanks to Lisa Gray and Lauren Kern for their thoughtful editing. And thanks to Erin Mayes and DJ Stout at Pentagram Design, Austin, for working overtime on design and graphics.

Many thanks to Jay P. Francis for his tireless recipe testing and retesting and his perfect Tex-Mex taste.

Thanks to archivist Tom Shelton at the University of Texas at San Antonio's Institute of Texan Cultures for his many historical insights. And to Rayna Green, curator of Julia Child's Kitchen at the Smithsonian Institute's National Museum of American History for helping to bring the heros of Tex-Mex into the national spotlight.

Thanks to the *Houston Press* and New Times Corporation for permission to borrow freely from my previously published articles.

Thanks for the advice and suggestions of Latin American scholar Justin Wartell at Indiana University, and of librarian Adan Benavides Jr. at the Benson Latin American Collection at the University of Texas at Austin. Special thanks to Texas-Mexican Railway historian Arturo Dominguez for his research; to Marfa historian Cecilia Thompson for all her help; to Mexican-American historian Thomas Kreneck at Texas A&M, Corpus Christi, for explaining the Mexican-American generation; to John T. Edge of the Southern Foodways Alliance at Ole Miss for his Southern tamale tales; and to historian and Mexican food authority Jeffrey Pilcher for his comments and advice on the history of Mexican and Tex-Mex cuisine. Thanks to Eddie Wilson for remembering the birth of hippy Tex-Mex. Thanks also to my fellow Tex-Mex journalists Ron Bechtol and John Morthland for their stories. And many thanks to journalist, musicologist, and all around good guy Joe Nick Patoski for his Tex-Mex music article and bar-hopping advice.

And thanks to my darling Kelly Klaasmeyer and my daughter, Julia Walsh, for eating nothing but Tex-Mex for so long.

An order of cheese
enchiladas at
Brown's *Mexican Foods*
in San Antonio

Contents

INTRODUCTION

TEX-MEX: THAT LOVABLE UGLY DUCKLING

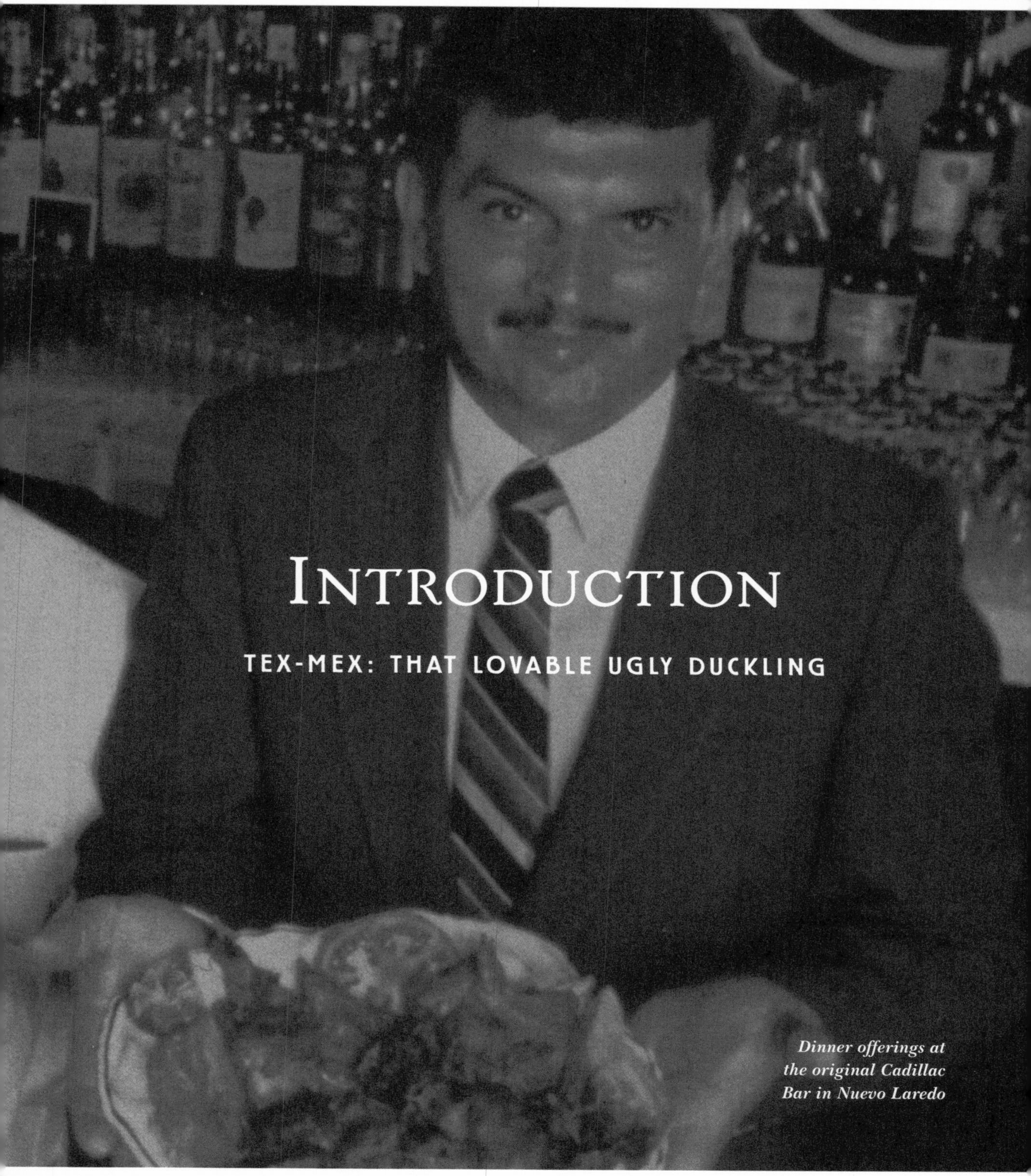

*Dinner offerings at
the original Cadillac
Bar in Nuevo Laredo*

TEX-MEX IS THE UGLY DUCKLING OF AMERICAN regional cuisines. Since it was called Mexican food for most of its history, nobody even thought of it as American until about thirty years ago. That was when the first authoritative Mexican cookbook in the United States, Diana Kennedy's *The Cuisines of Mexico,* was published.

Kennedy trashed the "mixed plates" in "so-called Mexican restaurants" north of the border and encouraged readers to raise their standards. The English-born Kennedy was the wife of the late Paul Kennedy, a *New York Times* correspondent posted in Mexico City. She had spent little time in the United States at the time of the book's publication in 1972 and evidently wasn't familiar with the Tejano culture.

Hugely popular in the United States, *The Cuisines of Mexico* was a breakthrough cookbook, one that could have been written only by a non-Mexican. It unified Mexican cooking by transcending Mexico's nasty class divisions and treating the food of the poor with the same respect as that of the upper classes. But while admirably egalitarian in her attitude toward the food of Mexicans, Kennedy lambasted the food of Texas-Mexicans.

In a later book, *The Art of Mexican Cooking,* Kennedy wrote, "Far too many people outside Mexico still think of them [Mexican foods] as an overly large platter of mixed messes, smothered with a shrill tomato sauce, sour cream, and grated yellow cheese preceded by a dish of mouth-searing sauce and greasy deep-fried chips. Although these do represent some of the basic foods of Mexico—in name only—they have been brought down to their lowest common denominator north of the border, on a par with the chop suey and chow mein of Chinese restaurants twenty years ago."

Tex-Mex entered the lexicon of the food world within a year of *The Cuisines of Mexico*'s publication. The first time it was used in print in relation to food, according to the *Oxford English Dictionary,* was in this 1973 quote from the *Mexico City News,* an English-language newspaper: "It is a mistake to come to Mexico and not try the local cuisine. It is not the Tex-Mex cooking one is used to getting in the United States."

If you go to the library to look up Tex-Mex, you will find lots of definitions. But unfortunately they are all different. The dictionaries don't agree on whether Tex-Mex means

DEFINING "TEX-MEX"

- *Oxford English Dictionary:* "Designating the Texan variety of something Mexican. First use in print, *Time* magazine, 1941 '. . . Tex-Mex Spanish, that half-English half-Spanish patois of the border . . .' "
- *Merriam-Webster's Collegiate Dictionary, Tenth Edition Dictionary:* "Of, relating to, or being the Mexican-American culture or cuisine existing or originating in esp. southern Texas."
- *Food Lover's Companion:* "A term given to food (as well as music, etc.) based on the combined cultures of Texas and Mexico."

Americanized Mexican food in general or specifically the kind from Texas.

Some food writers put San Francisco's steak burritos, San Diego's fish tacos, and Tucson's chimichangas in the Tex-Mex category. That's because they use the term Tex-Mex to mean Americanized Mexican food, regardless of its place of origin.

There is no consensus on what Tex-Mex means in Texas either. Middle-aged Anglos tend to describe it as a specific subset of the larger genre of Mexican food—one that involves yellow cheese enchiladas with chopped raw onions and chili gravy as served in San Antonio around 1955.

Why the confusion? Because for many years, the people who owned the restaurants where Tex-Mex was served refused to use the term at all. Tex-Mex was a slur. It was a euphemism for bastardized, and it was an insult that cost Mexican-Texan families who had been in the restaurant business for generations a lot of business.

TEX-MEX WAS STILL CALLED MEXICAN food when its popularity began to spread beyond Texas to other parts of the country. But the biggest fans of Tex-Mex have always been in the West and Midwest. Texas-Mexican food first became popular in the Midwest in 1893, when a San Antonio chili stand was set up at the Chicago World's Fair. Chili con carne was being canned in Oklahoma and St. Louis by 1910. Cincinnati's first chili joint opened in 1922. And more chili joints sprang up across the country, becoming Depression-era havens for cheap food. Meanwhile, tamale vendors popularized another kind of Mexican food across the country. In *The World on a Plate,* food historian Joel Denker tells us tamales were among the most common foods on the streets of Chicago in the early 1900s and were far more popular than hamburgers.

Because of their greater familiarity with its traditions, food writers and cooking authorities from the western half of the country think

TEJANO

"In Spanish, a Texan of Mexican descent is called a tejano *or* tejana *(with a lowercase* t). *Hispanics in Texas identified themselves as Tejanos as early as January 1833, when leaders at Goliad used the term. Contemporary historians use the term to distinguish Mexican Texans from residents of other regions and to distinguish them from the Texans, as Anglo-American Texans were called, during the period between the end of the Spanish era in 1821 to Texas Independence in 1836.*

"The term 'Tejano' gained greater currency following the Chicano movement of the mid-1960s with corresponding changes in nuance and usage. It now encompasses language, literature, art, music, and cuisine. Tex-Mex is a related term that is not synonymous."
—**Adán Benavides**
from the Handbook of Texas Online

of Tex-Mex more sympathetically than do their New York counterparts.

"I love Tex-Mex. I grew up on it," says Rick Bayless, author of *Authentic Mexican* and *Mexico One Plate at a Time.*

In his cookbooks, Bayless, who comes from Oklahoma, pays tribute to Tex-Mex as a distinctive regional cuisine. "When people cook from the heart, there isn't a right, or wrong, way to do it," he told me. Bayless said that when writing *Authentic Mexican*, his first cookbook, which was published in 1987, he wanted to include Tex-Mex as well as New Mexican and California Mexican. But his New York editor didn't share his point of view.

In *Eating in America: A History* (1976), the late Chicago food writer Waverly Root defines Tex-Mex as a unique regional cuisine: "Tex-Mex food might be described as native foreign food, contradictory through that term may seem. It is native, for it does not exist elsewhere; it was born on this soil. But it is foreign in that its inspiration came from an alien cuisine; that it has never merged into the mainstream of American cooking and remains alive almost solely in the region where it originated . . ."

Today, most people agree that Tex-Mex isn't really Mexican food. And for reasons I hope this book will explain, Tex-Mex has started to shed its negative connotations. In the last five years, some of the same Texas-Mexican restaurants that once shunned the term have begun to claim they invented Tex-Mex!

Meanwhile, historians are beginning to study "Tex-Mex" more seriously. As it has become more widely understood to describe an American regional cooking style, it has also begun to be used retroactively. Culinary folklorists now trace Tex-Mex cooking all the way back to the state's Native American peoples and to Juan de Onate's colonists who first brought European livestock to El Paso in 1581.

"Tex-Mex foods are a combination of Indian and Spanish cuisines, which came together to make a distinct new cuisine," writes

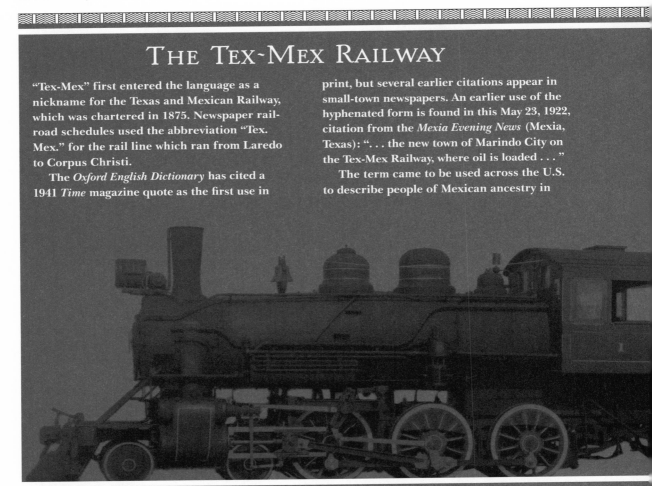

THE TEX-MEX RAILWAY

"Tex-Mex" first entered the language as a nickname for the Texas and Mexican Railway, which was chartered in 1875. Newspaper railroad schedules used the abbreviation "Tex. Mex." for the rail line which ran from Laredo to Corpus Christi.

The *Oxford English Dictionary* has cited a 1941 *Time* magazine quote as the first use in print, but several earlier citations appear in small-town newspapers. An earlier use of the hyphenated form is found in this May 23, 1922, citation from the *Mexia Evening News* (Mexia, Texas): ". . . the new town of Marindo City on the Tex-Mex Railway, where oil is loaded . . . "

The term came to be used across the U.S. to describe people of Mexican ancestry in

Joe S. Graham in the Texas State Historical Society's Handbook of Texas Online.

For all these reasons, I thought this might be a good time for a Tex-Mex cookbook. For the past ten years, I have been gathering scraps that I thought might shed some light on the story of Tex-Mex cooking. From restaurants and museums, garage sales and presidential libraries, I've collected recipes, snapshots, menus, postcards, and advertisements for canned chili. And I've interviewed a bunch of colorful veterans of the Tex-Mex restaurant business. In this book, I have put those scraps together. The result is not a complete picture but a fragmented collage made up of one man's gleanings.

It's been more than thirty years since *The Cuisines of Mexico* was published, and many of its baroque Mexican dishes seem like museum pieces now, while at the same time, Tex-Mex has achieved worldwide popularity.

We can all thank Diana Kennedy for inadvertently granting Tex-Mex its rightful place in food history. By convincing us that Tex-Mex wasn't really Mexican food, she forced us to realize that it was something far more interesting: America's oldest regional cuisine.

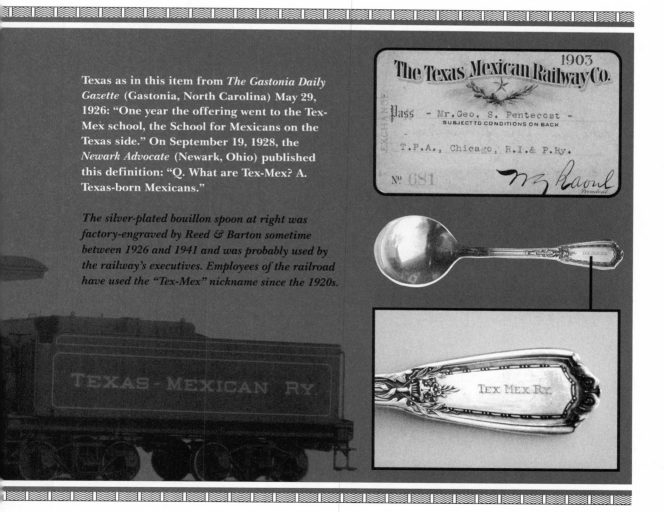

Texas as in this item from *The Gastonia Daily Gazette* (Gastonia, North Carolina) May 29, 1926: "One year the offering went to the Tex-Mex school, the School for Mexicans on the Texas side." On September 19, 1928, the *Newark Advocate* (Newark, Ohio) published this definition: "Q. What are Tex-Mex? A. Texas-born Mexicans."

The silver-plated bouillon spoon at right was factory-engraved by Reed & Barton sometime between 1926 and 1941 and was probably used by the railway's executives. Employees of the railroad have used the "Tex-Mex" nickname since the 1920s.

Women preparing tortillas,
San Antonio, 1938

CHAPTER 1

TALKING TEX-MEX

TERMS, TOOLS, AND TECHNIQUES

THE RECIPES IN THIS BOOK WERE CHOSEN TO tell the story of Tex-Mex cooking. Unfortunately, many of the ingredients have been banned from the kitchens of American food lovers for years. Lard, Velveeta, and processed foods are used here in heaping quantities. Such is the heritage of Tex-Mex, a cuisine without pretensions.

Likewise, the restaurants that appear in this book aren't necessarily serving the most popular version of Tex-Mex food anymore. Some of the historic eateries I have described long ago fell out of fashion. Others are out of business. And many of Texas's most famous Tex-Mex restaurants aren't even mentioned. If I have left out your favorite Tex-Mex joint, I apologize. If it makes you feel any better, I've left out many of my own favorites too.

The featured dishes come from Texas-Mexican restaurants and Tejano home cooks. You won't find recipes for burritos, chimichangas, and a few other popular items in these pages. I don't have anything against these foods; it's just that they aren't from Texas.

To make sure we're all on the same page regarding definitions of Tex-Mex dishes and ingredients, here's a glossary of terms and a chile pepper identification guide.

DISHES

BOTANAS
In Mexico and much of Texas, botanas means appetizers and a botanas platter is a sampler plate. But in Lower Rio Grande Valley Tex-Mex restaurants, a "botanas platter" is something altogether different and exceedingly popular. It's a huge pile of tostadas and nachos topped with fajita meat and guacamole, served with tortillas and salsas on the side. The communal platter feeds several people.

BURRITOS
Burritos are often categorized as Tex-Mex by those who use the term to mean Americanized Mexican food. But while burritos have long been popular in Arizona and California, they weren't seen in Texas until very recently. Burritos originated in the Mexican state of Sonora. They are made by wrapping one of the large flour tortillas typical of that area around a filling.

CHALUPAS
The word means canoes. True Mexican chalupas are made by pressing tortilla dough into an elongated boat shape before cooking. Tex-Mex chalupas are usually made by frying tortillas into a flat shape, then topping them like tacos. Typically, Tex-Mex chalupas come with a meatless topping of beans and cheese. Sometimes the word is used interchangeably with tostadas, which means fried tortillas.

CHILAQUILES
Chilaquiles are tortilla chips or scraps cooked in a sauce, often with meat and cheese. Chilaquiles are very similar to migas.

CHIMICHANGAS
According to legend, these deep-fried burritos were invented in Tucson when someone dropped a burrito in a deep-fryer. The name means whatchamacallits. Like burritos, chimichangas are considered Tex-Mex by those

who use the term to describe all Americanized Mexican food.

ENCHILADAS

The word means chilied. Tortillas enchiladas are corn tortillas "softened" in hot oil and then dipped or cooked in a chile sauce. Originally, they were served without fillings and topped with a little Mexican white cheese. Tex-Mex enchiladas are typically rolled with a filling of either meat or cheese, then garnished with a little more sauce and cheese. Stacked enchiladas, which are typical of El Paso and West Texas, are chilied tortillas served like a pile of pancakes with cheese and onions in between and garnished with more sauce and cheese.

ENCHURITO

The name of this modern aberration suggests that it is half burrito and half enchilada. Usually, it's a burrito topped with enchilada sauce and cheese and eaten with a knife and fork.

ENVUELTOS

Literally, "surrounded or enveloped" in English, envueltos usually describes tortillas wrapped around a filling and then either fried or cooked in a sauce.

FAJITAS

Faja means "belt or girdle," so fajita literally means "little belt." It refers to the piece of meat called a skirt steak in English. Originally, in Tex-Mex cooking, fajitas meant grilled skirt steak chopped and served with flour tortillas and condiments to make tacos. But customers who didn't understand the Spanish thought it referred to the whole spread of grilled meat, condiments, and tortillas and began asking for "chicken fajitas."

FRIJOLES REFRITOS

Frijoles refritos, cooked beans mashed in hot oil, is the most common preparation in Tex-Mex cooking. Though generally translated as "refried beans," some argue "well-fried beans" is a more accurate translation.

Frijoles means "beans" in Spanish. The most common variety on Tex-Mex tables is the pinto bean. Pinto means "painted" in Spanish, a reference to their dappled coloring. The modern pinto bean is a hybrid related to the anasazi bean cultivated by early Native Americans.

GORDITAS

Gorditas ("little fat ones" in Spanish), are made with masa (tortilla dough), which is patted into a circle. The dough is dropped into hot oil where it puffs up. It is then split open to form a pocket. A filling, often beans or shredded meat and cheese, is placed in the pocket.

MIGAS

The word means "crumbs" in Spanish. Bread crumbs or chunks of stale bread fried with garlic are used in the Spanish versions of migas, while tortillas are used in Mexico. In Tex-Mex cooking, migas is a popular breakfast dish made with scrambled eggs and crushed tortilla chips or fried tortillas scraps. Optional ingredients include onions, serrano chiles, and cheese.

NACHOS

In their simplest form, nachos are tortilla chips topped with cheese and jalapeño slices and broiled until the cheese melts. Guacamole, sour cream, and many other toppings may be added.

PANCHOS

In the Lower Rio Grande Valley, when you spread refried beans on the nachos before adding the other ingredients, they become panchos.

QUESADILLAS

These are tortillas sandwiched or folded over a filling of cheese and other ingredients and

BODEGAS DE LA GLORIA Nº 1
M. ELIZONDO. PROP

FRIJOL

GALLETAS

AZUCAR

CAFÉ

...XAS
1918

Warehouse for Matilde Elizondo's store, San Antonio, 1918

toasted on a greased or ungreased griddle until the cheese melts. Tex-Mex quesadillas are nearly always made with flour tortillas.

SALSA PICANTE

Salsa picante or picante sauce is the chunky, tomato and chile sauce also known as "hot sauce" in English. In Tex-Mex restaurants, it refers to the omnipresent table sauce that is spooned onto tacos, eggs, and guacamole and used as a dip for tortilla chips. Pepper sauce is a vinegar-based solution dispensed from a shaker bottle, such as Tabasco sauce. Salsa ranchera is blander and made with more tomatoes.

TACOS

Mexican tacos are just tortillas wrapped around a filling. Tex-Mex tacos more often take the form of tortillas fried into a U-shaped shell. Puffy tacos are made by frying raw tortillas so that the masa puffs up as it fries. Crispy tacos is sometimes used as another name for puffy tacos and sometimes used to mean a freshly fried tortilla that doesn't puff up. Original or old-fashioned tacos are made by filling corn tortillas and then frying them with the filling inside.

TAMALES

Mexican tamales are made with masa (tortilla dough) that is mixed with lard and flavorings and spread on a corn husk, topped with a filling, and then rolled up and steamed. Tex-Mex tamales may be made Mexican-style with masa, or Southern-style with cornmeal mush or cornbread crumbs. Southern-style tamales are often wrapped in parchment paper or wax paper instead of corn husks.

TOSTADAS

The word means "toasted." Tostadas are generally fried tortilla quarters in Mexico. In Tex-Mex, tostadas are more often fried tortilla chips, or whole fried tortillas topped like tacos.

CHILE PEPPERS

Merriam-Webster's Collegiate Dictionary, Eleventh Edition, is the standard guide to spelling for most American cookbooks. In that dictionary, the preferred spelling for a capsicum pod is "chili." At one time, this was also the standard spelling in Texas. But you never knew if the writer was talking about the dish or the pepper.

To avoid this confusion, in the last few decades, Southwesterners have adopted the convention of using "chili" to refer only to the dish. This book departs from Merriam-Webster's spelling by employing the Southwestern convention of using chile or chile pepper to refer to the pods, and chili or chili con carne to refer to the dish.

Unfortunately, the names used for specific chiles vary across the United States. The big green poblano chile, and its dried form, the ancho, are central to the Tex-Mex cooking style. Poblano and ancho are well-known names in Central Mexico, Texas, and most of the United States and are also the names used in such standard reference materials as Mark Miller's *Great Chile Poster* and in nearly all Mexican cookbooks.

But the poblano is confusingly called a pasilla or ancho in both the fresh and dried form on the Pacific Coast of Mexico. Since most of the Mexican-Americans in Southern California come from the Pacific states, their nomenclature is used in Los Angeles.

But grocers on the Eastern Seaboard buy their chiles from the L.A. Produce Terminal. So, in an odd migration of misunderstanding, food stores in New York, Boston, and Washington, D.C., often use the Oaxacan nomenclature for chile peppers.

Here we will attempt to get it all straight.

FRESH CHILES

Fresh chile peppers are usually harvested in the green stage. Fully ripened red chiles are most often used for drying, but they also turn up fresh in the supermarket for a brief period in the fall. The following fresh chile peppers, listed from mildest to hottest, appear in this book:

Anaheim

The name comes from a chile cannery opened in Anaheim, California, in 1900 by a farmer named Emilio Ortega, who brought the pepper seeds to California from New Mexico.

Also known as the long green chile by New Mexicans and West Texans (until it turns red and becomes the long red chile), the Anaheim has a pleasant vegetable flavor and ranges from slightly warm to medium-hot. To use the Anaheim, you generally roast it and remove the blackened skin.

In New Mexico, the long green chile is further subdivided by region of origin. The two most common names encountered are Hatch and Chimayo. Hatch chiles are grown in the southern part of New Mexico (around the town of Hatch) from certified seed sources and are graded according to heat. Mild green Hatch chiles are often roasted and peeled, then eaten like a vegetable. Cultivars like Big Jim, Sandia, and Espanola Improved are often referred to by name.

Chimayo chiles are the older, more traditional chiles grown in the northern part of New Mexico (around the town of Chimayo) from seeds saved from the last harvest. Chimayo chiles are treasured for their superior flavor and unpredictable heat, but they are becoming increasingly rare.

Poblano (also called Ancho or Pasilla)

Fatter and wider than the Anaheim, the poblano is darker green and has a richer flavor. It is one of the most commonly used

chiles in Central Mexican cooking, both in its fresh and dried forms (see ANCHO). Poblanos are named after the Mexican city of Puebla, where they probably originated. They are generally slightly hot and are usually roasted and peeled before use. Poblanos are the peppers most commonly used for Tex-Mex chile rellenos.

Jalapeño

Hot, green, and bullet-shaped, the jalapeño is the classic Tex-Mex hot pepper and one of the world's best-known chiles. Originally grown in Mexico, it is named for Jalapa, a town in the state of Veracruz. The fresh jalapeño has a strong, vegetal flavor to go with the heat. The jalapeño is most widely consumed in its pickled form. Besides hot sauce, a bowl of pickled jalapeños is the most popular condiment on the Tex-Mex table.

Serrano

Similar to the jalapeño, the serrano is hotter and smaller. Most Mexicans claim that serranos have a fuller, more herbaceous flavor. Since the vast majority of jalapeños are pickled, the serrano is actually the most widely used fresh chile pepper in Mexico and Texas.

Pequin

Also known as piquin, chilipiquin, or chiltepin, this tiny chile grows wild throughout southern Texas and northern Mexico. Although "pequin" seems to be a corruption of the Spanish *pequeño*, meaning "small," the Spanish name itself is probably a corruption of *chiltecpin*, a Nahuatl word meaning "flea chile," a refer-

Francisco Riojas was sixty-two when this photo was taken in 1948. He began selling serranos and jalapeños in San Antonio's Haymarket Square in 1923.

ence to both its size and sting. Because its seeds were spread by birds rather than cultivation, pequins are considered the oldest chiles in North America. In northern Mexico, they are collected in the wild and sold in markets, where they fetch more than almost any other kind of chile. They are sometimes dried and preserved for year-round use. A pequin bush can be found in almost any backyard or vacant lot in south Texas, and pequins are very common in Tex-Mex home cooking. Because they are not grown commercially, they are seldom found in restaurant cooking or in grocery stores. If you find some, you can substitute three or four fresh pequins for one serrano or half a jalapeño.

Habanero

The world's hottest pepper, the habanero, also known as the Scotch bonnet, should be treated with respect. It has a wonderful apricot-like flavor and aroma but must be used in small quantities and handled with care. The habanero came to Mexico from the Caribbean and is named after Havana, Cuba (*habanero* means "someone from Havana").

Rajas

Roasted peppers that have been seeded, peeled, and cut into strips are called rajas. They're used as an ingredient in some recipes and as a condiment for fajitas.

DRIED CHILES

The following dried chile peppers, listed from mildest to hottest, are used in this book:

Ancho (also called Pasilla)

The dried form of the poblano chile, the ancho is very dark brown and wide. (In fact, the word *ancho* means "wide" in Spanish.) Anchos are the fleshiest of the dried chiles, and their pulp combines a little bitter flavor with a sweetness reminiscent of raisins. They are usually mild, although occasionally one will surprise you with its heat. Mulattos are closely related and a suitable substitute.

Guajillo

Tapered with a smooth, shiny, reddish skin, the guajillo has a tart, medium-hot flavor. When soaked and pureed, it gives foods an orange color. Dried Anaheims are also sometimes called guajillos, but they are generally milder.

Pasilla

Long and skinny with a black, slightly wrinkled skin, the pasilla has a strong, satisfying flavor and can range from medium-hot to hot. The name comes from the Spanish *pasa*, meaning "raisin," a reference to the appearance of the skin. On the west coast of Mexico, and hence in Los Angeles, they also call fresh green poblanos "pasillas."

Red Chile (Chile Colorado)

This is the dried form of the Anaheim, or New Mexican long red chile. In West Texas and New Mexico, red ripe chiles are hung in strings called "ristras" and dried in the sun on the sides of homes and barns. The chiles are then sold whole or in pulverized form. Connoisseurs buy red chiles by appelation; Hatch red chiles (from the area around Hatch, New Mexico) are available in varying heat levels. The increasingly rare Chimayo red chiles (from peppers grown around the northern New Mexican village of Chimayo) are grown from seeds handed down from father to son. Chile guajillo is a suitable substitute.

Chipotle

 This is the smoke-dried jalapeño. Small, wrinkled, and light brown, chipotles have an incredibly rich, smoky flavor and are usually very hot. Smoking jalapeños to preserve them has been common in Mexico since long before the Spanish arrived. The original Nahuatl spelling, *chilpotle*, is also sometimes seen.

We prefer to use dried chipotles, but you can also buy them canned, and canned chipotles are acceptable in most recipes. Obviously, you can't make chile powder from canned chipotles, but you can use them for purees. Canned chipotles are already soaked in some kind of sauce, usually a vinegary adobo. Just stem and seed them and puree them with some of the sauce from the can.

Chile de Arbol

Literally, "tree chile," the chile de arbol is a small shiny red chile about 3 inches long with a thin tapering body. It has a high heat level and is often chopped and simmered with tomatoes to make a hot table sauce.

CAUTION: HANDLING CHILE PEPPERS

It's wise to wear rubber gloves when handling jalapeños, serranos, and especially habaneros. Get a little juice from the cut-up pepper on your face or in your eyes, and you can count on ten minutes of sheer agony. If you don't have rubber gloves, use a piece of plastic wrap to hold the pepper while you cut it. Clean the knife and the cutting board immediately with hot soapy water. If you get pepper juice on your hands, try soaking them for a few minutes in a mild bleach solution.

GLOSSARY OF EQUIPMENT AND INGREDIENTS

BEAN MASHERS

Mexican bean mashers look like miniature billy clubs, and some Mexican restaurant owners, such as Carolina Borunda Humphries, once wielded them to keep the peace. A potato masher works just as well on refried beans, but not as well on drunk and rowdy customers.

CABRITO

The Spanish first brought cattle, sheep, and goats to Texas in 1580. Cabrito, Spanish for "kid goat," remains a favorite delicacy of the northern Mexican and Texas ranching regions more than four hundred years later.

CAZUELAS

These clay pots were buried in the coals of a wood fire and used to cook beans, soups, and stews.

COMAL

A flat cast-iron pan without sides, the comal is traditionally used to cook tortillas. You can substitute a cast-iron skillet. Roasting tomatoes, peppers, or garlic in a comal is a typical step in making salsa. In this case, "roasting" means placing the ingredient in a dry, ungreased comal and heating it until lightly charred.

CORN HUSKS (HOJAS)

These dried leaves from the corn plant, also known as shucks, are used to wrap tamales. Don't economize on them; buy the expensive hojas that are already cleaned. The cheaper brands contain lots of corn silk.

LARD

"Lard has half the cholesterol of butter and

Angelita Davila counts out handmade tortillas at the El Triunfo tortilla factory in San Antonio, 1937.

one third the saturated fat," Rick Bayless has been telling cooking classes and TV viewers for the last decade or so. He's preaching to the choir in Tex-Mex country. The highest sales of lard in the United States are in the Hispanic neighborhoods of West Texas. It's always been part of Tex-Mex, and in some recipes, it's irreplaceable.

But as Bayless also explains, all lard is not created equal. Cooks once bought fresh lard at the meat market or rendered it themselves from pork fat. Unfortunately, this fresh lard has been largely replaced by the shelf-stable hydrogenated lard sold in tubs or loaves. Hydrogenated lard contains unhealthy trans fats and has little or no flavor.

Luckily, fresh lard has been making a comeback. You can find it in Mexican meat markets and ethnic groceries and even on the Internet. But the cheapest, tastiest, healthiest lard is the kind you make at home. And it's incredibly easy (see page 90).

LIMES

The limes called for in this book are Mexican limes—the little ones also known as Key limes. If you are substituting the larger Persian limes, you may need to reduce the amount by about half.

MASA

Masa, the dough used for tamales and corn tortillas, is made by treating dried corn kernels in a solution of lime (calcium oxide, a chemical). Corn treated with lime (or "slaked") is called nixtamal. Nixtamal is then ground into fresh masa. There are small tortilla factories in Mexico, Texas, and elsewhere where fresh masa can still be bought. It is wonderful stuff, but it has a very short shelf life; it begins to spoil within a few hours. Refrigerated, it can last up to a few days.

Masa harina is a flour made out of dried masa fresca that can be kept indefinitely. By adding water to it, you get a reconstituted masa that is not quite as sticky and flavorful as the fresh stuff, but it's still passable. Fresh masa is rapidly disappearing, largely as a result of Mexican government policies that favor the industrial giant Maseca. Even Carlos Fuentes, one of Mexico's greatest writers, has complained about how bad the tortillas in Mexico City have become.

METATE

The ancient grinding stone of Mesoamerica, the metate was once the most irreplaceable tool in the Mexican kitchen. Used primarily to grind lime-treated corn into masa dough for tamales and tortillas, it was also sometimes pressed into service for other uses such as mashing beans. The rounded handpiece is called a mano.

The metate became obsolete when people stopped slaking and mashing their own corn and began buying prepared masa or powdered masa mix. The molcajete took over the metate's mashing functions.

MOLCAJETE

The three-legged stone mortar or molcajete is the Cuisinart of ancient Mexican cooking. (The pestle is called the tejolote.) Although it has been replaced by the more convenient electric appliance in much of Mexico, the molcajete is still considered superior to the food processor or blender for making salsas, guacamole, and other blended mixtures that need to retain some of their chunkiness. And in the case of guacamole, it also serves as an attractive serving dish.

Molcajetes are easy to find in Mexican markets and are usually cheap. They must be seasoned before using, however, as the porous rock often contains grit. First, rinse as much of the grit out of the mortar as you can, then grind a couple of fresh chile peppers. Discard the pepper mash and put the molcajete in a hot oven or in the sun until it dries out. The molcajete always retains a little of the flavor of the last thing you ground in it.

PILONCILLO

This Mexican raw brown sugar is more flavorful than regular brown sugar. It is sold in a cone and must be grated or dissolved in water before use.

MEXICAN OREGANO (*LIPPIA GRAVEOLENS*)

Mexican oregano is a member of the verbena family and is more pungent than Mediterranean oregano. It can be found dried in Mexican markets and some supermarkets in the Southwest, but it is difficult to find fresh. Planting a little in your garden is the best guarantee of having some on hand (see seed sources, page 267.)

NOPALITOS (PRICKLY PEAR CACTUS PADDLES)

The Spanish name for the prickly pear cactus is *nopal;* the plural is *nopales.* The baby cactus paddles, called *nopalitos,* are eaten as a vegetable. But before they can be sliced and cooked, they must be scraped clean of the tiny barbed spines called glochids. Cleaning cactus pads requires gloves and careful handling. A spineless variety of prickly pear is now cultivated in Texas, and it is an excellent product. If you can't find spineless nopalitos, look for the packaged variety. (Pickled nopalitos are not a suitable substitute.) Many grocery stores that cater to Mexican communities sell 10-ounce packages of pre-cleaned, pre-sliced nopalitos in the produce section. These are well worth the extra cost. If you decide to clean your own and get a barb stuck in your finger, take this advice from cactus expert Dr. Peter Felker of Texas A&M University: "Use a pair of tweezers! Your first inclination when you can't get hold of the little things with your fingers is to try to pull them out with your teeth. If you do that, odds are you will end up with a cactus barb stuck in your tongue. And that's a mistake you won't make twice."

NORTEÑO

Spanish for "northerner," in Mexico the word refers to a resident of the northern desert states where the country's cattle ranches are located. Mexico's norteño culture is closely linked to the cowboy culture of the American Southwest, which lies just across the border.

PRICKLY PEAR FRUIT

The *Opuntia ficus-indica,* better known as the prickly pear, provides the most common of Mexico's cactus fruits. The fruit is called a *tuna* in Mexico and comes in a wide variety of colors. The purplish red tuna is the one we use in our margarita recipes. Prickly pear fruit is cultivated on plantations in Mexico and is much larger than the fruit of wild cacti. Like the paddles, the fruit has clusters of barbs and must be handled carefully. You will usually see a pair of tongs beside a bin of prickly pear fruit in a grocery store—use them to select the fruit. Wear rubber gloves to clean it when you get home.

TOMATILLOS

Husk-covered tomatillos, which are tart and nearly always cooked before eating, are essential to Tex-Mex and Mexican cooking. They are widely available in grocery stores. Look for firm, unblemished tomatillos with tight husks. Many Mexican cooks say that the smaller tomatillos are more flavorful.

TORTILLAS

Corn tortillas are among the oldest foods in Mesoamerican culture. They are made of the corn dough called masa. Flour tortillas were invented in the Mexican state of Sonora, that nation's largest wheat-producing region. Many grocery stores stock a wide variety of tortillas these days. There are plain and flavored flour tortillas, fluffy white corn tortillas, and old-fashioned corn tortillas. The old-fashioned corn ones, sometimes called enchilada tortillas, are somewhat leathery but hold up well in cooking. Use these for frying

USING A TORTILLA PRESS

1. Cut two squares from a plastic grocery bag. Put the 2 together.

2. Fold the Plastic sheets in half, then in half again.

3. Folf the square in half diagonally to form a triangle. Then fold the triangle in half to form a skinny triangle.

4. Lay the triangle across your tortilla press from the middle to the edge and cut the plastic with a 1/2 inch of overlap.

5. Unfold into two 8 1/2 - 9" circles

6. Place a ball of masa dough between the plastic sheets and roll or press in a tortilla press

7. Peel the plastic apart and remove the tortilla

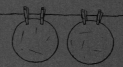

8. You can wash and dry the sheets and use them again if you like.

and save the flour tortillas and fluffy white corn tortillas for serving at the table.

Homemade tortillas

Homemade flour tortillas are pretty easy to make without special equipment. But Puffy Tacos and a few other recipes in this book require fresh homemade corn tortillas. For these, you will need a tortilla press (see Mail-Order Sources, page 267) and powdered masa harina mix (see masa, page 13).

Heating tortillas

Storebought flour or corn tortillas need to be heated before serving. The easiest method is to wrap them in foil and stick them in a 350°F oven for five to ten minutes. Corn tortillas can

also be wrapped in a paper towel or clean dish towel that has been slightly dampened and then put into the oven or microwave. The moisture from the towel will steam them slightly and improve their texture as they warm up.

When you only need a few flour tortillas, it's even easier to put a few into an ungreased skillet over medium heat and to flip them quickly as they warm, shuffling the tortillas until each side has been in contact with the skillet for ten seconds or so.

TORTILLA PRESS

This hinged contraption is used to flatten tortillas evenly. It is necessary to line a tortilla press with two sheets of plastic to prevent the masa dough from sticking (see diagram above).

Mexican cowboys branding cattle

Old-fashioned Breakfasts

THE SPANISH MISSIONS AND THE COWBOY CULTURE

IT'S EARLY SUNDAY MORNING AT MI TIERRA CAFÉ AND Bakery, the sprawling San Antonio bar, restaurant, and *panadería* where the heart of Tex-Mex beats 24/7. No matter the hour, waitresses in red, white, and green dresses and waiters in black bowties stand ready to deliver a hot cup of coffee, a plate of huevos, and hot fresh tortillas.

The walls of Mi Tierra are covered with photos of the old days of San Antonio. Pete Cortez, an immigrant from Guadalajara, opened the restaurant in 1941 on the Mercado Square. It was only a few years earlier, in the late 1930s, that the chili queens, San Antonio's most famous purveyors of Tex-Mex, had finally been banned by public health authorities from selling their tacos and enchiladas in the very same square.

I spread a hot flour tortilla with some creamy refried beans, then dip the first bite into

The bakery case at Mi Tierra restaurant in San Antonio

an egg yolk and the thin but *piquante* ranchera sauce. The tortilla bulges when I bite it, and a creamy rush of smooth beans, rich egg yolk, and fiery hot sauce takes over my palate. My waiter, Francisco, makes sure I never see the bottom of my coffee cup.

The combination of tortillas, beans, and hot sauce takes my imagination back to the very beginnings of Tejano culture. Three hundred years ago, when some of Texas's native people first took up residence in Spanish missions, did their breakfast taste the same?

MISSION FOODS

In the San José Mission, there is an exhibit of mission-era foodstuffs. The Indians of South Texas were hunter-gatherers. They lived on *nopales* (prickly pear pads), tuna (prickly pear fruit), the beans of the mesquite tree, which were ground into flour, pecans, wild onions, and wild game, all of which they continued to eat during the mission era. The chile pequin also grew wild in South Texas, as it still does today.

Spanish transplants included; tomatoes, potatoes, sugar cane, rice, and squash. At the height of the mission era, around seven long-

horn cattle were rounded up each week from outlying mission ranches and slaughtered for meat. Goats from Rancha de las Cabras, another outlying livestock ranch, supplemented the beef.

The cash crop of the San Antonio missions was cocineal, a valuable red dye made from an insect that inhabits the prickly pear cactus. For their own use, the Franciscans imported chocolate, almonds, saffron, cloves, cinnamon, and copper plates and pots. The priests also imported large quantities of wheat and corn.

After breakfast, I drive out to the south edge of town, just past Interstate 410, and turn into the parking lot of Mission San Francisco de la Espada, where ten o'clock Mass is about to start. The ancient wood-beamed church fills quickly. The priest and the deacon are members of the Franciscan order, as were the Spanish priests who built this church in the 1740s.

In the ancient San Antonio missions, indigenous tribes of South Texas, each with its own languages and customs, came together. The Franciscan fathers and Spanish soldiers taught them how to ride horses, herd livestock, and cultivate food crops. The Spanish-speaking Indians who emerged from the mission culture of Texas and northern Mexico gave birth to the Tejano ethnicity.

As the congregation files to the communion rail, I muse about the connection between the flat wafers the priest is passing out and the flour tortillas I had for breakfast. Wheat and the hand-operated mills needed to grind it into flour were first brought to Texas by Franciscan priests who needed wheat flour to make communion wafers.

At the nearby San José Mission, I visited with docent Mike Casey, a volunteer who operates the national park's newly reconstructed grist mill. The enormous quartzite burrstone wheel, believed to be of French origin, was found on the grounds of the San José Mission and has been put back into service for demonstration purposes. The stone is turned by water pressure from the mission's *acequia* system, a series of irrigation canals built by the Spanish. Casey tells me the original grist mill probably operated between 1794 and 1808 and was used exclusively for wheat.

The Alamo, the most famous of the San Antonio missions, is now a State Historic Site in the center of downtown. The other four San Antonio missions are administered by the National Park Service. San José, which still offers colorful mariachi masses on Sundays, was

The Juan de Onate statue

Tex-Mex Thanksgiving

The first Thanksgiving feast in America was celebrated in El Paso twenty-three years before the Pilgrims arrived at Plymouth Rock. Spanish explorer Juan de Onate held the festival to give thanks for safe passage across the Rio Grande River on April 20, 1598. Onate brought six hundred colonists and seven thousand head of livestock from Mexico to Texas. The culture of the Spanish missionaries and colonists would shape Texas foodways forever.

In 1998, the City of El Paso commissioned a statue of Onate to commemorate the 400th anniversary of the event.

JANIE GARZA

Janie Garza outside Mission Espada

"I was born on the grounds of Mission Espada in 1944. My dad was the caretaker. There was always a community living in the compound and just outside it. We are still a community, even though the National Park owns it now.

My mom didn't cook Mexican food. She cooked Tex-Mex. Always pinto beans, and lots of nopalitos (young, tender nopal cactus pads). I still eat nopalitos all the time. When I was a little girl, my dad and his friends fished in the river. They set out their lines at night, and every morning they got catfish. Crawfish lived in the acequias, and we ate them fried. They taste just like fried shrimp. We picked mulberries and raspberries that grew around. There was an onion field where we picked little onions. An agarita bush grows right in front of the church. It has little berries that we made jelly with. The agarita is very thorny; you can't pick the berries. You have to lay a cloth on the ground under it and hit the tree, and the berries fall into the cloth. We also picked up pecans down by the river. Those were all things that we found around this area, and we still eat them today."

the most successful of the missions and was surrounded by a thriving village. Missions Concepción, San Juan, and Espada were moved from unsuccessful sites in East Texas to the San Antonio River in the 1730s and 1740s. While San José and Espada still function as Catholic churches, the buildings, grounds, collections, and exhibits belong to Mission National Park, which was established in 1978 and covers about 819 acres.

WHEN THE SPANISH BEGAN COLONIZING Texas, they expected to apply the same model that had succeeded in Mexico. There, Indian natives had adopted Catholicism and the Spanish language, transforming themselves into loyal peasants. But in Texas, the model didn't work.

Texas was home to three different Spanish mission regions. The earliest colonists arrived in the 1580s and settled in the regions from El Paso east to Big Bend and north to Santa Fe, New Mexico. Here the Patarabueye and Pueblo didn't need to be converted to the concept of crop cultivation. They were already agricultural tribes who grew corn, cotton, and beans in irrigated river-bottom land.

In the late 1600s, Spanish colonizers targeted the Caddo Indians in East Texas. But the Tejas Caddo, who were also successful farmers, lived quite comfortably in the forests and river bottoms and had little need of

Mexican cowboy eating after round-up, Marfa, 1939

European help. After Spanish soldiers infected Caddo women with venereal diseases, the Indians avoided the Spanish entirely. The would-be colonizers eventually gave up and withdrew to the San Antonio region to concentrate their efforts on the nomadic Indians of the south plains.

The Pueblo revolt of 1680 marked a turning point in the Spanish colonial experiment. The Spanish were pushed out of present-day New Mexico, all the way south to El Paso. The rebellion also resulted in the theft of hundreds of Spanish horses. Although the Spanish retook Santa Fe ten years later, the transfer

LOS CABALLEROS NORTEÑOS (THE NORTHERN KNIGHTS)

At the end of the sixteenth century, Texas was part of El Norte, the northern limit of New Spain. Spanish explorers seeking gold and silver were the first Europeans to explore the desolate frontier. Missionaries followed, trying to convert the natives. Thanks to the introduction of cattle, sheep, and goats by the Spanish missions, an economy based on livestock trading developed in the arid prairies as the herds thrived and multiplied.

Beginning in the 1600s, El Norte became a destination for a certain sort of rugged fortune hunter. In the rigid caste system of early Mexico, mestizos, people of mixed Spanish and Indian heritage, had few opportunities. Seeking a better life, a few of the hardiest headed north. In the beginning, these "norteños" (Spanish for "northerners") worked as freelance vaqueros, rounding up "wild" cattle and selling them at a profit. Later the vaqueros struck arrangements with large landowners and worked on or managed rancheros.

Like the gauchos of Argentina, the horseman who herded livestock in El Norte developed an outdoor cooking style that revolved around the roasting, stewing, and barbecueing of meat. Native American beans and corn were staples and wild chile pequins supplied the seasoning.

The norteños prided themselves on their horsemanship, and called each other "caballero" ("cavalier" or "knight" in Spanish). Their daily dress was the hats and boots they rode in. Indifferent to the authorities in Mexico City, they patterned their code of conduct on the militaristic rules of chivalry as practiced by the knights of the Iberian peninsula. Entrepreneurial and fiercely independent, the vaqueros, and the Texas cowboys who eventually emulated them, developed mythic reputations.

ANGLO AND TEJANO FOODS

In 1835, when Juan N. Almonte wrote his "Statistical Report on Texas," there weren't a lot of things to count. Between Goliad and San Antonio, a distance of thirty-eight leagues, he couldn't find a single inhabitant. Between San Antonio and Austin, only a few houses were seen at intervals.

Though the Brazos region was the most successfully cultivated, it offered the least comfort for outsiders. "Each settler lives independent of the whole world, having at home everything which he needs for himself but nothing for travelers," Almonte wrote of the Americans.

When it came to food, Almonte found major differences between the Tejano and Anglo communities. His survey left us with a very interesting pair of grocery lists to compare:

"The food most generally used among the Mexicans in Texas is the tortillas, beef, venison, chickens, eggs, cheese, and milk, and sometimes coffee, chocolate, tea and sugar may be secured," he reported. *"Among the Americans, the most common is bacon, and cornbread, coffee sweetened with bee's honey, because they have no cane sugar, butter, buttermilk, and sometimes crackers."*

No wonder the Anglos became so fond of Texas-Mexican food.

---

of horses to the Apache and, later, the Comanche warriors couldn't be undone. In the hands of the Native Americans, the Spanish horse culture gave rise to what has been called the most effective light cavalry in world history. By 1759, the mounted Indians were defeating large Spanish armies.

Ironically, the success of the Spanish missions in San Antonio was a direct result of the horse theft. Fearing invasion by the mounted Apaches, the peaceful nomadic tribes of the South Texas prairie sought protection at the Spanish missions along the San Antonio River. Protected by the Spanish forts called *presidios,* the South Texas missions were successful economic centers between 1745 and the end of the century.

But the Apaches and Comanches had put an end to any Spanish dreams of a lasting em-

Five Comanche men, circa 1890

pire. When independent Mexico enacted the constitution of 1824, the Spanish withdrew, abandoning the Texas missions. The lands and livestock were given to the mission Indians, and the churches become local parishes.

American history books generally refer to the Spanish colonization of Texas and the Southwest as a failure. In political terms, perhaps it was. But the legacy of the Spanish era includes the old Spanish highways, the names of many of our towns and cities, the cowboy tradition, and the cooking techniques and ingredients of what would become Tex-Mex and New Mexican cuisine. Modern urban Texans may feel little connection to this ancient history. But if you dig far enough below the surface of any significant part of Texas culture, you inevitably encounter the bedrock of the Spanish colonial period.

MOLCAJETE SAUCE

1/2 onion, finely
chopped

1 1/2 tablespoons fresh
lime juice

6 Roma or other
tomatoes

2 jalapeño chiles,
stemmed, seeded, and
halved lengthwise

1 garlic clove

1 cup chopped fresh
cilantro

Salt

The original version of this basic Tex-Mex salsa was made in a mortar of coarse stone called a molcajete. The traditional recipe calls for chiles and tomatoes to be roasted in a comal, a flat cast-iron griddle, then ground together in the molcajete with a tejolote or pestle. The tiny chile pequin, which grows wild in Texas, was once the most common chile pepper used in this sauce.

You can use a food processor instead of the molcajete, but don't skip the roasting step. You'll be amazed by how much it improves the flavor. You can serve this everyday table sauce with almost anything.

MAKES ABOUT 3 CUPS

Soak the onion in the lime juice for 15 minutes in a small bowl. "Roast" the tomatoes, chile halves, and garlic clove in an ungreased skillet over high heat, turning as needed until slightly charred on all sides. Pulse in a blender; the mixture should remain chunky. Transfer to a bowl and add the onion, lime juice, and cilantro. Salt to taste. Use immediately, or cover and refrigerate for up to 1 week.

FRIJOLES

It's best to cook beans slowly so they become completely tender without burning. Nowadays, the easiest way to do this is in a crockpot. Just be sure to heat them thoroughly before eating.

2 cups dried pinto beans (1 pound)

MAKES 6 CUPS COOKED BEANS AND 4 CUPS BEAN BROTH

Sort the beans to remove any stones or grit and rinse in a colander. Place the beans in a pot with 8 cups water, bring to a boil, and cook on low heat for 6 hours or until tender. Stir a few times so that the beans cook evenly and don't burn. Add water as necessary. Cooked beans will keep in the refrigerator for up to a week.

To cook in a crockpot:
Cook for 2 hours on high and 6 hours on low heat. Add water as necessary.

COWBOYS AND VAQUEROS

The word *vaqueros* (literally "cow men") comes from *vaca*, the Spanish word for cow. The early Anglo cowboys were called buckaroos, a mispronunciation of *vaqueros*. Literally translated, *vaquero* became the English word "cowboy."

Other words that came to us from *vaquero* culture include alamo (which means "cottonwood tree"), bandana, bandido, bronc, camino, compadre, cantina, canyon, coyote, dinero, hombre, hoosegow (from the Spanish *juzgado*, meaning "courthouse"), lariat, lasso, loco, mosey and vamoose (both from *vaminos*, Spanish slang for "let's go"), ramada, rodeo, savvy (from the Spanish *saber*, "to know"), sierra, todo, and vista.

Texan herdsmen, 1859

Mi Tierra's Frijoles Charros (Cowboy Beans)

1 teaspoon lard or
vegetable oil

4 slices bacon, minced

1/2 onion, chopped

2 fresh jalapeño or
serrano chiles,
stemmed and chopped

2 garlic cloves,
minced

6 cups Frijoles and
bean broth (page 25)

1 tablespoon salt, or
to taste

1/2 teaspoon ground
cumin

Chopped fresh
cilantro

In the days of the vaqueros, a pot of beans was often all there was for breakfast. Adding a little bacon and chile made plain beans into a delicious meal.

MAKES 6 CUPS

Heat the oil and fry the bacon and onion together in a skillet over high heat until the onion is golden. Add the chiles and garlic and continue cooking for a minute more, until the chiles are softened. Stir the cooked mixture into a soup pot or crockpot containing the frijoles. (Include the bacon grease, if desired.) Add the salt and cumin and simmer for 10 minutes or more to combine the flavors. Serve in a bowl, garnished with cilantro.

Beans a la J. Frank Dobie

"On the oldtime ranches of the border country, where I grew up, frijoles were about as regular as bread, and in some households they still are." —J. Frank Dobie, *A Taste of Texas*

The father of Texas letters, J. Frank Dobie, always insisted beans should be cooked plain and appreciated without a lot of extras. At his most extravagant, he would mash a couple of wild chile pequins on his plate, mix the beans with the chiles, and top them with a little chopped onion.

FRIJOLES REFRITOS

The mashed potatoes of Tex-Mex, refried beans are served with almost everything. If you already have unseasoned cooked beans, this is the easiest way to heat up a couple of portions. If you don't have time to cook a pot of beans, start with canned pinto beans. (Two 16-ounce cans are perfect for this recipe.) If you do the refrying steps yourself, you'll still get a great homemade flavor.

MAKES 3 CUPS

1/4 cup lard or vegetable oil

3 cups drained cooked pinto beans, broth reserved

1/2 teaspoon salt, or to taste

1/2 cup reserved bean broth

1/8 teaspoon ground black pepper

Melt the lard in a large skillet over medium-high heat. Allow to heat for another minute, then add the beans and mash them for 2 minutes with a fork or potato masher. Stir in the salt. Add the bean broth and the black pepper and continue mashing until the beans reach the desired consistency. Tex-Mex beans are generally chunky rather than soupy.

VARIATIONS

Full-flavor Frijoles:
When the lard or oil is hot, add 1 cup chopped onions and 3 minced garlic cloves and sauté until soft. Add the beans and proceed as directed.

Breakfast Frijoles:
Use bacon grease instead of lard.

Ox Eyes

2 tablespoons
vegetable oil

2 jalapeño chiles,
stemmed, seeded, and
minced

1/2 onion, chopped

1/2 green bell pepper,
seeded and chopped

One 15-ounce can
pureed tomatoes

Salt

4 eggs

4 flour tortillas,
warmed

"Ox Eyes" or "Eggs in Hell" are among the colorful names for eggs poached in hot sauce. This old recipe is a special favorite of campfire cooks. If you already have some hot sauce made, you can just dump it in the skillet and start from there. Serve immediately with Frijoles Refritos (page 27), additional warmed flour tortillas, and Café de Olla (page 37).

SERVES 2

Heat the oil in a deep sauté pan or skillet over medium heat. Add the chiles, onion, and bell pepper and sauté until wilted, about 3 minutes. Add the tomatoes and bring to a boil. (The sauce should be quite runny and fill the pan to a depth of at least an inch. If it is too solid, add a little water.) Salt to taste.

Stir the sauce well and then gently break the eggs into the pan. Cover and allow to cook for 4 minutes or until the egg whites are well set but the yolks are still soft, or to desired doneness.

To serve, put 2 tortillas on each plate. Gently lift the eggs out of the pan and place one on each tortilla. Spoon the sauce around the eggs.

*A campfire breakfast
of Ox Eyes, flour tortillas,
and Café de Olla*

CISCO'S HUEVOS RANCHEROS

One 14.5-ounce can
peeled tomatoes

1 medium garlic clove,
minced

3 medium serrano
chiles, stems removed

8 eggs

**The late Rudy Cisneros
in Tex-Mex heaven**

Cisco's is a little bakery on Austin's East Side where you can get huevos rancheros and a cocktail at 7 A.M. The walls of the back dining room are covered with photos of such famous former patrons as LBJ, John Connally, George Bush Sr., Willie Nelson, Ben Crenshaw, and Walter Cronkite. Here's their huevos recipe. Serve with bacon, Frijoles Refritos (page 27), and flour tortillas.

SERVES 4

Bring the tomatoes plus $1/2$ can water to a boil in a saucepan over medium-high heat and add the garlic and chiles. Remove the pan from the heat and allow the ranchero sauce to cool. Puree the mixture in a blender for 2 to 3 minutes. When ready to use, warm the sauce in a small pan. Fry the eggs to the desired doneness and ladle a generous amount of sauce over the top.

AMAYA'S MIGAS

1 tablespoon
vegetable oil

2 cups dime-sized
tortilla pieces or
crushed tortilla chips

$1/2$ cup chopped
tomato

$2/3$ cup chopped onion

1 jalapeño chile,
stemmed, seeded, and
chopped

2 eggs

$1/2$ cup Cheddar
cheese

"When I was a kid growing up in Corpus Christi, we used to eat migas for dinner during Lent," remembers Robert Amaya of Austin's Taco Village. "Migas or migajas, we called it. It was a meatless main dish made by frying torn-up tortillas with eggs. We use tortilla chips now instead of fried tortillas and we serve migas for breakfast." Serve with Frijoles Refritos (page 27) and tortillas.

SERVES 2

Heat the oil in a large skillet over medium heat and sauté the tortilla pieces or chips until slightly crisp, 1 to 2 minutes. Add the tomato, onion, and chile and cook for 5 minutes. Pour in the eggs and mix with a spatula, scraping up the eggs as they cook. When the eggs are partially set, add the Cheddar. Cover. Toss a few more times until the cheese melts.

EL CHICO'S CHORIZO

If you think you don't like Mexican chorizo, this recipe will change your mind. It is adapted from a cookbook published by El Chico restaurants in the 1970s. They started with ground pork, but that was before food processors became common. The fresh-ground flavor is much better. Choose fatty or lean chops, depending on your preference (I like the fatty kind for chorizo). Add more paprika if you like an intense orange color.

MAKES 1¼ CUPS

Combine all of the ingredients except the oil and onion in a food processor. Process until coarsely ground, about 20 seconds. Heat the oil in a skillet or sauté pan over medium-high heat. Stir in the chopped onion. Add the chorizo mixture and brown for 5 minutes or to desired doneness.

VARIATIONS

For lean chorizo:
Omit the oil, add the mixture to a cold skillet, turn the heat to high, and brown to taste.

Chorizo y Papas:
Add 1 cup boiled potato chunks and turn with a spatula over medium heat until the chorizo and potatoes are well combined and heated through.

Chorizo y Huevos:
Add 2 beaten eggs to 3 heaping tablespoons of hot cooked chorizo in the skillet and turn with a spatula over medium heat until the eggs are cooked to the desired doneness.

1/2 pound boneless pork chops, cut into 4 or 5 pieces

1 teaspoon chili powder

2 teaspoons paprika

1 teaspoon salt

1/4 teaspoon garlic powder

1/4 teaspoon ground cumin

2 tablespoons red wine vinegar

1 tablespoon vegetable oil

2 tablespoons chopped onion

A Mexican woman grinding on a metate in front of a jacal (a hut made of sticks) at a goat camp on La Mota Ranch in La Salle County, 1880s.

FLOUR TORTILLAS

4 cups all-purpose flour (15 ounces)

1/4 cup lard (2 ounces)

1 teaspoon salt

The amounts given here will vary dramatically depending on the dryness of your flour and the hardness of your water. San Antonio's drinking water percolates through the Edwards Aquifer and yields the fluffiest flour tortillas in the state. You will probably have to tinker with the amounts given here if you don't live in San Antonio.

MAKES 8 TORTILLAS

Put all the ingredients in the bowl of an electric mixer with 1 cup water and mix with the dough hook attachment until well blended, about 5 minutes. Alternatively, use a food processor with the dough blade or knead by hand. The dough should be moist and pliable. If it is still dry, add 1/4 to 1/3 cup water as needed.

Cover the mixing bowl with plastic wrap and allow the dough to rest for 30 minutes to 1 hour.

Form 8 balls with the dough. If the dough is too sticky, add extra flour. On a floured surface, roll each ball with a rolling pin to form 6- to 8-inch rounds.

In a large skillet, griddle, or comal, brown each tortilla over high heat for 1 minute on each side until puffy and freckled with brown spots.

NOTE

For fluffier tortillas, add 1/2 teaspoon baking powder.

Margarine may be substituted for lard. However, vegetable shortening is not a good substitute.

CORN TORTILLAS

Fresh masa makes the best corn tortillas, but it's extremely difficult to find, even in Mexico. Nearly everyone relies on powdered masa mixes such as Maseca or Quaker Masa Harina Mix these days. Here's the basic recipe.

MAKES 10 TORTILLAS

2 cups masa harina

Measure the masa harina into a bowl and add 1¼ cups warm water, stirring until a dough begins to form. Turn out onto a clean dry work surface and knead for about 5 minutes or until smooth.

Divide into 10 equal-sized balls.

Heat an ungreased comal, skillet, or griddle until very hot. Position each ball of dough between two pieces of plastic (see diagram) and press lightly into a 6-inch disc. Peel off the plastic. Cook each tortilla for 15 to 30 seconds on each side, until cooked through.

VARIATION

Puffy Tacos:
Divide the dough into 8 balls and make each tortilla about 5 inches wide and ⅛ inch thick. Proceed as directed (see page 185.)

Janie Garza's Nopalitos and Eggs

1 1/2 cups prepared nopalitos (see head note)

2 tablespoons vegetable oil

1/2 cup chopped onions

2 garlic cloves, minced

1/2 teaspoon chili powder

Salt

4 eggs, beaten

Nopalitos are young, tender prickly pear pads. They taste like tart green beans and have a wonderful crunch. Removing the thorns from the pads is a daunting task. You're better off to look for bags of pre-cleaned chopped nopalitos in the produce section of a Mexican market. If you avoid nopalitos because of the slime, you'll like this recipe—the scrambled eggs absorb it all.

SERVES 2

Bring 3 cups water to a boil in a medium saucepan over medium-high heat and add the nopalitos. Cook until they deepen in color, about 5 minutes, and drain. Heat 1 tablespoon of the oil in a medium skillet over medium heat and cook the onions until wilted, about 3 minutes. Add the garlic and drained nopalitos. Sprinkle with the chili powder and salt to taste. Add the remaining tablespoon of oil and the eggs. Scraping from the bottom of the pan, cook until the eggs are at the desired doneness and the nopalitos are incorporated.

Living History

Water still flows through the canals of San Antonio's ancient acequia system and until recently the system was still used for agricultural irrigation. In the 1930s, the Archdiocese of San Antonio, in cooperation with the National Park System, invited the Franciscan order to return to San Antonio's mission churches, resume their roles as parish priests, and play a part in preserving the living history of the San Antonio missions.

Like Janie Garza, many of the people who worship at Mission Espada church are descended from families who lived on the mission's grounds.

Café de Olla

Cowboy camp coffee was never filtered; the grounds were boiled in the pot. Chuckwagon cocineros used to say that to test coffee, you drop a horseshoe in the pot. If the horseshoe floats, the coffee is strong enough. This boiled coffee recipe comes in very handy for campfire cooking. The secret is getting the grounds to settle. Some of the old cocineros swore by eggshells for this purpose; others used a dash of cold water. If you forget that the grounds are still on the bottom and shake up the pot, you'll be picking this coffee out of your teeth all day.

MAKES 8 CUPS

Put the coffee, salt, and cinnamon with the water in a metal coffee pot over medium heat. Bring just to a boil and then reduce to a simmer (or move the pot to the side of the campfire) for a few minutes. Add the orange peel, return to the heat, and bring to a boil again. Set the coffee pot on the table. Add $^1/2$ cup cold water to settle the grounds and wait for 5 minutes without disturbing the pot. Pour carefully (or use a tea strainer). Add sugar to each mug to taste—or drink it black like a real *vaquero*!

8 heaping teaspoons best-quality coffee, medium ground

$^1/8$ teaspoon salt

1 cinnamon stick

8 cups spring water

Peel of $^1/2$ orange

Grated piloncillo or brown sugar

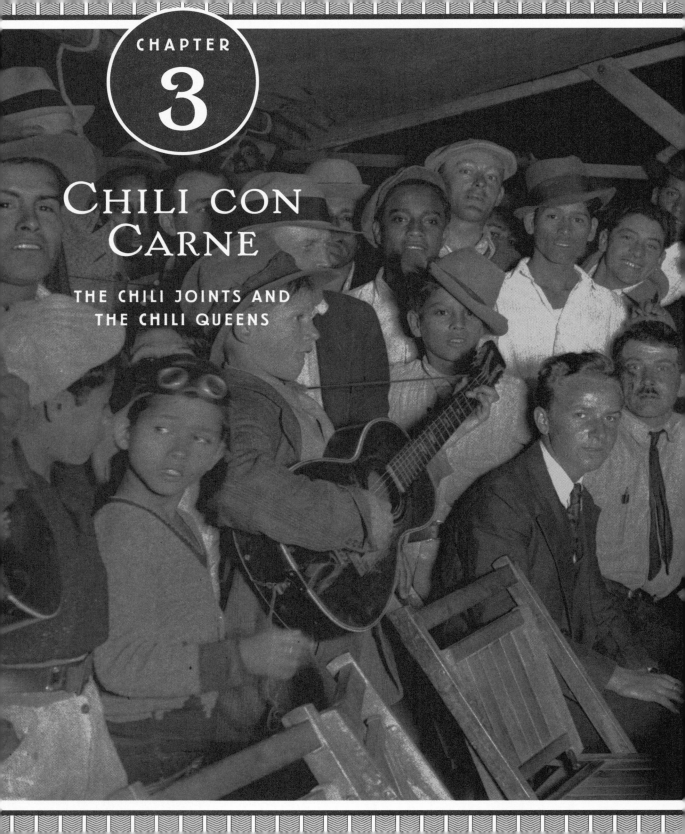

CHILI CON CARNE

THE CHILI JOINTS AND THE CHILI QUEENS

Chili Queens and their customers, Haymarket Plaza, 1936

THE SLOW-SIMMERED, COARSELY GROUND BEEF in the bowl before me has a healthy dose of chili powder and no beans, identifying it as true Texas-style chili. The meat is tender, and there's a strong aroma of cumin. I have to admit that it's an excellent bowl of chili. Which is kind of a surprise in a chain like Chili's.

The Chili's location in Bastrop, where I am eating this bowl of Texas red, has decorated its walls with chili cook-off posters and snapshots from chili cook-offs all over Texas. Every Chili's I've ever seen is decorated exactly the same way. It's a cookie-cutter format, but sadly, it's about all that's left of the American chili joint.

Opened by former cowboy cooks and other such dubious chefs, ramshackle chili joints once served up a bowl of red and a plate of crackers for a nickel. By the early part of the twentieth century, they were found all across the Midwest. Some variation on chili con carne was served in restaurants across the United States.

Chili con carne's fame began to spread across the country after the Columbian Exhibition of 1893 in Chicago. The Texas exhibit at this "world's fair" recreated a typical San Antonio chili stand and sold authentic Texas chili con carne to fair-goers. Within a few years, chili stands and chili joints began popping up all over the United States, and canned chili became a common item in food stores.

In most of the rest of the country, chili has one purpose—it is a hearty one-dish meal. But in Texas, chili has a wide variety of uses. It can be used straight or diluted as a sauce. It's a popular topping for tamales. To make it into a meal, you combine it with beans, tamales, tortillas, enchiladas, scrambled eggs, or any number of other things. Texans don't have anything against eating beans with their chili. They just have a lot of other ways to eat it.

"Chili con carne evolved from enchilada sauce," suggests Raul Molina, of the Molina's restaurant chain in Houston. Chile colorado, which literally means "red chile" in Spanish, was also the name given to red chile sauces and to red chile sauces with meat, such as the dish that came to be called chili con carne. At first there was little or no difference between red chile sauce and "chili." But as beef became cheaper, cowboys and chuckwagon cooks turned the red chile enchilada sauce into a meat-heavy main dish.

The invention of chili powder around 1900 made the dish very easy to prepare. The Texas

CHILI QUEENS VS. CHILE QUEENS

The English word "chili" and the Spanish word *chile* were used more or less interchangeably in historical accounts of San Antonio's chili queens (or chile queens). We use the "chili queen" spelling because most Southwestern food writers have adopted the convention of using the English word "chili" for the dish and the Spanish spelling "chile" for the pods.

Descendants of Canary Islanders laying flowers on an outdoor altar on the doorstep of the Spanish Governor's Palace, San Antonio, 1933

food companies that sold chili powders and canned chili advertised "authentic Mexican" flavor, and so most Americans assumed that chili con carne was of Mexican origin. All the food prepared and sold by the Spanish-speaking citizens of San Antonio was called Mexican food—with good reason.

With some notable exceptions, Texas-Mexican food at the time was more or less identical to the norteño food of northern Mexico's ranching region. This was the only part of Mexico most Texans knew. Few at the time realized Mexico City had an entirely different idea of Mexican cuisine.

In the late 1800s, the Mexico City elite considered beans, chiles, and corn products such as tortillas and tamales to be low-class street foods. Educated Mexicans have a special contempt for Tex-Mex chili con carne, which is defined in the *Diccionario de Mejicanismos* as a *"detestable comida que con el falso titulo de mejicana"*—that is, a detestable food falsely labeled Mexican. Clearly, something about the flavor of chili con carne was uniquely un-Mexican.

SOME ARGUE THAT THE EXOTIC TASTE OF Tex-Mex can be traced to the Canary Islands. In March 1731, fifteen families from the Canary Islands arrived in the struggling settlement of Bexar, as San Antonio was then known.

In mission-era San Antonio, Spanish soldiers and citizens were barred from fraternizing with the mission Indians. (Earlier missions in East Texas had failed because so many Indians died from European diseases.) Since Indians made up nearly the entire population of the missions, the Spanish community was completely lacking in social and commercial opportunities.

The settlement lacked colonists, but few Spaniards were interested in relocating to such a wilderness. So the government of Spain recruited families of colonists from the Canary Islands, a Spanish possession off the coast of Africa where land was in short supply. To entice the recruits, the Spanish crown offered male islanders who relocated the noble title *hidalgo*. The islanders expected to form the aristocracy of the new land called Texas, but when they got there, they were disappointed to discover that there was no peasant class to rule over, since the Mission Indians were kept segregated from the Spanish soldiers and citizens.

The Canary Islanders and their offspring supplied the community with most of its lead-

"Chili Stand" in front of a laundry, Haymarket Plaza, circa 1904

Chili Stand.

PORTRAIT OF A CHILE QUEEN

In 1894, the San Antonio *Daily Express* wrote an article describing "the ever-attentive, always jolly 'chile queen.' They are 'good fellows' these 'chile queens' and are able and willing to talk on any subject that may be named from love to law. As a general rule they are bright, bewitching creatures and put themselves to much trouble to please their too often rowdy customers . . ."

ers for many years. The Canary Islanders' influence on San Antonio culture continues to this day—especially when it comes to food.

It has been said that the Canary Islanders brought cumin *(comino)* to Texas. But shipping lists of items sent to the San Antonio missions indicate that cumin was among the spices already available to the Franciscans. If the Canary Islanders didn't actually introduce cumin to San Antonio, they did bring with them from North Africa a taste for cumin in amounts that most Spaniards would find overwhelming.

The Canary Islands were originally inhabited by the Guanche, a Berber people who came from Morocco. According to the American Spice Trade Association, the "lavish use of spices" characterizes Berber foods, and the cuisine's "flavor imprint" is made up of "cumin, coriander, saffron, chiles, ginger, cinnamon and paprika." The Canary Island women reportedly made a stew with cumin, chile peppers, wild onions, and the available herbs. These were cooked outdoors in copper kettles in the village plaza and shared with soldiers and passersby at sundown.

The Canary Islanders' taste for cumin-heavy seasoning and their tradition of outdoor socializing after dinner may be where the San Antonio chili stand tradition began. In the July 1927 issue of *Frontier Times* magazines, San Antonio commissioner Frank H. Bushwick talked about the chili queens and their original location in Military Plaza, where they worked before being moved to Market Square in 1887. "The chili stand and chili queens are peculiarities . . . of the Alamo City. They started away back there when the Spanish army camped on the plaza," Bushwick said.

"Chili stands, that used to come out with the stars and fringe the horizon of Military Plaza, were an institution that was distinctively San Antonian," wrote James P. Newcomb in 1901. "The fame of the Chili Queen became worldwide." The chili stands

SOME OF THE CHILE QUEENS' FRIENDS

"Every class of people in every station and position in life who come to this city visit the places (chili stands) and partake of the piquant eatables . . ."
— San Antonio

Daily Express, June 17, 1894

shared the public squares with vegetable vendors. The vendors arrived before dawn and sold their wares until just after noon. The chili queens, who often worked as laundry women by day, set up their food stalls in the evening.

In the beginning the food vendors simply ladled their stews from cazuelas or clay pots. But by the late 1800s an elaborate sort of portable restaurant had evolved. Three ten-foot planks were propped on sawhorses in the shape of a J, then covered with red-and-white-checkered oilcloth, explained occasional San Antonio resident William Sydney Porter, better known as O. Henry. The tables were decorated with vases of paper flowers and lit by laundry lamps. Patrons could add seasonings from red clay condiment dishes that contained oregano and chopped onions, among other things. In O. Henry's day, a bowl of chili with bread and water sold for ten cents.

In his bizarre tale "The Enchanted Kiss," O. Henry describes the "delectable chile-con-carne . . . composed of delicate meats minced with aromatic herbs and the poignant chile colorado—a compound full of singular savor and a fiery zest . . ."

Many chili queens went on to open small cafés in the front rooms of their homes. These impromptu eateries were known as *fondas*. "Sadie, the acknowledged 'queen' of all 'queens' on account of her beauty, her vivacity and her aptitude at repartee, has opened up a fonda, taken unto herself a husband and is taking life quietly and easy," reported the San Antonio *Daily Express* in 1894.

San Antonio's Mexican Quarter, or El Laredito, as it was known, wasn't just a place to eat chili, it was the most exciting late-night scene in the state of Texas. Some favorite fondas were on the edge of the city's red light district. About a place called Madame Garza's, San Antonio author Charles Ramsdell, wrote: "It was frequented by pimps, gamblers, and courtesans as well as by the best people. The two worlds had a rare opportunity to study each other over a bowl of chili."

The Canary Island women and their outdoor dinner parties made San Antonio more hospitable for the Spanish military. Likewise, the flirtatious chili queens spiced up the lives of lonely Anglo cowboys, Texas Rangers, and American military men at a time when women were scarce and San Antonio was the only town on a vast and empty frontier.

BEYOND CHILI

San Antonio's chili stands (or chile stands, as they were often referred to in print) offered a lot more than chili con carne. This 1931 article for the Texas Folk-Lore Society describes a typical menu.

Few tourists can have forgotten the "chile stands" of San Antonio, Texas, once a most interesting feature of the life of that charming city, but abolished within the past two or three years in deference to the "progressive" spirit of certain councilmen.

At these one was always tolerably sure of getting a cup of excellent hot coffee, or one of equally good chocolate, for the making of which the Mexicans are deservedly famous; tea, strange to relate, was never to be had, and milk only infrequently.

But "chile con carne," "tamales," "tortillas," "chile rellenos," "huevos revueltos," "lengua lampreada," *many other kinds of* "pucheros" *and* "ollas" *with leathery cheese, burning peppers, stewed tomatoes and many other items too numerous to mention at this time, were always on sale.*

Puchero *is a stew of any kind; it resembles an* "olla"; *when made of tripe, it is called by the name* "menudo."

Huevos revueltos *are eggs fried on both sides, and served with chile sauce.*

Cabra lampreada *and* lengua lampreada *are goat meat or tongue fried in egg.*

Frijoles, it goes without saying, appear on every one of these tables."—John G. Bourke, "The Folk-Foods of the Rio Grande Valley and of Northern Mexico," in *Southwestern Lore*, ed. J. Frank Dobie. Texas Folk-Lore Society, no. 9 (1931).

A TRIP TO THE
MEXICAN QUARTER CHILI STANDS

During the Great Depression, the Works Progress Administration (WPA) hired writers to chronicle American life. Among their projects was *America Eats,* an unpublished book about food. In this excerpt titled "Mexican Quarter Chili Stands," we get a vivid picture of what it must have been like to eat a "combination plate" at a San Antonio chili stand. Since the chili stands disappeared in the early 1930s, the mythic experience described here would probably be typical of the 1920s.

No tourist in San Antonio has seen the city until, at night, he has visited the chili stands on Haymarket Plaza, not far from the city's heart at the nearer edge of the great Mexican quarter.

One follows his nose past the Municipal Market in search of the source of an aroma which, once sniffed, is never forgotten—the fragrance of burning mesquite wood. He turns the corner and runs squarely into Old Mexico, as abruptly as walking onto a Hollywood movie set. Tables are spread outdoors along the whole block and behind them women and girls tend fires and charcoal braziers above which Mexican foods are stacked. Three Mexican minstrels, brave in embroidered costumes and high-peaked straw hats, pluck their guitars tentatively, ready to serenade.

A Mexican family, plainly in modest circumstances, sits at the first long table, giving itself a night out. He wears his Sunday best and his wife her best reboza [sic] (shawl), one end of it thrown gracefully across her shoulder. There are patches on the clothes of the three small children, but the general effect is one of being scrubbed and starched. The waitress comes to take the order and finally takes it, but only after a long conver-

sation that covers the balminess of the air, neighborhood news, the high cost of living, and remedies for colds. Everything here moves slowly and with graceful ease.

The children have tacos, tasty favorite of shine boy and banker alike—a tortilla folded and fried crisp and stuffed with seasoned meat and chopped greens. After much deliberation the parents fix upon enchiladas—tortillas dipped in chili sauce, covered with chopped onion and grated cheese and done up jelly roll style. And now the husband—this obviously is an occasion for special celebration—glances significantly at the expectant musicians. They come to stand close behind the family. Plaintive tenors blend with plaintive guitars in a song about a little princess who, from all accounts, was deeply in love.

Now there is a new note—a sort of suppressed excitement. The grapevine has brought word that tourists are approaching and here they come, a party of five. The three serenaders look at them a bit wistfully; had they waited a little longer they would have caught these rich folk. But the newcomers are not to lack for music. As they seat themselves, two small boys—the elder cannot be ten years old—pop up from nowhere, vest-pocket fashion plates of the hidalgo of a century ago. Their costumes are stunning, their guitars almost as large as themselves. Two serenades go on at once, so softly that they complement each other.

One of the party of five—the bellwether of this flock—is an elderly gentlemen cut on the pattern of New York and points East.

"No chili con carne," he says. "We ate that in Kansas City."

The waitress looks a bit injured. In the hands of its friends, chili con carne is a soul-warming dish, but in Kansas City, St. Louis, New York,

Chili stands in Military Plaza, circa 1880

New Haven and Hartford, it may be only a soupy gravy, wholly without any convictions of its own and sometimes even containing such foreign matter as spaghetti. The Easterner's attention is upon a fire from which floats lazily the fragrance of mesquite mingled with what seems to be the spice of the Indies.

"Some of that," he points out, "and that—and that."

His womenfolk look at him with the admiration that is due to the brave.

Some of that and that and that turns out to be two tacos, two enchiladas, and two tamales on each plate, the whole buried under chopped salad greens. The visitors start hesitatingly and gain confidence as they go.

Other tourists are arriving, some of whom will try the food although most of them will only look on—and usually add to the receipts of the serenaders, whose groups increase on especially balmy and busy nights. But all of them who patronize the stands will probably depart as soon as they have eaten, which is a matter not wholly to be understood by the Mexican customers. Neither to them or the proprietors of the chili stands does it seem reasonable that even Yanqui customers, whose ways are strange, should hasten to be on their way as soon as they have spent their money. Women are now in a mood for gossip, men for reminiscence. Eating is a social affair; and time is not the all-important thing in life.

—Texas Writers' Project, WPA

Venison Chili

1/2 teaspoon salt, plus more as needed

1 cup coarsely ground venison shoulder meat or beef chuck cut in 1/2-inch cubes

1 ancho chile pod

Mesoamericans were stewing meat with chiles long before the arrival of Columbus. Of course, the Indians didn't have skillets or garden vegetables. But if you think browning the meat and adding garlic, tomatoes, and onions is absolutely essential to making chili, give this three-ingredient recipe a try.

SERVES 1

Heat 1 cup water and the 1/2 teaspoon salt in a saucepan over medium-high heat. Add the meat and ancho pod. Bring to a boil and then reduce to a simmer. Remove the ancho stem after 20 minutes and remove the large pieces of ancho skin after 40 minutes. Mash the softened ancho with a spoon and stir, mixing the chile and meat together. Salt to taste.

Tangia (Berber Chili)

2 garlic cloves, minced

1/2 teaspoon paprika

1/2 teaspoon ground black pepper

1/2 teaspoon turmeric

1 teaspoon ground cumin

1/2 teaspoon powdered ginger

1/2 teaspoon salt

1 1/2 pounds leg of lamb, cut into 1/2-inch dice with fat removed

2 large onions, quartered

1/2 cup beef broth

This traditional Moroccan "bachelor stew" made of meat chunks, onions, and a spice mix that includes chile powder (paprika) and cumin is probably similar to the stews the Canary Islanders brought to San Antonio in the late 1700s.

SERVES 4

Preheat the oven to 350°F. Combine the garlic, paprika, black pepper, turmeric, cumin, ginger, and salt in a bowl. Add the meat and toss until well coated. Lay the onion quarters in the bottom of a baking dish and add the broth. Put the meat on top of the onions. Bake for 2 1/2 to 3 hours, until the meat is very tender.

CARNE CON CHILE

Jorge Cortez at La Margarita in San Antonio remembers when his family made this Mexican beef and chile stew with big chunks of meat. The ingredients are nearly the same as in chili. "But we never called it chile con carne, we called it carne con chile," he says with a laugh.

MAKES 4 CUPS

Heat the oil in a large skillet or Dutch oven and brown the meat well, 5 to 10 minutes, until any water evaporates. Add the onion and cook until wilted, about 5 minutes. Add the garlic, flour, cumin, bay leaves, black pepper, and salt. Stir constantly for about 2 minutes or until the flour is browned. Add 2 cups water and the ancho pods. Cover and simmer for 20 minutes. Continue cooking, stirring, and adding more water until the ancho dissolves completely and the meat is tender. Remove any large pieces of ancho skin. Serve in a bowl with tortilla chips or as a sauce over enchiladas or tamales.

1/4 cup vegetable oil

1 pound 2 by 1/4-inch sirloin strips

1/2 cup chopped onions

3 garlic cloves, minced

1 teaspoon flour

1 teaspoon ground cumin

2 bay leaves

1 teaspoon ground black pepper

1 teaspoon salt

2 ancho chile pods

Jorge Cortez

CHILE PUREE

5 garlic cloves,
unpeeled

2 ounces ancho chiles,
seeded and stemmed
(6 to 8, depending on
size)

1 ounce guajillo (for a
reddish puree) or
pasilla (for a darker,
sharper-tasting
puree) chiles, seeded
and stemmed

1 1/2 teaspoons salt

2 tablespoons
vegetable oil or lard

1/2 teaspoon sugar,
optional

In San Antonio, Tex-Mex chile sauces always start with ancho chiles. But the best chile sauces combine at least two types of chiles for a well-rounded flavor. Customize the recipe for the peppers you prefer or have available. This puree makes a great base for chili con carne and enchilada sauces.

MAKES 4 CUPS

Put the garlic cloves in a large skillet, griddle, or comal and toast them over high heat, turning several times to char the peels. Remove them from the heat and allow to cool. Remove the peels.

Bring 8 cups water to a boil in a pot. Turn off the heat.

Rinse the chiles to remove any dust from the skin. Put them in the hot water. Place a plate on top of the chiles to submerge them and allow them to soak for 1 hour.

Remove the chiles and put them in a blender with the garlic. Add the salt. Add 3 cups fresh water and process on high for 5 minutes.

Pour the puree through a strainer into a bowl or large measuring cup, using a spatula or wooden spoon to push it through. Extract as much puree as possible and discard the skin left in the strainer.

Heat the oil in a skillet or pot over medium-high heat. Reduce the heat to low and add the strained chile puree. Simmer for 5 minutes, stirring with a spoon to prevent sticking. Remove the pot from the heat and allow the puree to cool.

Taste the puree for bitterness; you may need to add sugar to balance the flavor. Reserve the puree for use in other recipes.

CASA RIO CHILI CON CARNE

The earliest chili con carnes were stews; the meats weren't browned. The raw meat was simply combined with the liquids in earthen cazuelas, or "ollas," and placed over a fire. This 1940s recipe from the Casa Rio restaurant is based on the old technique.

MAKES 9 TO 10 CUPS

Heat $5^{1}/2$ cups water in a soup pot over high heat. Add the meats, salt, cumin, pepper, garlic, chiles, and sugar and bring to a boil. Reduce to a simmer and cook for 35 minutes. Add the chili powder and simmer for 30 minutes more.

Combine the flour and the melted shortening in a bowl and stir until smooth. Add to the cooked chili and cook until thickened, 2 to 3 minutes.

2 pounds pork, cut into $^{1}/2$-inch dice

1 pound beef, cut into $^{1}/2$-inch dice

2 tablespoons salt

3 tablespoons ground cumin

1 tablespoon ground black pepper

6 garlic cloves, minced

2 medium serrano chiles, finely chopped

5 ancho chile pods, seeded, stemmed, and minced

1 teaspoon sugar

$^{1}/4$ cup chili powder

$^{1}/4$ cup flour

$^{3}/4$ cup melted vegetable shortening or lard

Casa Rio's tables along the San Antonio River

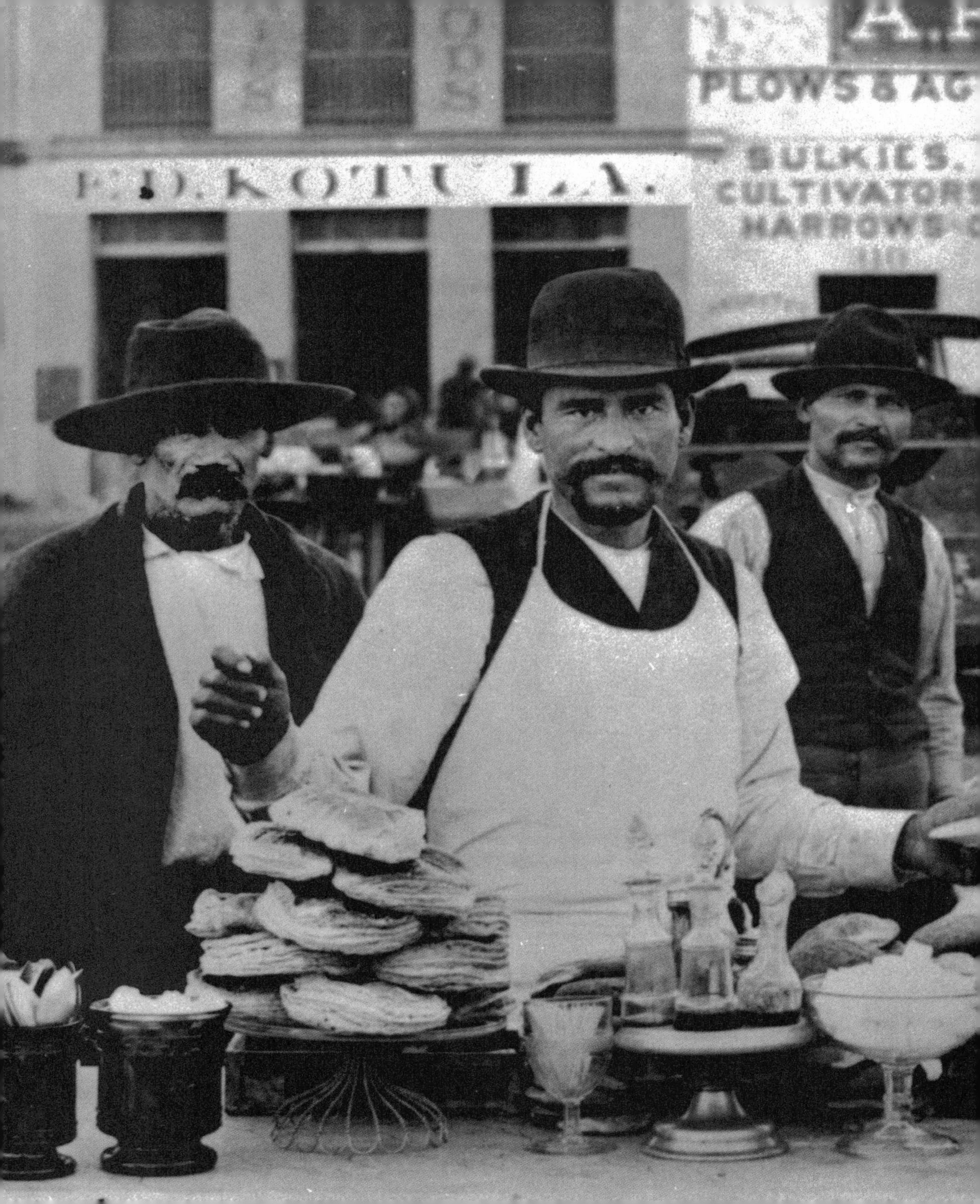
F. D. KOTULA.
PLOWS & AG
SULKIES.
CULTIVATORS
HARROWS

Men selling a variety of foods at a chili stand in Military Plaza, circa 1887

Lady Bird Johnson's Pedernales Chili

4 pounds chili meat (beef chuck ground through the chili plate of a meat grinder or cut into 1/4-inch dice)

1 large onion, chopped

2 garlic cloves

1 teaspoon dried Mexican oregano

1 teaspoon ground cumin

2 tablespoons chili powder

1 1/2 cups canned whole tomatoes and their liquid

2 to 6 generous dashes of liquid hot sauce

Salt

During the ranch era, the Dutch oven and cast-iron skillet became common cooking utensils. The new cookware made it possible to brown the meat before cooking the chili, which improved the color and flavor. Here's a classic cowboy chili recipe that Lady Bird Johnson used to give out.

MAKES 12 CUPS

Sauté the meat, onion, and garlic in a large skillet over medium-high heat and cook until lightly colored. Add the oregano, cumin, chili powder, tomatoes, hot sauce, and 2 cups hot water. Bring to a boil, lower the heat, and simmer for about 1 hour. Skim off the fat while cooking. Salt to taste.

PUCHERO

Though our imaginations are drawn to chili con carne and combination plates, that certainly wasn't all that the chili queens served. Old-fashioned Mexican soups like this one were also a common offering. Pucheros are also found in the Canary Islands, where they often include fruit and other sweet items.

SERVES 8 OR MORE

Combine 4 quarts cold water, the soup bones, and garlic in a large soup kettle. Bring to a boil, reduce the heat, and simmer for 1 hour. Remove any scum that may rise to the surface. Remove the soup bones. Add the vegetables and salt and simmer until everything is tender, 30 to 45 minutes, adding water to maintain a constant level. Serve in soup bowls.

Put the garnishes on a plate and pass around at the table so soup eaters can garnish their own bowls.

For the garnish

$^{1}/_{4}$ cup minced fresh cilantro

$^{1}/_{4}$ cup chopped onion

$^{1}/_{4}$ cup chopped jalapeño chile

1 lime, quartered

---

3 pounds soup bones

6 garlic cloves, minced

One 15-ounce can chickpeas, drained

1 acorn or butternut squash, peeled, seeded, and cut into 1-inch cubes

2 ears corn, cut into 2-inch rounds

3 carrots, peeled and cut into 1-inch pieces (about 1 cup)

$^{1}/_{2}$ head cabbage, quartered

2 jalapeño chiles, chopped

2 celery stalks, cut into 1-inch pieces (about 1 cup)

2 sweet potatoes, cut into 1-inch cubes (about 2 cups)

2 Mexican green squash, cut into $^{1}/_{2}$-inch slices (about 1 cup); zucchini may be substituted

1 small onion, quartered

1 plantain *(platano macho)* (about 7 ounces), peeled and cut into 1-inch slices

1 cup fresh string beans cut into 1-inch pieces

2 tablespoons salt

*Cowboy dishing
chili, Marfa, 1939*

CHILI QUEEN ENCHILADAS

For the sauce
1 tablespoon lard or vegetable oil

1 cup chopped onions

2 cups Chile Puree (page 50)

1 teaspoon salt

^{1}/$_2$ teaspoon dried Mexican oregano

For the enchiladas
Oil for frying (about 1 tablespoon)

12 corn tortillas

^{1}/$_2$ cup crumbled Mexican white cheese, such as *queso fresco*

^{1}/$_2$ cup chopped onions

We barely recognize the original version of the enchilada today—a tortilla dipped in chile sauce and folded over on a plate with a garnish of cheese and onions. That's the way the chile queens served them.

MAKES 12 ENCHILADAS TO SERVE 4

Melt the lard in a skillet over high heat and sauté the onions until soft, 3 to 5 minutes. Add the chile puree and stir for a few minutes, blending well. Add the salt and oregano and 1 cup water. Bring to a boil, reduce the heat, and simmer for 5 minutes. Reserve in the skillet.

In another small skillet over high heat, pour enough oil to cover the bottom. Using tongs, quickly fry each tortilla for about 30 seconds on each side. Dip the fried tortilla into the chile sauce and immediately transfer to a plate. Fold the chilied tortilla in half. Repeat until each plate has 3 folded tortillas. Top with crumbled cheese and chopped onions. Serve immediately.

In an effort to comply with sanitary regulations, the Chili Queens were moved to screened tents in Haymarket Plaza, shortly before they were outlawed in the late 1930s.

Sam Huttleston's Chili

The once common "chili joint" has all but disappeared from the American restaurant scene. According to Bill Bridges, author of The Great American Chili Book, *the greatest of the Texas chili joints was Lang's in Dallas. There were actually two chili joints called Lang's, owned by brothers. "When my dad reminisced about Lang's, I swear a tear came to his eye," says Bridges. The meat shortages of World War II put Lang's and other chili joints out of business. According to Bridges, this recipe, from a Texas real estate man named Sam Huttleston, is the closest anybody has ever come to recreating Lang's chili.*

SERVES 6

Toast the cumin seeds in a skillet. Using a bean masher or a smaller pan, crush the seeds coarsely and reserve in a dish.

Heat the oil in the same skillet over medium high-heat and sauté the onion and garlic until the onion is soft, 3 to 5 minutes. Sear the meat with the onion and garlic until the pink color is gone.

Put the meat mixture in a stewpot over medium heat. Add the reserved cumin seeds, paprika, and chili powder, stirring to mix well, and add enough water to barely cover. Salt to taste. Simmer for 1 to 2 hours, adding water as necessary to maintain a thick but liquid consistency.

Brown the flour in a dry skillet by stirring for a few minutes over medium-high heat. When the meat is tender, make a slurry by adding water to the browned flour and stir it into the meat. Continue cooking for 10 minutes or until the chili is the desired thickness.

2 tablespoons whole cumin seeds

1 tablespoon vegetable oil

1 large onion, diced

3 garlic cloves, minced

3 1/2 pounds chuck, cut into 1/4-inch dice

2 tablespoons paprika

6 tablespoons chili powder

Salt

2 tablespoons flour

TRUCK STOP CHILI

1/4 pound bacon

3 pounds trimmed
beef brisket, cut into
1/4-inch cubes

1 pound onions,
chopped

1 1/2 tablespoons
ground cumin

3 1/2 tablespoons chili
powder

2 teaspoons paprika

1 teaspoon dried
Mexican oregano

1 teaspoon ground
black pepper

1/2 teaspoon dried
thyme

1/2 teaspoon salt

4 large garlic cloves,
minced

One 13.75-ounce can
beef broth

One 28-ounce can
plum tomatoes in
puree

2 dried chipotle chiles

Here's a more elaborate diner-style chili made with bacon and chipotles. It tastes great all by itself, over tamales, with a side order of beans, or as an enchilada sauce for Truck Stop Enchiladas (page 61).

MAKES 9 TO 10 CUPS

Cook the bacon in a large skillet until crisp. Remove the bacon and reserve. Over high heat, brown the beef in the bacon drippings left in the skillet and set the meat aside. Over medium heat, sauté the onions in the remaining drippings for 8 to 10 minutes, until lightly browned.

Toast the cumin in a small skillet over medium heat, stirring constantly for 1 minute or until fragrant.

Add the toasted cumin, chili powder, paprika, oregano, black pepper, thyme, salt, and garlic to the cooked onions and sauté for 1 minute. Crumble in the bacon, add the beef broth, 1 cup water, tomatoes, chiles, and the beef. Bring to a boil, reduce the heat, cover partially, and simmer for 3 hours or until the meat is very tender, adding water as needed to maintain the desired consistency.

TRUCK STOP ENCHILADAS

Margie Alexander is a modern-day chili queen. She's spent fifteen years as a waitress at the Texas Grill, an old-fashioned roadside diner on Highway 90A in Rosenberg. There she tempts hungry truck drivers with chili-slathered enchiladas like these, stuffed with Cheddar and sprinkled with raw onions.

MAKES 24 ENCHILADAS

Preheat the oven to 400°F. Heat the oil in a small skillet over medium heat. Dip each tortilla in the oil. Then place the tortilla in a Pyrex baking pan and put $1/4$ cup of the cheese, $1/4$ cup of the chili, and a tablespoon of the onions across the middle. Roll up the tortilla and place seam side down in the Pyrex pan. Continue filling and rolling the tortillas until the pan is full. (You will need about three pans.) Pour $1/2$ cup chili on top of the enchiladas. Sprinkle generously with cheese and bake until the cheese on top begins to bubble, about 10 minutes.

Remove from the oven, top with the remaining chopped onions, and serve immediately.

$1/2$ cup vegetable oil

24 corn tortillas (see page 35)

2 pounds Cheddar or American cheese, grated

Truck Stop Chili (page 60)

2 large onions, chopped

Margie Alexander

CHAPTER 4

EARLY COMBINATION PLATES

THE ORIGINAL MEXICAN RESTAURANT

A modern-day combination plate at Johnny's Mexican Restaurant in San Antonio

THE ROOSEVELT SPECIAL AT THE ORIGINAL

Mexican Restaurant in Fort Worth consists of one beef taco, one bean chalupa, and an enchilada with a fried egg on top. That, the waiter tells me, is what Franklin Delano Roosevelt ordered when he visited the restaurant in 1936. If it was good enough for FDR, I tell him, it's good enough for me.

I suspect the taco shell was fried fresh in FDR's day, but the taco in my Roosevelt Special comes on a pre-formed shell. The bean chalupa is pretty good, though. And the combination of fried egg, cheese enchilada, and chili con carne is sensational. And I get to wash it down with a frozen margarita, a pleasure FDR missed out on.

Elliot Roosevelt, FDR's son, lived in Benbrook just outside Fort Worth. When his famous father came to visit, the younger Roosevelt took him to Fort Worth's favorite Mexican restaurant. Founded in 1926 by the Dineda family of Waco, the Original catered to Fort Worth's elite. Newspaper publisher Amon Carter, the city's prime mover and shaker, was among the crowd who hung out here.

The Original Mexican Restaurant on Camp Bowie Boulevard in Fort Worth is not connected to the Original Mexican Restaurant of Galveston, which opened in 1913, or the now defunct Original Mexican Restaurant of Houston, which opened in 1907, or any of the other "Original" Mexican restaurants around the state. Rather, all of them were copies of the original Original—the granddaddy of the genre, the Original Mexican Restaurant of San Antonio.

That first "Original Mexican Restaurant" opened at 117 Losoya Street in 1900, according to the story that appeared in the San

Otis M. Farnsworth

Antonio *Express* on May 15, 1915. The headline read: WHERE MEXICAN COOKING HAS BEEN MADE FAMOUS: A SAN ANTONIO RESTAURANT KNOWN ALL OVER THE COUNTRY.

According to the story, the restaurant was opened by a Chicagoan named Otis M. Farnsworth. The visiting Anglo got the idea for the venture after native San Antonians took him to a humble little eatery in the Mexican quarter.

Wrote the unidentified journalist: "At the little restaurant on the West Side where Mr. Farnsworth was escorted by friends, he noticed that a number of well dressed people were lined up on the sidewalk waiting their turn at one of the three small tables boasted by the café and the idea at once struck him that if the best class of people traveled to the other side of town and were willing to stand on the walk and wait their turn to be served that a thoroughly modern café serving Mexican dishes exclusively would prove a successful venture."

The Original Mexican restaurant was the first restaurant to be located along the San Antonio River in the area now known as the Riverwalk. The restaurant was so popular that it expanded into the adjoining properties at 117 and 119 Losoya. In 1915, the restaurant completed a roof garden and finished off a lower floor in the riverfront property.

With the exception of the cashier, every

employee of O. M. Farnsworth's restaurant was Mexican, according to the newspaper story, and the Mexican cooks were "the best possible to secure in the land below the Rio Grande." For the rest of the century, the "truly Mexican" decorations devised for the restaurant would be imitated by Texas-Mexican restaurants. Fresco and frieze work designed by artist Herbert Bernard depicted rural Mexicans in sombreros in a field of prickly pears with a San Antonio mission in the background.

Men were required to wear a jacket at Farnsworth's Original Mexican Restaurant, winter and summer, despite the fact that air conditioning had yet to be invented. That practice was abandoned when "sports shirts" came along in the early 1930s, remembers Farnsworth's son Alan, who ran the restaurant with his twin brother, Otis, after their father retired in 1942. When Otis Jr. died in 1961, Alan sold out.

"The Original Mexican Restaurant is believed to be the first in the United States to offer in Spanish a menu of authentic Mexican dishes and to be the originator of the Mexican plate that San Antonians still consider their signature dish today," wrote Ella K. Daggett Stumpf in the San Antonio *Express-News* in 1988.

Stumpf was referring to the "Regular Supper," which consisted of tamales, frijoles, chili con carne, enchiladas, tortillas de maís, sopa de arroz (Spanish rice) and café. When the restaurant opened in 1900, the price

was fifteen cents. By World War I it had reached thirty-five cents. At the outbreak of World War II, the regular supper went for forty-five cents.

Was the Original's "Regular Supper" the first Tex-Mex combination plate? Maybe, but the Original certainly wasn't the first Mexican eatery in Texas; the fondas, home kitchens, and chili stands on the West Side of San Antonio are more worthy candidates for that claim. But the Original lived on long after the fondas disappeared.

In 1910, when the reforms of the Progressive era brought about the first health inspections and rules for safe food handling, hole-in-the-wall restaurants and street vendors began to die out. Permanent Mexican restaurants with more hygienic facilities took their place. For some fifty years, the Original reigned as the oldest Mexican restaurant in San Antonio.

Farnsworth's Original was the most profitable Mexican restaurant of its day. It was a bold new concept in marketing, a Mexican restaurant created by an Anglo for an audience of fellow Anglos. The Original Mexican Restaurant approached Texas biculturalism from the American side of the equation. It was a restaurant that made it easier for Anglos to feel as if they were experiencing Mexican culture.

Packaging the colorful Mexican culture of Texas and marketing it to a mainstream audience was an idea that dawned on many people at about the same

The menu of the Original Mexican Restaurant

REGULAR SUPPER, 45c
Consists of

Tamales		Frijoles
Chile con Carne		Tortillas de Maiz
Enchilada		Sopa de Arroz
	Café	

SPECIAL SUPPER, 75c
Chile con Queso

Chile con Carne	Tamales	Sopa de Arroz
Frijoles	Enchilada	Chile Relleno
	Dulce	Café

SPECIAL SUPPER, $1.25
Chile con Queso
Ensalada de Aguacate

Chile con Carne		Sopa de Arroz
	Frijoles	Tamales
Táco		Chile Relleno
	Enchilada	
	Dulce	Café
	Té	

SHORT ORDERS

Chile con Carne	15	Chiles Rellenos	25
Frijoles	10	Mole Poblano	
Frijoles con Tortillas	15	Pollo con Arroz	
Sopa de Arroz	10	Chile con Queso	25
Sopa de Arroz con Tortillas	15	Pollo con Calabaza	
		Guajolote	
Tamales	20	Albondigas de Arroz	
Tamales con Salsa	25	Fritoque	25
Enchiladas	25	Pescado	
Enchiladas con Huevos	35	Ensalada de Aguacate	25
Huevos con Salsa	25	Té	05
Huevos Rancheros	25	Leche	06
Tácos	25	Café	05
Tortillas de Maiz	05	Chocolate	10
Chalupas	25		

"All prices listed are our ceiling prices or below. By Office of Price Administration regulation, our ceilings are based on our highest prices from April 4, 1943 to April 10, 1943. Records of these prices are available for your inspection."

time. The San Antonio chili stand at the Texas Exhibit of the Columbian Exposition in Chicago in 1893 had created such a sensation that consumers across the country were clamoring for "Mexican food" and in particular, chili con carne. Several businessmen set out to make their fortune on San Antonio–style Mexican food. Their various efforts proved synergistic.

In 1893, in the village of New Braunfels, near San Antonio, a German immigrant named William Gebhardt was operating a café joined to a bar called Miller's Saloon. Chili con carne was his most popular item. He relied on dried chiles that came from the far-off San Luis Potosi region of Mexico, as did the San Antonio chili stands. These were available during a limited season after the harvest, so a restaurant owner had to buy and store a year's supply of chiles. Gebhardt set out to powder ancho chiles and bottle them so they could be made available year-round.

He was probably inspired by Hungarian paprika powder, which had been used to season "paprika gravy" in Germany and Central Europe since the sixteenth century. The Hungarian processing method had evolved from hand grinding to watermills in the early 1800s. In 1859, the Palfy brothers of Szeged invented a machine that turned dried pepper pods into a fine powder.

But paprika is a generic product; Gebhardt hit on the idea of a marketing a spice mix that would remain proprietary. Legend has it that

Gebhardt first ground chiles in a meat grinder and then dried them in an oven. He ground the pulverized chile peppers, cumin seeds, oregano, and black pepper in an old hammer mill, feeding a little of this and a little of that into the contraption until he was satisfied with the flavor. What came out was put

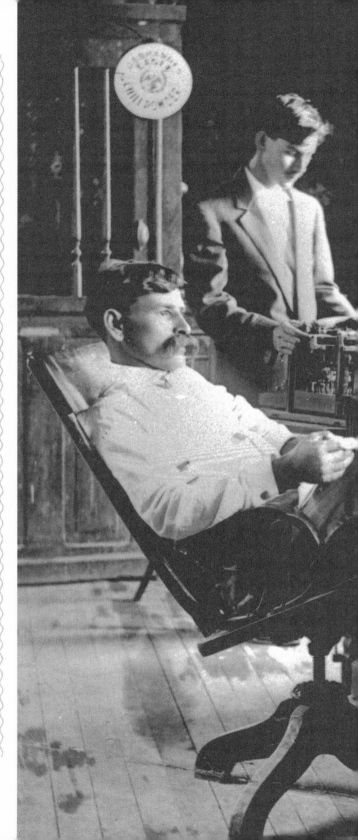

*William Gehbardt seated
at his rolltop desk*

one teaspoonful of *Gebhardt's Eagle Chili Powder*; bake from one hour to one hour and a half, basting occasionally. May be served hot or cold.

Alvóndigas Mexicanas—*Mexican Meat Balls*

Take equal parts of boiled beef and pork, say one pound; chop fine; add salt, a small piece of soaked bread, one egg well beaten and one teaspoonful of *Gebhardt's Eagle Chili Powder*; mix thoroughly and make into balls, putting in each a piece of hard-boiled egg; in a dish of hot lard or butter put five or six crushed tomatoes, a little chopped onion, broth, salt, and *Gebhardt's Eagle Chili Powder*; let boil a few moments and then put in the balls; when the meat is cooked it is ready for serving.

Tajadas de Rés y Ostras—*Beefsteak and Oysters*

Broil a very thick steak fifteen minutes. Put some oysters in a hot pan without any broth, stir over the fire briskly a few minutes, salt the steak and sprinkle with *Gebhardt's Eagle Chili Powder* (not too strong), then cover the steak with the oysters; bake in hot oven fifteen minutes. Remove the platter, keeping the oysters on top of the steak.

Chorizo Con Chili—*Hamburg Steak or Chili Sausage*

Grind the meat very coarse and add to each piece of meat one and one-half tablespoonful of *Gebhardt's Eagle Chili Powder*, one button of finely chopped garlic and salt. Then add a little high grade vinegar. Mix and let stand over night. Grind again the next morning, after which it can be either fried or broiled as desired.

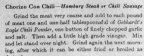

Guisado de Chili—*Chili Stew*

Cut two pounds of beef in slices, salt it and place in a pot in which you have heated two tablespoonful of lard; add one medium-sized chopped onion and stew about thirty minutes; now add one quart of warm water, one-half pint canned or two large mashed tomatoes, four sliced Irish

10

potatoes and one tablespoonful of *Gebhardt's Eagle Chili Powder*, and cook slowly until done.

Picadillo—*Mexican Hash*

Boil one-half pound of meat and chop fine as for hash, then take one tomato and one or two buttons of garlic and chop fine. Put tomato and garlic in a frying-pan, let cook for a few minutes, then add the meat and one-half teaspoonful of *Gebhardt's Eagle Chili Powder* and one onion cut fine, stirring well, and salt and pepper to suit taste. Then add broth in which meat has been boiled and boil or steam for about twenty minutes.

Goulash Americano—*American Goulash*

Cut into small squares one pound of beef, add chopped tallow, salt and one tablespoonful of *Gebhardt's Eagle Chili Powder* and mix the whole. Now put into graniteware pot two tablespoonful of butter, melt, and when brown add four or five slices of bacon and two or three finely sliced onions; cover the pot and let fry until the onions and bacon commence to brown; then add the meat and let cook about ten minutes, stirring frequently. Now add one pint of hot water and one button of chopped garlic and let cook until meat is tender. Always keep the pot covered as close as possible.

Goulash—

Put in a saucepan a large lump of butter, put on a quick fire, and when butter boils add two or three onions and three or four slices of bacon, cover the pan carefully and let the onions and bacon get nice and brown; then take veal and cut into small pieces; put into the pan, with a little salt and a generous portion of *Gebhardt's Eagle Chili Powder*, covering the saucepan tight. Do not put a drop of water in, but cook until tender and serve.

Higado Con Chili—*Liver with Chili*

Scrape liver fine, cut in small pieces with a sharp knife; cut up an onion fine, heat a little lard or butter in a thin frying-pan; put in liver with onions and keep stirring until done; sprinkle flour over liver; salt and

11

Early Gebhardt recipe booklet

in little-necked bottles and then packed for retail.

In 1896, Gebhardt opened a factory in San Antonio and became a traveling peddler selling his chili powder from the back of a wagon. He received U.S. trademark number 32,329 for Eagle Chili Powder in 1899. Today the company is owned by Beatrice Foods.

The first "Mexican cookbook" in the United States was published by Gebhardt in 1911. The recipes used Gebhardt chili powder in a wide range of applications. The pamphlet promised consumers "that real Mexican tang."

Gebhardt had plenty of competition across the state of Texas. In Fort Worth, DeWitt Clinton Pendery developed another brand of chili powder in the 1890s that he called "Chiltomaline." Pendery's company still sells spices in Fort Worth. In Austin, a chemist named T. Bailey Walker came up with yet another chili powder formula and formed the T. B. Walker Manufacturing Company in 1901.

Walker was one of the first to can chili con carne and tamales. The company, which would later be known as Walker's Austex, was located on Guadalupe Street in Austin between 4th and 5th Streets, on what is now known as Republic Square. Thanks to the aroma of chili con carne in the air, that part of Austin was called Chili Square in the early 1900s. Walker marketed the Mexene brand of chili powder with a label that showed the devil stirring a pot of chili.

Powdered chiles are rarely used in Mexican

cooking, but chili powder became central to the Tex-Mex cooking style. Bottled chili powder reduced the costs of making Mexican food in a restaurant. And it saved restaurant owners the trouble of buying, transporting, and storing Mexican chile peppers.

Chili powder standardized the flavor of Texas-Mexican food and forever set it apart from the fare south of the border. Since it already included cumin and other spices, chili powder made cooking chili con carne, the use for which it was originally intended, remarkably simple. But chili powder's unanticipated uses turned out to be its true destiny: you could add the stuff to just about anything edible and call the result Mexican food.

The adventurous Anglos who crossed over to San Antonio's West Side to eat Mexican food expected exotic chile-based sauces. But when Mexican restaurants began to market themselves to the Anglo mainstream, milder seasonings had to be devised for the tender palates of young children, old ladies, and faint-hearted visitors from out of town.

Chile-based sauces were too hot and too strange for most Anglos' tastes. Yet the enchilada sauce had to have some modicum of Mexican flavor or else its "authenticity" would be questioned. The answer to the culinary dilemma was a cultural crossover called "chili gravy." At its blandest, chili gravy resembles the flour-based brown gravy you might find on a Salisbury steak or a roast beef plate at a Southern cafeteria, but with a sprinkling of chili powder added. The taste of chili gravy explains Tex-Mex more eloquently than words ever will.

"Mexican-Americans don't eat chili gravy at home," Albert Villareal of San Antonio's

Albert Villareal

Casa Rio restaurant tells me. Many early Tex-Mex restaurants made chili gravy by thinning chili con carne with water and then adding roux as a thickener. Casa Rio's recipe was even simpler, Villareal explains: "You cooked flour in lard until it turned light brown, added chili powder and comino. Then you started adding chicken stock and whipping it with a whisk."

Villareal was born in 1931. At sixteen he started working as a busboy at the Anglo-owned Casa Rio and eventually worked his way up to head cook, a position he held for twenty-three years. Located on the Riverwalk, Casa Rio began the custom of setting up tables along the river for al fresco dining. They also began offering gondola rides on the river. Casa Rio's menu was fashioned after that of its neighbor, the Original Mexican Restaurant. Eventually Casa Rio would buy out the Original.

"In the beginning, customers would complain. They said the food was too hot," Villareal says. "So we had to change it. We stopped using serranos. The cooking was different back then. Refried beans were beans and lard, period. Mash the beans in hot lard, add a little flour to make them extra thick, that's it. If you put a spoonful on a towel, they wouldn't stick because of all the lard. Tamales were the same thing, if the dough sticks to your finger, there's not enough lard. It's not the same today. No more lard. We use vegetable oil. The lard tasted better.

"Way back, your enchilada tortillas were red," Villareal continues. "We dipped the tortillas in hot lard, which makes them a little crispy on the edges—nice with the gravy, cheese, and onions. The cheese was Wisconsin [Cheddar], but once in a while, the Wisconsin wouldn't melt and you had to use American.

SELECTED
MEXICAN
RECIPE

RARE RECIPES

AUSTEX

AUSTEX

Cooking . . . .
OUTH OF THE RIO GRANDE

Compliments
Walker's Austex Chile Co
AUSTIN · TEXAS

MEXICAN
for AMERI

GEBHARDT'S

Gebhardt's
EXICAN
OOKERY
MERICAN HOMES

INTERNATIONAL
RECIPES

With the
Magic
SEASONING

Good Cooks
Use to Impart
Zest and Flavor
to World-Famed
Dishes

MEXENE
CHILI POWDER
SEASONING

Magic
MEXENE
All-Purpose
SEASONING

MEXICAN
COOKERY
FOR
AMERICAN
HOMES

GEBHARDT
SAN ANTONIO

WALKER'S AUSTEX CHILE COMPANY
CHILE CON CARNE • TAMALES • MEXENE CHILE POWDER SEASONING

MEXENE • AUSTEX • MEXENE • AUSTEX

MEXENE ROOM

Tested and Approved
by the
Bureau of Foods, Sanitation and Health
Conducted by
GOOD HOUSEKEEPING MAGAZINE

PACKERS OF
QUALITY FOOD PRODUCTS
NATIONALLY ADVERTISED

NRA
CODE

CHILE
SPECIALISTS
OF AMERICA

The red enchiladas gave the otherwise brown Mexican plate some variety," Villareal says. "But then people started complaining about red dye number 3.

"The stuff on a Regular Plate wasn't what we ate at home," says Villareal. "There are two different kinds of Tex-Mex. We never had enchiladas or chili con carne growing up. We never had avocados either, except when the neighbor had some on his tree. My dad was from Monterrey. He liked to cook meat over charcoal. My dad would eat beef for breakfast, lunch, and dinner, just like in Monterrey. We had beef strips with tomatoes and onions on flour tortillas, and beans in broth.

"Mexican-Americans never ate at the Anglo Tex-Mex restaurants," says Villareal. There were Mexican restaurants where Mexicans ate, he tells me. "I remember when I was a little kid we went to the farmers' market in El Mercado, and there were food stands that sold tacos. You could get lengua with hot sauce, tripas, carnitas—my favorite was beans. At home, you can do anything you want. But at the restaurant you have to make it the way they expect it."

GEBHARDT'S AND THE ORIGINAL MEXICAN Restaurant helped put the "Tex" in Tex-Mex. They were also among the first to make a point of proclaiming their authenticity. There had never been any reason for the chili queens or the Tejano fondas on San Antonio's West Side to guarantee "genuine Mexican food." But after Anglos got into the business, it became mandatory.

Texas-Mexican restaurants forever after promised authenticity and delivered whatever their audience actually wanted. Today, the Tex-Mex combo plate seems hopelessly old-fashioned. But I like to eat one now and then to remind me of the evolution of Tex-Mex from its bland beginnings at the turn of the century to the hot and spicy version we favor today. It's American culture evolving before your very taste buds.

Homemade Chili Powder

5 whole ancho chile
pods (approximately
2 ounces), stemmed
and seeded

1 teaspoon dried
Mexican oregano

1/2 teaspoon garlic
powder

1/2 teaspoon ground
cumin

"We used to use Gebhardt's Chili Powder," says Albert Villareal of Casa Rio restaurant. "Now we grind our own." It's easy to make chili powder yourself, and when you do, you can add more or less ancho seeds to make it hotter or milder and adjust the cumin and garlic powder the way you like it, he says.

MAKES 1/4 CUP

Spread the chile pods out flat. Toast the chiles in a comal or cast-iron skillet over medium heat until they become aromatic, then remove and cool.

Cut the chiles into small strips with scissors. In a spice or coffee grinder, grind the strips in several batches until powdered. Combine the powdered chile, oregano, garlic powder, and cumin in a bowl. Grind the coarse powder in batches for an additional 2 minutes or until finely ground.

Store in an airtight container until ready to use.

Chili Gravy

1/4 cup lard or
vegetable oil

1/4 cup flour

1/2 teaspoon ground
black pepper

1 teaspoon salt

1 1/2 teaspoons
powdered garlic

2 teaspoons ground
cumin

1/2 teaspoon dried
Mexican oregano

2 tablespoons chili
powder

2 cups chicken broth
or water

The lifeblood of old-fashioned Tex-Mex, chili gravy is a cross between Anglo brown gravy and Mexican chile sauce. It was invented in Anglo-owned Mexican restaurants like the Original.

MAKES 2 CUPS

Heat the lard in a skillet over medium-high heat. Stir in the flour and continue stirring for 3 to 4 minutes, until it makes a light brown roux. Add all the dry ingredients and continue to cook for 1 minute, constantly stirring and blending the ingredients. Add the chicken broth, mixing and stirring until the sauce thickens.

Turn the heat to low and let the sauce simmer for 15 minutes. Add water to adjust the thickness.

ORIGINAL CHEESE ENCHILADAS

Dipping the tortillas in hot lard gives these old-fashioned enchiladas a rich distinctive flavor. If you are afraid that lard is bad for your health, please read the note on lard on page 11.

MAKES 8 ENCHILADAS TO SERVE 4

Preheat the oven to 450°F. Heat the lard in a small skillet over medium high heat for 3 minutes. Using tongs, place a tortilla in the hot fat. If the tortilla doesn't bubble immediately, the lard is not hot enough. Heat the tortilla for 30 seconds or until soft and lightly brown. Remove with tongs and allow to cool before handling.

Have the cheese, onions, chili gravy, and tortillas handy for assembly. Roll $1/4$ cup cheese and 1 tablespoon chopped onion in a tortilla. Place 2 rolled tortillas, seam side down, on an ovenproof plate with a high lip. Ladle $1/2$ cup chili gravy over the top. Sprinkle $1/4$ cup cheese over the tortillas. Repeat for all four plates. Bake in the oven for 10 minutes or until the sauce bubbles and the cheese is well melted. Remove from the oven and serve immediately. Garnish with the remaining chopped onions.

VARIATION

Enchilada Plate:
Spoon Refried Beans (page 27) and/or Mexican Rice (page 163) onto plates before placing in the oven.

Enchilada Tray:
Place all 8 tortillas in an ovenproof casserole and divide and garnish after baking.

$1/2$ cup lard or vegetable oil

8 corn tortillas (see page 35)

3 cups shredded Cheddar cheese

$1^1/2$ cups chopped onions

$1^1/2$ cups Chili Gravy (see page 74)

ORIGINAL ART

This group portrait of a private party held on New Year's Eve, 1925, provides a glimpse of the interior of the Original Mexican Restaurant. The murals on the upper walls were painted by the German artist Herbert Bernard. His depiction of Mexican peasants in sombreros would inspire the decorators of Mexican restaurants for decades to come. The uniformed men at the party are members of a philanthropic organization known as the Committee of the Christian Union.

Spanish Sauce

2 tablespoons butter

1 onion, finely chopped

1 green bell pepper, seeded, stemmed, and chopped

1 garlic clove, minced

2 tablespoons flour

¹/₂ teaspoon salt

¹/₂ teaspoon chili powder

1¹/₂ cups chopped ripe, seeded tomatoes

1 cup meat stock or water

Tex-Mex Spanish sauce is a tomato sauce with onions and a touch of chili powder added. It is lighter than chili gravy. This recipe comes from a 1932 Gebhardt's pamphlet.

MAKES 3 CUPS

Melt the butter in a saucepan over medium heat. Add the onion, bell pepper, and garlic and sauté until soft. Add the flour, salt, chili powder, tomatoes, and meat stock. Reduce the heat and simmer for 10 minutes or more, stirring frequently until the softened tomatoes melt into the sauce.

Variation

Huevos con Salsa:
Spoon 3 tablespoons Spanish sauce over 2 scrambled eggs.

Chalupa:
On a flat fried tortilla, spread refried beans and top with chopped tomatoes, chopped lettuce, and 3 tablespoons Spanish sauce.

Pollo con Arroz

Chicken cooked with rice is an old-time comfort food in many cultures. The Mexican version uses a whole fresh-killed chicken. The modern Tex-Mex version is often made with a package of economical chicken thighs.

SERVES 4 TO 6

Rinse the chicken and allow to dry. Heat the oil in a large sauté pan over medium-high heat and brown the chicken for 5 minutes or until nicely colored, then remove it and set aside. Add the rice, onion, and garlic, stirring constantly until the onion is soft and the rice has changed color, about 5 minutes. Stir in the tomato and 2^1/2 cups boiling water, and add salt and pepper. Return the chicken to the pan. Cover and simmer for 30 minutes or until the rice and chicken are done.

2^1/2- to 3-pound chicken, cut up, or chicken thighs

^{1}/4 cup vegetable oil

1 cup raw rice

^{1}/2 onion, chopped

1 garlic clove, minced

^{1}/4 cup tomato puree

1^1/2 teaspoons salt

1^1/2 teaspoons pepper

Fritoque

Pronounced free-TOKE-ay, this dish is found on the World War II–era menu of the Original Mexican Restaurant in San Antonio. The recipe is adapted from The Texas Cookbook, *published in 1949 by Arthur and Bobbie Coleman. It tastes like a bowl of beans with crushed nachos in it. If you don't have dried red chiles you can use pickled jalapeño slices.*

SERVES 2

Mix the beans, tostadas, and chiles. Place the mixture in individual baking dishes and divide the cheese evenly, sprinkling over each. Place in a hot oven just long enough to melt the cheese.

2 cups cooked Frijoles (page 25)

1 cup broken tortilla chips (tostadas)

2 small dried red chiles (see page 10), crushed, or jalapeño slices, to taste

^{1}/2 cup grated Cheddar or American cheese

Variation

Chiltoque:
Substitute 2 cups chili con carne for the frijoles.

Hot Tamales!

Mexican, Tejano, and Southern-Style

Workers on the tamale
assembly line at the Gebhardt
Chili Powder Company

ON A SUNNY SUNDAY AFTERNOON IN EARLY November I pulled up to a big brick house on 9th Street in Taylor, Texas. It was hard to find a place to park; the cars and trucks of the Lopez family were overflowing the driveway and the street. The Lopez clan had invited me to join them for their annual Christmas tamalada. November is a little early for Christmas, but not for the Christmas tamalada.

A tamalada is a tamale-making party, usually a family get-together when everyone pitches in to make a big batch for the holidays. When I arrived at 8 A.M., every flat surface in the kitchen was spread with corn husks. While I watched, the Lopez family assembly line cranked out a hundred dozen tamales in five hours.

"On Christmas morning, after the presents are opened, we'll all gather here again to eat menudo [tripe stew], buñelos [cinnamon pastries], and tamales," said Steve Lopez, the leader of the assembly line. "It's a family thing, we come together to make tamales, and we come together again to eat them."

"We love to eat tamales after midnight mass," said his sister-in-law Cruz Lopez.

Black and Mexican cotton pickers in Mississippi

Brother-in-law Ygnacio Dominguez comes down to Taylor every year from Grapevine, Texas, a three-hour drive, to help with the tamale-making.

"I'll be back to help with the eating too," he says with a smile as he smears masa on a corn husk. Ygnacio is teaching one of the kids how to spread the masa properly. He nods at the little one fumbling with the spoon. "Preserving our culture, that's what this is all about."

As the tamales come out of the steamer, we all stop to test the flavor. They are creamy with pork fat and steaming hot; the taste is a little like mashed potatoes combined half and half with butter, stuffed with a little meat, and covered with gravy.

Tamales are one of the oldest foods of Mesoamerica; Spanish observers in the era of Columbus found the natives eating tamales made with seafood and meat dipped in chile pepper sauces. Of course, the ancient recipes changed with the introduction of European livestock.

Now tamales are most commonly made with pork and lard. The Lopez family uses easy-to-handle pork butts, but Tex-Mex restaurants more often use a pig's head, which is boiled until the meat and lard cook away. It's a very inexpensive and efficient way to make tamales. The broth is used to wet the masa, and the lard is whipped into the mixture until it is fluffy. Then the masa is spread on a corn

░▒▓ (decorative border pattern) ▓▒░

TEJANOS VS. MEXICANS

The life of Juan N. Seguín illustrates the bicultural dilemma that Tejanos have faced throughout their history. A member of a long-established Tejano family, his father was an *alcalde* (civil official) of San Antonio and an ally of Stephen F. Austin. When war with Mexico was declared, Seguín raised a company of sixty-five Tejanos and fought in the Battle of Gonzales in 1835, after which Austin granted him a captain's commission. Seguín and his Tejano unit eventually joined up with Sam Houston's army to defeat the Mexicans at the Battle of San Jacinto. Seguín became the only Tejano in the Senate

Juan Seguín

of the Republic. Despite his poor English, he was the chairman of the Committee on Military Affairs. Upon his return to San Antonio, he was elected mayor. But hostilities between Anglos and Mexican-Texans began to erupt as the Anglos questioned the loyalties of anybody with a Spanish surname. Fearing for his safety, Seguín resigned as mayor in 1842 and crossed the border into Mexico with his family.

Seguín retired in Nuevo Laredo, where he died in 1890. His remains were returned to Texas in 1974 and buried in Seguín, the town named in his honor.

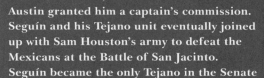

shuck, a little of the meat is placed in the middle, and the tamale is rolled up and steamed.

But tamales also took on other forms north of the Rio Grande. Masa harina, which is made from corn treated with lime, wasn't as easy to find as plain cornmeal. So in Texas, tamales made of cornmeal became common. Parchment paper or wax paper often replaced the less convenient dried corn husks. The tamales common in Louisiana and Mississippi are most often made with cornmeal, cooked mush, or corn bread. To this day, most of the tamales canned in Texas are made with cornmeal.

After Texas achieved its independence, Tejano cooking and Mexican cooking grew further apart. Spanish law had forbidden the Texas colonists from trading with the French in Louisiana or with the American states. So before independence, most of the items in the Tejano pantry were either local or shipped from Mexico.

By 1845, Texas had joined the Union, and American staples began to outnumber the Mexican ones. But by that time the Texians, as Anglo-Texans called themselves, had already developed a taste for tamales, chiles, frijoles, and the rest of the Tejano repertoire.

In 1861, Texas joined the Confederacy. Tejanos fought on both sides in the Civil War, but most of the Tejanos who chose to fight joined the Confederate forces. The most famous Tejano Confederate troop—the 33rd Texas Cavalry, commanded by Colonel Santo Benavides—fought several battles along the border against Union-supported Mexican forces. The 33rd was ill-equipped and had to find its own rations in the desolate region of South Texas that it patrolled. So it can be said with certainty that throughout the Civil War,

San Antonio resident Maria Moreno loads up on corn shucks to get ready for holiday tamale-making, 1948.

at least one Confederate regiment ate nothing but Tex-Mex.

Corn was the main ration of the Confederate soldier, usually in the form of corn bread or corn cakes, which were known as corn pone. Perhaps Tejano Confederate soldiers introduced tamales to their Southern comrades, since tamales made from cornmeal became well known all across the South after the Civil War. The tamale-making tradition was certainly practiced by itinerant Mexican farm workers who took over much of the cotton picking after slavery ended. "Hot tamales" became hugely popular in the African-American communities of Louisiana and Mississippi.

Waves of Mexican immigrants fleeing the Mexican Revolution after 1910 made money selling tamales and chili gravy from roving carts. The tamale vendors spread from San Antonio to cities as far away as Chicago and New Orleans. Tamales became the most common street food in Texas and eventually in much of the South and Midwest as well.

A common arrangement had the women of a Mexican-Texan household up early in the morning to make tamales. Then the man of the house would set off with the well-stocked cart to sell the tamales in the streets. Mr. and Mrs. Delfino Martinez were one such couple. Martinez left Mexico to avoid conscription in Pancho Villa's army around the turn of the century and ended up in Austin. He sold his wife's tamales on Congress Avenue until 1925, when the pair opened the first Tex-Mex restaurant in Austin, El Original, just off Congress Avenue. Their son, Matt Martinez, founded Matt's El Rancho, Austin's quintessential Tex-Mex restaurant. Today, the fourth generation of the Martinez family is still in the business of selling Tex-Mex food.

The street tamales of the early 1900s were generally made with masa and lots of lard, with very little meat inside. Their chili gravy was a thin sauce often made of chili powder mixed with the pork broth. Tortillas and enchiladas, which were simply fresh tortillas

LOS CONFEDERATOS TEJANOS

Brothers Refugio and Cristóbal Benavides both became captains in The Benavides Regiment, as the 33rd Texas Cavalry was known. The Benavides were widely heralded as heroes throughout the Lone Star State. Another brother, Colonel Santos Benavides (not shown), was the highest ranking Tejano in the Confederate Army. He commanded the 33rd Texas Cavalry, which was never defeated in battle. The regiment invaded northern Mexico in retaliation for Unionist-inspired guerilla raids into Texas and drove off a Union force that attacked Laredo in 1864.

(left to right): Refugio Benavides, Atanacio Vidaurri, Cristóbal Benavides, and Juan Z. Leyendecker, officers of the Benavides Texas Cavalry, 33rd Texas, CSA

◢◣◢◣◢◣◢◣◢◣◢◣◢◣◢◣◢◣◢◣◢◣◢◣

GET 'EM WHILE THEY'RE HOT!

Like the Italian fruit sellers of New York and the cockle sellers of London, many tamale sellers became famous for their distinctive cries. Several famous popular songs are based on hot tamale men's slogans, including Robert Johnson's "Hot Tamales," which included the lyric: "Hot tamales and they're red hot, yes she got 'em for sale!"

A few of the cries once heard on city streets in Texas include: "Hot tamales and enchilollies, get 'em while they're hot!

"Hot tamales, floatin' in gravy, suit your taste and I don't mean maybe!"

A two-part cry began: "Hot tamales, two to a shuck." When the shuck proved to contain only one tamale, the vendor sang out: "One fell out and the other one stuck."

◸◹◸◹◸◹◸◹◸◹◸◹◸◹◸◹◸◹◸◹◸◹

dipped in chili gravy, were also available from the same vendors. In Houston and East Texas as well as other Southern cities, blacks began to adopt the Mexican tamale-vending business, creating their own African-American style tamales in the process.

Texans have a special fondness for tamales, and if you know where to look, you can still find homemade tamales in most Texas towns. You might see them wrapped in aluminum foil on the counter of a convenience store, in a Mexican bakery, or along the side of the road. There's an enterprising tamale vendor in Houston who goes from bar to bar selling a dozen for five dollars. You can even see signs advertising homemade tamales in the front yards of private homes, especially around Christmas time. But compared to a hundred years ago, when tamales were everywhere, today's tamale sellers are few and far between.

One of the last of the old-time tamale men in Texas was named Walter Berryhill, who sold tamales in Houston's upscale River Oaks neighborhood in the early 1960s. Every good tamale salesman had a gimmick; Berryhill's was that he dressed in a white jacket and top hat.

Like most African-American tamale vendors, Berryhill sold cornmeal tamales drenched in his own version of chili gravy. He rigged his pushcart with a propane burner in order to comply with health department temperature regulations and so was able to keep selling tamales long after most tamale men had disappeared. When Berryhill retired in the mid-1960s, a lawyer named Bob Tarrant bought his recipe and his pushcart, mainly because he liked the tamales. Decades later, Tarrant met Chuck Bulnes, who was running a business called Texas Tamales and proposed that they open a restaurant with Berryhill's tamale recipe.

Berryhill's tamale cart is now chained to a pole at the corner of Westheimer and Revere in Houston in front of the restaurant called Berryhill's Tamales. The tiny restaurant has a bar and a couple of bar-height tables inside, plus a few more tables outdoors. They sell five kinds of tamales based on Walter Berryhill's recipes. The meat tamales taste good with the mild chile gravy poured over the top, but I suspect Walter Berryhill would have the same complaint about these tamales that I do. They don't have enough lard in them.

Berryhill's current owner, Jeff Anon, tells me that the restaurant substantially reduced the amount of lard when adapting Berryhill's original recipe. "Lard gives tamales a gelatinous sort of texture," he admits. But no matter how wonderful it makes the tamales taste, modern Americans loathe lard, so the recipe had to be compromised." The tamales aren't served in chili gravy anymore either.

"We put the chili gravy on the side because when people opened the tamale, they got it all over their clothes," Anon said. "But it's still Walter Berryhill's chili gravy."

Hot tamale vendor
at the Victoria train
station, late 1800s

A Christmas Tamalada

100 DOZEN

Masa

If you are making the full recipe you will need to divide the masa into batches or use a large commercial mixer.

1^{1}/$_{2}$ cups salt

^{1}/$_{2}$ cup garlic powder

2 cups chili powder

^{1}/$_{3}$ cup ground cumin

50 pounds prepared masa

1 tablespoon baking soda

Reserved broth from the pork roasts

9 pounds lard

Meat Filling

Steve Lopez makes the pork filling the night before the tamalada. Mixing the spices with the cooked pork as you grind it helps ensure an even blend.

70 pounds boneless pork butt (about 10 large roasts)

4^{1}/$_{2}$ cups chili powder

^{3}/$_{4}$ cup ground cumin

1 cup garlic powder

1^{1}/$_{4}$ cups salt

I carefully wrote down Steve Lopez's recipe, but the quantities are a little daunting. It takes a lot of pots to handle seventy pounds of pork butts or fifty pounds of masa. So here's Steve's recipe for a hundred dozen tamales and a scaled-down version for an easier to handle ten dozen.

Put the pork roasts in a large pot or pots and cover with water. Bring the water to a boil and then turn down to a simmer. Simmer the meat for 3 or 4 hours, until very tender. Shred the meat and grind in a meat grinder. Combine all the spices and sprinkle each batch of ground pork with spices. Mix well. Save the broth the pork was cooked in.

Combine the salt, garlic powder, chili powder, cumin, prepared masa, and baking soda in an electric mixer bowl. With the mixer on low, slowly add the pork broth to make a moist dough. Increase the mixer speed to medium and begin adding the lard spoonful by spoonful. Beat the mixture until the masa has a spongy light texture, at least 10 minutes. Drop a spoonful of masa into a glass filled with water. It should float. If it doesn't, add additional lard and re-test.

Making the Tamales

10 DOZEN   100 DOZEN

120 tamale wrappers   **1,200 tamale wrappers**

Soak the tamale wrappers (corn husks) overnight in water with a weighted plate on top. Or simmer the wrappers in hot water for 15 to 20 minutes and then let them stand a few hours until they are softened.

To make the tamales, spread 2 heaping tablespoons of masa in the middle of each wrapper. Put 1 heaping tablespoon of meat filling in the center of the square. Pick up the sides of the wrapper and bring them together so that the masa forms around the filling. Roll the loose ends together and fold the bottom over. If the wrapper is too small, roll the tamale in an additional husk.

Stand the tamales upright, sealed side down, in the steamer section of a steamer pot and steam for 1 to 1¹/₂ hours, replenishing the water as necessary. (Put a coin in the bottom of the pot. If you can't hear the coin rattling, it's time to add more water.) Serve hot out of the steamer with coffee, hot chocolate, or cold beer.

To store the tamales, freeze them uncooked.

10 DOZEN

Masa

2¹/₂ tablespoons salt

2 teaspoons garlic powder

3 tablespoons chili powder

1¹/₂ teaspoons ground cumin

5 pounds prepared masa

¹/₄ teaspoon baking soda

Reserved broth from the pork roasts

1 pound lard

Meat Filling

7 pounds boneless pork butt

7 tablespoons chili powder

1 tablespoon ground cumin

1¹/₂ tablespoons garlic powder

2 tablespoons salt

STEWED CHICKEN

3 pounds chicken
breasts with skin and
bone

1 onion, quartered

4 garlic cloves

2 tablespoons
powdered chicken
bouillon

6 whole black
peppercorns

1 bay leaf

1 teaspoon ground
cumin

Salt

You can use this filling for the chicken tamales, chicken enchiladas, and chicken tacos in this book. Save the broth for making masa or enchilada sauce. It will keep refrigerated for a week.

MAKES ENOUGH STUFFNG FOR 24 TAMALES

Bring 8 cups water to boil in a large pot. Add the chicken and all the remaining ingredients. Reduce the heat to medium and simmer for 40 minutes. Taste the broth for seasoning. Remove from the heat and allow the chicken to cool in the broth. Remove the chicken and shred, discarding the bones and skin. Strain the chicken broth and reserve for another use.

HOMEMADE LARD

5 pounds (or more)
pork fat

The idea here is pretty simple. You melt pork fat without browning it, then strain it to remove the bits of meat, called cracklins. Many people melt lard on the stove, but the cracklins tend to sizzle and spit, causing nasty burns. The slow oven method is safer and easier. Cracklins are delicious in a taco or a salad. Ask your butcher for pork fat for rendering lard; it should be nearly meatless.

MAKES 4³/4 POUNDS LARD AND 1 CUP CRACKLINS

Preheat the oven to 200°F. Cut the fat into 1-inch cubes. Cut away any large pieces of meat and reserve for another use. Spread the fat cubes in a roaster pan and place in the oven for 2 to 3 hours, until completely melted. Remove the pan from the oven—be careful not to splash yourself—and pour the melted fat through a colander lined with cheesecloth. Put the fat into clean jars and allow to cool, then store in the freezer until ready for use. Lard will keep for several months frozen.

MEXICAN-STYLE TAMALES

Here's a recipe for enough masa to make a batch of twenty-four tamales. You can fill them with anything you like. Just use a broth appropriate to the filling. If you know where to get fresh masa and you want to substitute it for the masa harina, skip ahead to the step where the lard is added.

MAKES 24 TAMALES

Combine the salt, masa harina, and baking powder in the bowl of an electric mixer. With the mixer on low, slowly add the broth and make a moist dough (if using fresh masa, add the baking powder and salt, but don't add any broth or water). Increase the mixer speed to medium and begin adding the lard spoonful by spoonful. Beat the mixture at least 10 minutes, adding air in the process, until the masa has a spongy light texture. Drop a spoonful of masa into a glass filled with water. It should float. If it doesn't, add additional lard and re-test.

To make the tamales
Follow the instructions on page 89 in the Tamalada recipe for soaking the husks, spreading the masa, filling them, and steaming the tamales.

VARIATIONS

Chicken Tamales with Salsa Verde:
Spoon 2 tablespoons Stewed Chicken (page 90) into the masa on each tamale and top with 2 teaspoons of the Salsa Verde (page 94) before folding and steaming.

Pork and Red Chile Tamales:
Spoon 3 tablespoons Chile Colorado con Puerco (page 113) into the masa on each tamale before folding and steaming.

1¹/2 teaspoons salt

4 cups dried masa harina or one pound fresh masa

1 teaspoon baking powder

3¹/2 cups warm broth or water

1 cup lard, at room temperature

24 corn husks

On a campaign stop at the Alamo in 1976, President Gerald Ford posed for photographers while eating a tamale. Unfortunately, the president didn't realize you are supposed to remove the corn shuck first.

SALSA VERDE

24 tomatillos, husks
removed

6 serrano chiles,
stemmed and seeded

1/2 medium onion

4 garlic cloves

Salt

Made with tomatillos instead of tomatoes, this sauce has a refreshing tartness. It makes a great enchilada sauce and is also used in Chicken Tamales with Salsa Verde (page 91). Refrigerated, it's also a classic Tex-Mex table sauce.

MAKES ABOUT 3 CUPS

Boil the tomatillos, chiles, onion, and garlic in a large saucepan in enough water to cover for 15 minutes or until they are softened. Reserve a cup of the cooking water. Allow the cooked vegetables to cool, then puree in a blender until smooth. The sauce should be quite liquid; add a little of the cooking water if it is too thick. Salt to taste.

VARIATION

Green Table Sauce:
Chill in the refrigerator and add 2 tablespoons chopped fresh cilantro just before serving.

NOTE:
You can leave the seeds in the serranos for a much hotter sauce.

CORNMEAL TAMALES

As tamales spread across Texas and the rest of the South, they underwent some changes. Easy-to-find cornmeal replaced the Mexican lime-slaked masa and paper squares were often used to roll up the tamales instead of the traditional corn shucks. Anglo tamale-eaters preferred beef to the traditional pork, so beef tamales became common.

MAKES 36 TAMALES

Combine the ground beef, seasonings, yellow cornmeal, and tomato sauce in a large bowl and mix well. Make 36 balls of approximately 2 tablespoons of the mixture, or 1 1/2 ounces per ball. Roll each ball into a cigar shape about 5 inches long. Fill a 9 by 12-inch casserole or cake pan with the dredging mixture. Dredge the individual meat "cigars" in the cornmeal until well coated. Place each cornmeal-coated "cigar" in a piece of paper and roll up the paper around the filling. In a large steamer pot, lay two layers of tamales and steam for 1 hour, covered. Serve hot.

VARIATION

Mississippi Corn Bread Tamales:
Add 1/2 cup water and a teaspoon of salt to 10 cups corn bread crumbs and work into a paste. Cover the meat "cigars" with the paste individually instead of dredging. Proceed as directed.

3 pounds ground beef

1 1/2 teaspoons ground cumin

1 tablespoon garlic powder

1 1/2 teaspoons cayenne pepper

1 teaspoon ground black pepper

1 tablespoon salt

1 1/2 teaspoons onion powder

1/4 cup chili powder

4 tablespoons sugar

1/2 cup yellow cornmeal

Two 8-ounce cans tomato sauce

36 pieces parchment or wax paper cut into 5-inch squares

For dredging:
4 cups yellow cornmeal mixed with 2 teaspoons salt

Cornmeal Tamales Cooked in Chili Gravy

Three 8-ounce cans tomato sauce

1 tablespoon garlic powder

1 teaspoon cayenne pepper

1 tablespoon onion powder

3 tablespoons chili powder

1 tablespoon sugar

36 Cornmeal Tamales (page 95), uncooked

MAKES 36 TAMALES

Combine the tomato sauce, garlic powder, cayenne, onion powder, chili powder, and sugar in a bowl with 2 cups water and mix well. Layer the rolled tamales in a Dutch oven and cover with the sauce. Add additional water so that the tamales are covered by liquid. Bring to a boil over medium heat, then reduce to a simmer. Cover and cook for 1 1/2 hours, replenishing the water as necessary.

Serve the tamales in the sauce.

Lily Guerrero sells tamales at her roadside stand.

TAMALE PIE

Corn shucks are messy and many home cooks aren't very comfortable using lard anymore, so tamales aren't as common as they used to be. Instead, convenient casseroles like this tamale pie, made with packaged corn bread mix, have gained popularity with suburban homemakers. It's like one giant tamale made with corn bread on the bottom, corn bread on the top, and chili con carne in the middle.

SERVES 8

Preheat the oven to 350°F. Heat the oil in a large frying pan and brown the meat over medium-high heat. Stir in the onions, pepper, and chile and cook for 3 to 5 minutes, until limp. Add the tomato sauce, corn, chili powder, salt, cumin, garlic, and oregano. Simmer for about 10 minutes, stirring occasionally.

Meanwhile, prepare the corn bread mix according to the package instructions, adding a little extra milk to thin it to the consistency of pancake batter. Spread about half the batter in the bottom of a greased 9 by 12-inch baking pan. Gently spoon the meat mixture in evenly over the top. Spoon the remaining corn bread mix over the meat mixture. (Don't worry if it doesn't cover the meat completely.) Sprinkle olives and cayenne over the top.

Bake for 30 minutes. Remove from the oven and allow to cool for at least 15 minutes before slicing.

1/4 cup vegetable oil

2 pounds lean ground beef

2 cups chopped onions

1 green bell pepper, chopped

1 serrano chile, minced

One 8-ounce can tomato sauce

One 8-ounce can corn

1/4 cup chili powder

1 1/2 teaspoons salt

1 tablespoon ground cumin

1 tablespoon garlic powder

1 tablespoon dried Mexican oregano

2 packages corn bread/muffin mix (preferably Pioneer brand)

1 small can sliced black olives, drained

1/2 teaspoon cayenne pepper

CHAPTER 6

WEST TEXAS ENCHILADAS

THE OLD BORUNDA CAFÉ

Carolina Borunda at her wood-burning stove in the Old Borunda Café in Marfa

P

ANCHO BORUNDA, THE PROPRIETOR OF BORUNDA'S

Bar & Grill in Marfa, is standing there, stroking his long

white beard, waiting for me to say something. He has just

delivered an enchilada platter complete with rice, beans,

and a *chile relleno*. The enchiladas are red, and they're

stacked, with cheese and chopped raw onions liberally sprinkled in be-

tween the three tortilla layers. In fact, you can barely make out the tor-

tillas under all the cheese and red chile sauce.

Pancho traces the lineage of his enchilada recipe in a direct line to the Old Borunda Café, a legendary Marfa restaurant that opened in 1887 and closed in 1987. His new place, Borunda's Bar & Grill, is located right around the corner from where the Old Borunda Café once stood.

Pancho Borunda learned to cook under the tutelage of his aunt, Carolina Borunda, the matriarch of the Old Borunda Café. "She never wrote down any recipes. She told me to just sit and watch her cook," remembers Pancho. "Then she said, 'Let's see what you have learned.' So I cooked her a whole dinner."

"Did she like it?" I asked.

"Well, she didn't throw it out the window," he says with a chuckle. "But she said my enchilada sauce was too dry. I think I've fixed that, though."

"Where's the fried eggs?" I have to ask. I feel guilty bugging Pancho about it, but the Old Borunda's stacked red enchiladas were famously served with two sunny-side up eggs on top. The enchiladas in front of me are egg-naked.

Pancho Borunda

"A lot of people are watching their cholesterol now, so we only serve the eggs when somebody requests them," Pancho apologizes.

"Well, I'm requesting them," I announce. Pancho scoops up my plate and heads back to the kitchen. Lord knows I didn't drive eleven hours across the state of Texas to worry about my cholesterol. I came to the isolated hamlet of Marfa to learn about the Old Borunda Café's famous enchiladas.

Although we all use it as a noun, "enchiladas" is actually an adjective in Spanish. The real name of the dish is *tortillas enchiladas,* or "chilied tortillas," and it refers to the original method of preparation, which called for tortillas to be dipped in chile sauce and lightly fried. *Tortillas enchiladas* were called enchiladas for short, and now we only remember the nickname.

The earliest enchiladas, in Texas as in Mexico, were served in the street and usually consisted of nothing more than a tortilla dipped in chile sauce, sometimes sprinkled with cheese and chopped onions. In West Texas, as in New Mexico, a stack of these chili-dipped

The Old Borunda Café in Marfa

enchiladas with cheese and onions in between became the classic restaurant style.

In Mexican cafés and coffee shops, as in most Tex-Mex restaurants, the "enchilada plate" would eventually evolve into a dish that featured a couple of chilied tortillas wrapped around some kind of stuffing. Some old-fashioned West Texas enchilada purists look down on the rolled tortillas as some kind of modern heresy.

Pancho's stacked red-chile enchiladas with fried eggs on top arrive. As I saw away at the short stack of enchiladas, the ferociously hot enchilada sauce and the bland runny eggs ooze together. This rich sauce soaks into the starchy tortillas, softening them as I go. A strand of molten cheese pulls away from the pile with every bite.

Enchiladas like these were served by Tulia Borunda at the Old Borunda, which was originally known as Tulia's when it first opened by the railroad tracks at what is now the corner of Dean and El Paso streets in Marfa. But ac-

cording to *The History of Marfa and Presidio County* by Cecila Thompson, Tulia didn't serve enchiladas very often. In fact, Tulia Borunda didn't really specialize in Mexican food. Her regular offerings were steak and eggs, beans, potatoes, and coffee. The enchiladas were offered once a week.

I met with Thompson at a bookstore on Marfa's main street and she filled me in on Marfa and the Old Borunda's early history. Thompson was raised on a ranch outside Fort Davis and ate at the Old Borunda frequently. She was the one who told me about the fried eggs.

"The place was spotless, and the food was superb," she remembered. Everybody ate stacked red-chile enchiladas with fried eggs on top, sometimes with tacos on the side. The chicken tacos were made to order, stuffed first and then fried, then served with shredded lettuce and chopped tomatoes. There were no tortillas on the table, only white bread.

"White bread was considered a delicacy

A family eating dinner outdoors at their "ranchito" in the early 1940s

then—that was really uptown," said Thompson. "The better Mexican restaurants always had white bread when I was a kid."

Marfa is part of the West Texas region known as the Trans-Pecos, made famous as the jurisdiction of Judge Roy Bean, "Law West of the Pecos." The area is home to Big Bend National Park and an awesomely beautiful landscape. While the movie *Giant* was being shot here, its star, James Dean, ate regularly at the Old Borunda.

Marfa was just another nameless spot on a desolate though lovely plateau until 1883, when it became a water stop for the railroad. The wife of a railroad executive was given the honor of naming the place. She happened to be reading a Dostoyevsky novel at the time and picked the name Marfa, after a character in the book.

I ask Pancho about the nuances of enchilada history, but he shrugs his shoulders. He spent most of his career as a welder in the Pacific Northwest and only came back to Marfa a few years ago to open Borunda's Bar & Grill. "Let me call my cousin Stephanie," he says in answer to my many questions. "She used to work at the Old Borunda Café."

Stephanie Spitzer, eighty, the last surviving employee of the Old Borunda Café, kindly stops by Borunda's Bar & Grill to talk to me. First, she gives me the list of "begats" that starts with the founder, Tulia Gutierrez Borunda. Little is known about Tulia, except that she came from Mexico with her brother, probably via New Mexico. "Tulia's brother Cipriano Borunda had a *ranchito* where he grew chiles and produce for the restaurant," Stephanie Spitzer tells me. "His wife, my Grandma Carolina, used to have to fight off the Indians," she says. The Comanches were notorious for raiding farms and ranches and stealing food in those days. In 1910, Cipriano and Carolina took over Tulia Borunda's café and moved it out to the highway—Highway 90.

Marfa had a growth spurt around that time, thanks in large part to another Pancho—the

*After switching from **bandido** to revolutionary, Pancho Villa recruited thousands into his **División del Norte**. When a split among revolutionary leaders put Villa at odds with the U.S. government, Villa responded by raiding a border town in New Mexico. The U.S. Army invaded Mexico to punish him, but failed to catch him.*

legendary Pancho Villa. His real name was Doroteo Arango, and he was an accomplished cattle thief before he became a revolutionary. In his early years, Pancho Villa operated from Texas.

Pancho Villa's military campaigns consisted mainly of taking over *haciendas* in the Mexican state of Chihuahua, seizing all their horses and cattle, and trading the livestock in Texas for guns and money. The desolate river crossings in the Big Bend region, just south of Marfa, were perfect for this sort of activity.

For years, Villa was careful not to harm North American interests and in turn, American writers like John Reed romanticized him as the Mexican Robin Hood. Near the end of 1913, Villa's ragtag Division of the

North defeated a major army of "federales" in the border town of Ojinaga. The Mexican army fled across the Rio Grande and was taken into custody by the U.S. Cavalry and marched to Marfa.

After Villa destroyed the New Mexican town of Columbus in a 1916 raid, sentiment in the United States turned against the bandit. President Wilson ordered General "Blackjack" Pershing to pursue Pancho Villa into Mexico. The incursion was a fiasco. Villa was never caught, but Pershing's forces ended up engaging regular Mexican troops and taking many casualties.

During the hostilities, thousands of National Guard forces from as far away as Oklahoma were mobilized to protect the border. As the rail hub of all this military activity, Marfa grew, and the fame of the Old Borunda Café's enchiladas grew with it. When Cipriano and Carolina Borunda decided to retire, they turned to their daughter, also named Carolina, who'd grown up working in the restaurant.

"Their daughter, Carolina, was my aunt," Stephanie Spitzer tells me. "She took over the restaurant in 1932." The younger Carolina would run the Old Borunda for fifty-five years. A stern matriarch, she became the mother of West Texas Tex-Mex. Throughout its history, everything at the Old Borunda was cooked on a wood-burning stove, fueled exclusively with mesquite.

"There weren't any tacos or combination plates at the Old Borunda until Aunt Carolina took over in 1932." At the original place by the railroad tracks, Tulia served mostly steak and eggs, Stephanie tells me. Grandma Carolina just served enchiladas with eggs on top, tamales and beans, and that was it. The enchiladas were made with the dried long red chiles common to West Texas and New Mexico.

"No green enchiladas?" I wondered.

"No, but Cipriano grew green chiles. We called it 'chile macho,' " Stephanie tells me.

Stephanie Spitzer and Carolina Borunda

For the brief time of the year when green chiles were available, they were served stewed over Fritos corn chips. The chips served on the table were Fritos too, Stephanie tells me. You got Fritos and white bread when you sat down at the table.

"Carolina didn't have any recipes," Stephanie tells me. "You just had to watch her do it and then try it yourself."

"What do your think of the enchilada plate here?" I ask her. "Is it just like the Old Borunda's?"

Stephanie considers my plate carefully. "My aunt didn't like to put the beans on the plate because it looked messy," she says. The beans were served in a bowl on the side, she tells me. "And she didn't make rice. Tamales were all there was. She only made rice when she ran out of tamales."

"And what about the enchiladas?" I want to know.

"Carolina was kind to her customers," Stephanie says with a smile. "She didn't make them as hot as Pancho does. But people's tastes have changed." The Old Borunda's clientele was entirely Anglo, Stephanie explains. Mexican folks made this kind of food at home, she says; they didn't need to pay for it. And Aunt Carolina didn't serve any beer. Eventually, she would allow patrons to bring some, but no more than two bottles.

Pancho has a big wooden bean masher that used to belong to his Aunt Carolina. It looks like a stunted baseball bat. She used the bean masher to keep order in the place, I'm told. "It's not a honky-tonk," she told unruly patrons as she eighty-sixed them.

Carolina kept the Old Borunda Café open until its centennial in 1987. Carolina offered to let Stephanie Spitzer take over the place, but Stephanie declined because of her father's poor health. She has never regretted the decision. The Old Borunda is gone now, but the legacy lives on, in Pancho's new restaurant, Borunda's Bar & Grill, and in the taste buds of Texans.

OLD BORUNDA STACKED RED CHILE ENCHILADAS

Red Chile Sauce
12 red chiles, seeded and stemmed

1/2 onion

3 garlic cloves, minced

2 tablespoons vegetable oil

2 tablespoons flour

1 teaspoon salt

1/2 teaspoon dried Mexican oregano

1/2 teaspoon ground black pepper

For the enchiladas
3 tablespoons hot vegetable oil for dipping the tortillas

12 corn tortillas

2 cups shredded Monterey Jack or Cheddar cheese

1 cup chopped onions

4 eggs

These were the most famous enchiladas in Texas at the turn of the twentieth century. Pancho Borunda has never written this recipe down. He described the process to me, the way Carolina showed it to him. Are they just like the original? Well, why don't you whip up a stack and try them, then go out to Pancho's restaurant in Marfa and see if you can tell the difference.

MAKES 4 STACKS

Preheat the oven to 450°F. Fill a large pot with water. Bring the water to a boil over high heat and add the chiles. Reduce the heat and simmer, covered, for 15 to 20 minutes, until softened. Remove from the heat and allow to cool.

Place the chiles, onion, garlic, and 3 cups water in a blender and blend until well pureed, approximately 5 minutes on high. Strain the puree, extracting as much of the pulp as possible. Discard the remaining skin.

In a large skillet over medium-high heat, brown the flour with the oil for 2 to 3 minutes to make a blond roux. Reduce the heat to medium-low. Add the strained puree, salt, pepper, and oregano to the roux, stirring constantly until the mixture thickens. Set aside. (This may be used in other recipes calling for Red Chile Sauce.)

To make the enchiladas, heat the oil in a small skillet over medium-high heat for 3 minutes. Using tongs, place a tortilla in the hot oil for 30 seconds or until soft and lightly browned. Place on absorbent paper and allow to cool before handling.

Ladle a thin layer of sauce into a baking dish large enough to accommodate 4 stacks of tortillas. Place 4 tortillas in the dish and ladle some more sauce over each. Sprinkle with cheese and chopped onions, add another tortilla, and repeat. Top with a third tortilla, and sprinkle with the rest of the cheese and onions. Bake for 10 minutes or until the sauce bubbles and the cheese melts. While the enchiladas are baking, fry the eggs sunny-side up. Place each stack of enchiladas on a plate and divide the remaining sauce among the plates. Serve immediately with a sunny-side up egg on top.

VARIATION

Individual servings can be made to order in an ovenproof dish or pie plate.

Roasted Green Chiles

In late August and early September, chile sellers set up their giant propane-fired rolling drum roasters at grocery stores and farmers' markets in West Texas and New Mexico. Many people buy a whole year's supply of roasted peppers at this time of the year and freeze them. If you don't have a supply of roasted peppers in your freezer, it's easy enough to roast your own. You can use this technique for roasting poblanos too.

5 to 6 fresh green Anaheim chiles

Place the whole fresh peppers over a high gas flame and turn the peppers as needed to blister the skin on all sides. Don't allow the flame to burn too long in one place or you'll burn through the pepper. After most of the skin has been well blistered, wrap the warm pepper in a wet paper towel, place it inside a plastic bag, and set it aside to steam gently for 10 to 15 minutes. When you remove the towel, most of the skin should come off easily. Scrape off the rest of the skin with a butter knife. If you are making chile rellenos, remove the seeds carefully and try to keep the pepper intact (it's not easy). Otherwise, cut the pepper into strips or chop it up, depending on the recipe.

　　If you don't have a gas range, put the pepper in a skillet with a little vegetable oil and blister it over high heat on the electric burner. Proceed as directed.

Tulia Borunda's restaurant, the forerunner of the Old Borunda Café, circa 1900

CHILE MACHO (GREEN CHILE SAUCE)

4 cups chicken broth

2 cups chopped roasted green chiles (Anaheim; see page 107)

5 tomatillos, cooked and pureed

2 teaspoons minced onion

1 teaspoon dried Mexican oregano

1 garlic clove, minced

$1/2$ teaspoon salt

$1/4$ teaspoon white pepper

2 teaspoons cornstarch dissolved in 2 tablespoons water

Chile Macho was a seasonal treat at the Old Borunda. It was served only in August and September when the green chiles could be picked. Most chiles were allowed to ripen and turn red, then they were dried.

MAKES ABOUT 6 CUPS

Combine all the ingredients except the cornstarch in a large saucepan. Bring to a boil over medium-high heat, then reduce the heat and simmer for 10 minutes. Add the cornstarch and stir well. Cook for 5 to 10 more minutes, until well thickened. Serve over Fritos or as an enchilada sauce.

STACKED GREEN CHILE CHICKEN ENCHILADAS

This is what they're talking about when they say enchiladas in Marfa, El Paso, and the rest of West Texas. Green chile and chicken is a favorite combination.

MAKES 4 STACKS

Preheat the oven to 450°F. Heat the oil in a small skillet over medium-high heat for 3 minutes. Using tongs, place a tortilla in the hot oil for 30 seconds or until soft and lightly browned. Place on absorbent paper and allow to cool before handling.

Ladle a thin layer of sauce into a baking dish large enough to accommodate 4 stacks of tortillas. Place 4 tortillas in the dish and ladle some more sauce over each. Divide half the chicken filling among the first layer of 4 enchiladas and top with sauce and cheese. Add another layer of tortillas and top with the rest of the chicken, then more sauce and cheese. Finish with a third tortilla layer and sprinkle with some sauce and the rest of the cheese. Salt to taste. Bake for 10 minutes or until the sauce bubbles and the cheese melts. Place each stack on a plate and divide the remaining sauce among the plates. Serve immediately.

VARIATION

Individual servings can be made to order in an ovenproof dish or pie plate.

3 tablespoons vegetable oil

12 corn tortillas

Chile Macho (page 110)

2 cups Stewed Chicken filling (page 90)

2 cups shredded Monterey Jack cheese

Salt

Mexican hands
eating lunch on a
ranch in Menard

CHILE COLORADO CON PUERCO

Here's a West Texas version of chili con carne made with long red chiles and pork. Serve this over Fritos corn chips for a gourmet version of Frito Pie (page 204.)

MAKES 3 CUPS

Preheat the oven to 350°F. Remove the stems and seeds from the chiles and crumble them into a measuring cup. Add 2 cups hot water and allow them to soak until the pieces are soft, about 20 minutes. Put the chiles and the soaking water in a blender and puree.

Heat the oil in a large sauté pan over medium-high heat. Sauté the onion until soft, about 5 minutes. Add the garlic. Sprinkle the pork strips with salt and pepper and add to the pan. Stir until cooked through, about 5 minutes. Add the chile puree, tomatoes, and oregano and mix well. Reduce the heat to low, cover, and simmer for 20 minutes or until the pork is very tender, adding water as needed to maintain a saucelike consistency. Use as a sauce with enchiladas or tamales, or eat as a stew.

5 dried red chiles or 5 tablespoons pulverized red chiles

1 1/2 tablespoons vegetable oil

1 cup chopped onions

3 garlic cloves, minced

8 ounces boneless pork, cut into pencil-thin strips

Salt

Ground black pepper

1 cup crushed tomatoes

1 teaspoon dried Mexican oregano

CHAPTER 7

MEX-MEX

THE MYTH OF AUTHENTICITY

A Mexican bar near Market Square in Brownsville, circa 1910

L

OCATED ON HOUSTON'S KATY FREEWAY NEAR Voss, Las Alamedas is an impressive stone building with pillars and old wooden benches. Inside, the stone floors, mission furniture, and soaring high-beamed ceiling make the place look like a Spanish colonial hacienda in old Mexico. The restaurant's mission is to bring authentic upscale Mexican food to Texas. The owners are related to the owner of the famous Las Alamedas restaurant in Mexico City.

The hostess, Beatriz Gomez, is from Guanajuato. On the way to our table we banter a little in Spanish and I ask her if the food here is authentic Mexican or Tex-Mex. She tilts her open hand from side to side: "Media y media," she says, meaning "half and half."

The first two items on the appetizer menu, *ceviche Costeño* and *ostiones diabla* (oysters au gratin), seem authentically Mexican. The remaining six appetizers—crabcakes, a spinach-artichoke dip, fried calamari, *queso fundido* with flour tortillas, nachos, and shrimp stuffed with cream cheese—do not.

There are three purely Tex-Mex entrees: *fajitas de camarón, fajitas de pollo,* and fajita prime sliced. And then there is the "fancy" Mexican food: *huachinango Pontchartrain* with brown butter sauce and lump crabmeat, *pollo Cuernavaca,* "chicken breast topped with artichoke hearts in a mustard-pepper sauce," and *filete* forest, "mesquite grilled prime tenderloin smothered in a pepper-mustard garlic-wine sauce." This is Mexican food?

In fact, it's exactly the kind of Europeanized cooking that upscale restaurants in Mexico City serve. In the United States, this food seems completely ludicrous. Who wants to go

Mexican president Porfiro Díaz

to a Mexican restaurant to eat outdated Continental cuisine?

To understand this kind of Mexican food, you must first understand Mexico's historic class divisions. In the early 1900s, Europeans were the highest rank of the Mexican caste system; next came the Creoles, or *criollos,* colonists of supposedly pure European blood who were born in the Americas; then *mestizos,* people of mixed race; and at the bottom were the natives or *indios.*

In an article titled "Recipes for *Patria,*" Jeffrey M. Pilcher studies old Mexican cookbooks and describes how *criollo* culinary reformers once attempted to convert the Mexican masses from a corn-based diet to a European one:

"Mexican leaders of the nineteenth century hoped to build a modern patriarchal nation based on Western European models," writes Pilcher. "Cookbooks provided a valuable means of indoctrinating women into this new order by emphasizing European dishes and disparaging Indian foods . . . Corn became a symbol for disorderly and unsanitary elements of society such as street people and backward villagers."

These attitudes fragmented Mexican food along class lines. The vast majority of Mexi-

Nuns exiled by the revolutionary government of Mexico arriving in San Antonio, 1926

cans ate a corn-based diet that varied in form according to region. Meanwhile, elite Mexicans took guilty pleasure in consuming treats like enchiladas when they were out on the town. But at home, Mexican etiquette books advised them to keep such low-class Indian foods out of sight of guests.

In 1910, at a series of banquets held to commemorate the centennial of Mexican independence, not a single Mexican dish was served at any of more than a dozen state dinners. Guests of President Porfirio Díaz were served French champagne and food from Sylvain Daumont, a fashionable French restaurant in Mexico City. When the Mexican Revolution swept Díaz and his Francophile cronies from power, it also ended attempts by the *criollos* to restructure the country along European lines.

From 1910 through 1930, constant power struggles convulsed the country. The peso became worthless, and for the poor and middle classes, steady work was nearly impossible to find. During this period, some 1.5 million Mexicans—around 10 percent of the nation's entire population—emigrated to the United States. Most settled in Texas. Mexican-American scholars call this group "the Immigrant Generation."

As civic institutions in Texas strained under the load of so many new arrivals seeking jobs, medical assistance, and an education for their children, Anglo discrimination against Mexicans increased. Some of the newcomers, with their clumsy rural manners and lack of English, were an embarrassment to the better-established Tejanos.

Sign outside a retail business, San Antonio, 1949

During the era of immigration, segregation laws intended for blacks were unofficially extended to include Mexican-Americans. Unwelcome at Anglo barbershops, funeral homes, churches, theaters, and eating places, Mexicans developed their own parallel institutions.

In *barrios* such as San Antonio's West End and Houston's North Side, Mexicans and Mexican-Americans opened cafés, food stalls, and restaurants that catered to immigrants. And adventurous Anglos continued the tradition of venturing into "Mexican town," as the *barrio* was called, in search of "real" Mexican food.

Not all the new immigrants were poor, of course. Before the revolution began and the peso became worthless, some twenty-five thousand wealthy members of the Mexico City elite transferred their money to San Antonio. These wealthy *criollos* brought Mexico's racial

caste system with them to San Antonio. Like the elite of Mexico City, they looked down on poorer Mexicans and their native foods. And they were equally disdainful of the Anglicized Mexican food at places like the Original Mexican restaurant. To cater to them, yet another style of Mexican restaurant developed in San Antonio: upscale Mexican restaurants serving Europeanized food.

In 1949 *La Prensa,* San Antonio's Spanish-language newspaper, carried an ad for the Carta Blanca restaurant on Houston Street. There, Mexican food lovers were promised *"el más alto representativo de la cocina criolla autóctona y legítima"*—the highest form of native Creole cooking.

The "Immigrant Era" ended in the 1930s, but its effects changed the Texas-Mexican community forever after. The new arrivals remained in contact with their families and villages in the old country, and they gave the rest of the community a renewed sense of Mexican identity.

The elite Mexican attitudes about food are carried on by "authentic Mexican restaurants" such as Las Alamedas today. And although we don't call it "Mexican town" anymore, adventurous Anglo eaters still venture into the *barrios* where new immigrants live in search of the "authentic Mexican" food found in humble taquerias.

THREE TACO TRUCKS SIT SIDE BY SIDE IN the parking lot behind the Farmers Marketing Association on Airline Drive in Houston. The one in the middle, with "Taqueria Tacambaro" painted on the roof, is crowded with people at 1:30 P.M. Stand-up counters are mounted on three sides of the truck. They all face a short-order cook named Maria Rojas, who alternates stuffing gorditas, frying tortillas, and chopping meat behind sliding-glass windows. Maria is wearing a baseball cap that says Michoacán; a marijuana plant sprouts out of the second C. She is evidently proud of her homeland and its famous export.

The guy standing to my right is named Narciso Santos. I ask him in Spanish what kind of tacos he got. "*Tripitas y fajitas,*" he says with his mouth full. It looks like he got two with the chopped tripe and two with fajita beef. There is a nice-looking grilled jalapeño on his Styrofoam plate as well.

I ask Narciso if he has tried the other trucks. He makes a face and shakes his head. "*Éste es el famoso,*" he says, tapping a finger on the counter beside his Jarritos tamarind soda. Originally from Toluca, Narciso says he works in Conroe, but whenever he gets to Houston, he stops by this taco truck for lunch. I would guess that most of the well-dressed Mexican-Americans eating here aren't doing business at the market either.

I order one taco with grilled pork, which is called a taco al pastor, one of the fajita tacos that Narciso is having, and a bean-and-cheese

gordita. The taco al pastor is made with spicy pork that's crisped in a skillet and put into two folded-over corn tortillas, which are toasted on the griddle. Skirt steak and a big pinch of crumbly Mexican white cheese are placed in the middle of a flour tortilla on the griddle for the fajita taco. Maria calls this a fajita quesadilla, even though the Mexican cheese never melts enough to meld the tortilla together. The gordita is a thick masa cake split in half and stuffed with homemade refried beans and Mexican cheese.

Young combatant in the Mexican Revolution, circa 1914

Tortilla Delivery Service

Corn tortillas were once delivered door-to-door in San Antonio, just like milk. B. Martinez Sons Company had horse-and-buggy teams that ran twenty-five routes daily in San Antonio.

The tortillas are well toasted, so the tacos are wonderfully chewy. The meat is tender and spicy, and the green salsa that Maria douses it with is incendiary. Since my mouth is already on fire, I ask for a roasted jalapeño, which at this stage of the meal has a lot of flavor and not much heat.

When the crowd thins out at 2 P.M., I hang around and talk to Maria Rojas. She really is from Michoacán; I ask her if the stalls in the market of her hometown serve the same sort of food she's cooking. More or less, she says. In Michoacán, people eat tacos, but the meats

are different. They eat cabrito and stewed cabro (kid and adult goat), she tells me. There is no fajita meat, and there aren't any flour tortillas either.

I had come to the Farmers Marketing Association on a hunch. The taco trucks here, I figured, are the equivalent of the food stalls in the Mexican *mercado,* so maybe I could find some truly authentic Mexican food. Of course, I was wrong. Commercial Mexican food with no Tex-Mex influences is practically impossible to find in Texas. Various versions of "authentic Mexican food" have co-existed in Texas for nearly a century. But eventually, they all fuse with the native Tex-Mex style as the immigrants and their foods inch inexorably toward assimilation. But authenticity is highly overrated.

In 1972, Diana Kennedy's cookbook *The Cuisines of Mexico* drew a line in the sand between Mexican food and Tex-Mex; it also created a lot of confusion about what Mexican food really is. As the title suggests, Mexican cuisine is not a unified whole, but many different cooking styles. "Mole" in Puebla isn't the same as "mole" in Oaxaca, and in Mérida, there isn't any mole at all. Some of these cuisines of Mexico don't even share the same language, nor do they stay neatly within the borders of the country. Mayan-descended Yucatecan cuisine has much in common with the cooking in Guatemala and Honduras. And northern Mexican ranchero cuisine has ties to the cooking of Texas and New Mexico.

When Texas-Mexicans argued that the food tasted the same on either side of the Rio Grande and that Mexican authenticity was an arbitrary distinction, Kennedy's followers responded by substituting the term "interior Mexican" for "authentic Mexican." "Interior Mexican" refers to the corn-cultivating areas of the Mexican plateau and omits the northern desert.

After Kennedy's book came out, American diners became obsessed with the idea of authentic Mexican food, and "interior Mexican" restaurants began springing up everywhere. In Texas, they ranged from immigrant mom-and-pop joints located in former fast-food outlets to huge stone buildings that looked as if they came straight from colonial Mexico. Kennedy herself consulted on the menu at San Angel, a Houston restaurant that opened in 1972. Three years later San Angel's owners closed the establishment and moved to a larger space in Austin, where they founded Fonda San Miguel. Once again, Kennedy was their menu consultant.

"We started out to be really purist," remembers owner Tom Gilliland. "We wanted everything to be just like in Mexico. But we ended up becoming realists. We had to make some concessions. Diana made us commit to not serving chips and salsa, not only because it's not done in Mexico, but because the chips fill you up, and the hot sauce dulls your palate."

But patrons revolted. "Texans have this fixation about chips and salsa," Gilliland says. "We had customers saying that unless we gave them chips and salsa, they weren't coming back. So we finally gave up and gave them their damn chips and hot sauce. We just didn't tell Diana right away."

Fonda San Miguel's competitors didn't play by the same rules. "We began to see other restaurants that described themselves as 'interior Mexican' opening up," Gilliland recalls. "But some of them were just inventing their own dishes and naming them after Mexican cities." Many of the cooks were recent Mexican immigrants. They didn't care what Diana Kennedy said. They'd never heard of her.

The relationship between new Mexican immigrants, Anglos, and the Tejano community has always been complex. In his book *Ethnicity in the Sunbelt*, author Arnoldo De León explains that immigrants have had a love-hate relationship with more established Mexican-Americans.

American-born Mexican-Americans dislike the immigrants because they give the whole community a bad image. But the constant stream of fresh arrivals is crucial to perpetuating the unique culture of Texas-Mexicans. "They inject cultural ingredients that prevent the dilution of the *colonia*'s ethnicity," De León writes. "Certain foods are more popular among the immigrants than among the indigenous group," he goes on. "Restaurants and barrio food stores offer these and forestall the loss of the dish."

One day over lunch, I asked Rick Bayless, the chef and owner of Frontera Grill in Chicago and probably America's foremost au-

This 1924 photo taken in front of the Alamo City Employment Agency in San Antonio includes many newly arrived braceros, legal Mexican immigrants who were contracted to come to work as cotton pickers.

Deep-frying a pork skin to make chicharrones

buche (pork stomach), deep-fried *chicharrones* (crunchy fat), and several choices of stewed meats in long trays. There is a sign that says, "*barbacoa* $5.50, *barbacoa de cachete* $5.99." I know that Tejano barbacoa is made from a long-cooked cow's head, but I ask the guy in front of me what "cachete" means. He says it means cheek meat.

We strike up a conversation. His name is Marcello Martinez, and he says he works in an office off Highway 290. He has driven all the way to Matamoros Meat Market to buy his lunch. "It's that good," he says with a smile. Today he is ordering the pork and green chile stew. "It's kind of like pozole, but with potatoes," he says. "And it's very spicy." I ask him to identify the brown things that look like prunes in the *carne deshebrada* (shredded beef brisket). "They are big pieces of chipotle peppers," he says. "And they are unbelievably hot." Some restaurants offer things like barbacoa and carnitas on the weekends, but at Matamoros, you can buy them every day.

I order a carnitas taco and watch while the woman behind the counter chops the meat, blending the tender pork with its crunchy edges. It is an extraordinary amount of meat for a dollar and a half. I wonder if I should buy another pound to go. It's hard to find good carnitas in the middle of the week, and the crunchy pork, which is boiled in its own fat, is one of my favorite Mexican meats.

An Anglo construction worker steps up be-

thority on Mexican food, why Chicago had more "authentic Mexican food" than Texas.

"When somebody from Mexico moves to Texas, the Chicano community is there to teach them how things are done," he said. "But the Mexicans in Chicago are almost all first-generation. There's nobody here to show them what Americanized Mexican food is supposed to be like."

At Matamoros Meat Market No. 4 on Washington Avenue, I stand before a glass case filled with glistening pieces of roasted side me and asks for a fajita combo plate. The woman taking his order is straight from Mexico and doesn't understand. The young woman making my taco translates for her. "Fajita combo plato," she says. "Tortillas de harina," she adds without even asking. Some things are simply understood. After all, who eats fajitas with corn tortillas?

The Mexican woman ladles rice, refried beans, and fajita meat into the to-go carton. She adds a plastic cup with hot sauce, and some flour tortillas, and hands the Styrofoam lunch bucket to the tall blond Texan and smiles. "Gracias," he says.

She's learning Tex-Mex on the job.

SINCE THE 1940S, MEXICO'S RULERS HAVE embraced the mestizo view of the country's culture. Mexico's strength, according to this school of thought, is its unique blend of indigenous and European influences. Purely European foods have been replaced by dishes that combine European and indigenous ingredients as the culinary icons of this new national identity.

Mexico's regional cuisines receive more attention now; but the European bias remains. Mexican food writer and restaurant owner Patricia Quintana's website states: "The author of *Mexico's Feasts of Life* celebrates the haute cuisine of Mexico, eschewing tacos and burritos for regional cuisines that rival the delicate flavors found in European cuisines."

Elite Mexicans resent the idea that their country's complex cuisine is represented by tacos and enchiladas in the United States. In her book, Quintana writes, "Tex-Mex food is a regional cookery too, but the territory had few resources at the time the Americans began to adapt the peasant foods of the region, so it's all fairly simplistic."

In the United States, Quintana's views are championed by writers such as John Mariani. "One need not be chauvinistic to assert that New York has more interesting Mexican restaurants than most cities along the Rio Grande," opined an issue of Mariani's *Virtual Gourmet* newsletter. "At least they tend to be more authentically 'Mexican,' as opposed to Tex-Mex, which is what dominates most eateries in this country."

These writers are tilting at windmills. There are many fine interior Mexican restaurants in the United States. And there are even more wonderful Tex-Mex restaurants. But who says we have to choose one over the other? Discovering the sophisticated flavor of northern Italian cuisine didn't stop Americans from eating pizza; why should an appreciation for the cuisines of Mexico stop anybody from eating Tex-Mex?

The fact is chips and salsa, fajitas, margaritas, and nachos are increasingly popular in hip new restaurants in Guadalajara, Acapulco, and even Mexico City. It seems the better question may be: Once Mexicans taste Tex-Mex, will they lose interest in authentic Mexican cuisine?

ORAL HISTORY
DEBORAH CORTEZ

Third generation Manager/Co-owner,
Mi Tierra, San Antonio

"I realized that the food we served at Mi Tierra wasn't really Mexican food the first time my dad took me to Mexico. I was very young. We were in Guadalajara and I couldn't find anything there to eat. I wanted to go to Pizza Hut. I was in Guadalajara recently, and I saw chips and salsa, fajitas, and flour tortillas in a restaurant. Tex-Mex is catching on down there too."

DARIO'S CHILE RELLENOS

4 poblano chiles,
roasted, skin removed
(see Roasted Green
Chiles, page 107)

2 cups taco filling or
chicken filling (see
Ground Beef Tacos,
page 188, or Stewed
Chicken, page 90)

1 tablespoon
vegetable oil

4 eggs

1/2 cup Spanish
Sauce, warmed
(page 78)

1/2 cup sour cream

1 tablespoon chopped
pecans

1 tablespoon currants

Old-fashioned chile rellenos may be the pride of Mexican cuisine, but the whipped egg-white batter is tedious to make, and when fried, has an unappetizing color. The spongy batter also tends to absorb too much grease. This easy way to make chile rellenos was invented by Dario's, a Tex-Mex joint on Austin's East Side. Instead of a batter of beaten egg whites, they wrap the chile in a thin omelet. Dario's uses mild anaheim chiles, but getting the skins off the thin chiles while keeping them intact requires deep-frying. I've substituted poblanos, which are a little hotter, but much easier to work with.

SERVES 4

Slit the roasted skinless chiles down one side and remove the seeds and membrane, being careful not to tear the chile. Stuff with 5 to 6 tablespoons of the filling of your choice. Heat a large frying pan over medium-high heat and dribble a little oil into it. Beat an egg in a bowl with a tablespoon of water added. Pour the beaten egg into the hot frying pan and rotate the pan to spread the egg thinly. Place the stuffed chile on top of the egg with the stem protruding. With a spatula, flip the egg over the chile from the bottom, then from both sides, to cover it completely. Put a spoonful of Spanish sauce on the plate, then the chile. Top with a dollop of sour cream and garnish with a sprinkling of chopped pecans and currants. Serve immediately.

Tex-Mex Mole

Lots of Tex-Mex restaurants use bottled mole pastes from Mexico such as Doña Maria brand. Tricks of the trade include reconstituting the paste with chicken broth instead of water and boosting the flavor with peanut butter. Here's a simple homemade mole that tastes even better than the bottled paste.

MAKES ABOUT 2 CUPS

Heat the olive oil in a medium saucepan over medium heat. Add the garlic and onion and sauté until the onion is soft, about 5 minutes. Add the tomatoes, chiles, chocolate, sesame seeds, peanut butter, sugar, crackers, and chicken broth. Simmer for 5 minutes.

Transfer the mixture to a blender and puree until smooth. Salt to taste. If the mole has any grittiness, return it to the blender and puree again. Serve warm or cover and store in refrigerator for up to a week.

2 tablespoons olive oil

2 garlic cloves, minced

1/4 onion, sliced

2 tomatoes, peeled and quartered

1 ancho chile, stemmed and seeded

1 guajillo or pasilla chile, stemmed and seeded

1 ounce semisweet chocolate

1/4 teaspoon sesame seeds

1 teaspoon peanut butter

1/2 teaspoon sugar

2 saltine crackers

1 cup chicken broth

Salt

In the 1940s, Anglos and Hispanics rubbed elbows at the Mexican Manhattan restaurant.

El Azteca's Chicken Mole Enchiladas

6 tablespoons olive oil

1/4 cup diced onion

4 cups Stewed Chicken (page 90)

2 cups Tex-Mex Mole (page 127)

8 corn tortillas

4 slices *queso blanco* or Monterey Jack cheese

1/4 cup sesame seeds, toasted

In Oaxaca, these go by the name enmoladas. *The combination of chicken and mole sauce has been popular in Tex-Mex restaurants for many years.*

MAKES 8 ENCHILADAS

Preheat the oven to 300°F. In a medium skillet, heat 2 tablespoons of the olive oil over medium heat. Add the onion and cook until wilted, 2 to 3 minutes. Add the chicken and cook for another 2 or 3 minutes, until the chicken is heated. Remove from the heat and place in a bowl with 1/2 cup of the mole sauce. Toss well and set aside.

Wipe out the skillet and add the remaining 1/4 cup olive oil. Place over medium heat. When it is hot, dip a tortilla into the oil and cook for 10 to 15 seconds on each side, or until soft. Drain on absorbent paper. Repeat with the remaining tortillas.

Divide the chicken mixture evenly among the tortillas, roll them up, and place seam side down in a greased baking dish. Pour the remaining mole sauce over them. Arrange the cheese evenly on top.

Bake for 12 to 15 minutes, until bubbling hot. Remove from the oven, transfer to plates, and garnish with the sesame seeds.

POSOLE

Traditionally, this dish is made with dried posole and a pork shoulder. The posole can take as long as five hours to cook, by which time the meat and chiles have become extremely tender. This version uses easy-to-find canned hominy and still gets better as you cook it longer.

SERVES 6 TO 8

Bring 6 cups water to a boil and add the pork. Cook for 10 minutes. Reduce the heat to a simmer and add the rest of the ingredients (except the garnish). Salt to taste. Cook, covered, for $1^1/2$ to 2 hours (or longer), stirring and adding water if needed. Serve in soup bowls.

Pass around a plate of garnishes for everyone at the table to add to their soup.

$1^1/4$-pound pork shoulder, cut into slices (bones included)

$1^1/2$ cups roasted green chiles, chopped (see page 107)

3 garlic cloves, minced

1 cup chopped onions

2 tablespoons crushed red chiles

One 30-ounce can pozole blanco (white hominy)

1 teaspoon ground cumin

1 teaspoon dried Mexican oregano

Salt

Garnish plate
Lime wedges

Sliced radishes

Chopped onion

Chopped fresh cilantro

Baked tortilla strips

Tex-Mex Dry Rub

3 tablespoons salt

1/4 cup chili powder

1 tablespoon garlic powder

1 tablespoon onion powder

Here's an all-purpose seasoning blend for grilling and barbecueing. Try it on beef ribs or fajitas and serve the meat with flour tortillas.

MAKES 1/2 CUP

Combine all the ingredients, mix well, and store in an airtight container for up to 3 months.

Using 1/2 teaspoon per side of each steak, pat the dry rub into the meat on one side, turn, and rub into the other side.

Costillas (Beef Ribs)

6 pounds beef ribs

Tex-Mex Dry Rub (see above)

"Beef heads for barbacoa used to cost a dollar twenty-five each. Then around 1980, they hit nine dollars," says Robert Amaya of Taco Village in Austin. "I said never mind. I quit making them." Now Amaya serves beef ribs instead. He cooks them until the meat falls off the bone.

SERVES 6

Preheat the oven to 300°F. Cut the rack into individual ribs.

Lay the ribs fat side up in two 12 by 9 by 2 1/2-inch baking pans. Add 1 cup water to each pan. Bake for 2 hours. Increase the oven temperature to 450°F and turn the ribs meat side up. Sprinkle each rib with 1/4 teaspoon dry rub. Return to the oven and bake for an additional 45 minutes, until dark and crispy.

A Mexican neighborhood restaurant on San Antonio's West Side

BARBACOA

One 20- to 25-pound
cow's head, skinned
and cleaned

1 cup Tex-Mex Dry
Rub (page 132)

2 onions, cut in half

18-inch-wide heavy-
duty aluminum foil

Garnish plate
Fresh tortillas

Lime quarters

Chopped onion

Fresh cilantro

Salsa Verde (page 94)
or Molcajete Sauce
(page 24)

In Central Mexico, barbacoa means lamb or goat meat wrapped in maguey leaves and roasted on hot coals. In Texas, Mexican ranch hands adapted this interior Mexican style of cooking to roast cattle heads. They wrapped the cabezas in maguey leaves or, later, in aluminum foil and canvas and buried them in earthen pits with hot coals. As the years went by, restaurants had to stop burying the cabezas because of the health code. Now the heads are roasted and steamed in ovens.

"How do you make barbacoa at home?" I asked Paula Luna of Johnny's BBQ in Pharr.

"In an electric turkey-roaster oven," she said matter-of-factly. Here's her recipe.

MAKES ABOUT 2 POUNDS OF MEAT

Rinse the head out with a hose. Cut out the tongue and reserve. Sprinkle the dry rub all over the head and place forehead down in an 18-quart roaster oven (you may need to angle the head a little to get it to fit). Add 8 cups water and the onions. Cover. If the lid does not fit, cut two sheets of aluminum foil long enough to cover the top of the roaster with plenty to spare. Combine the two sheets by overlapping and folding them to make one 32-inch-wide piece of foil. Seal the roaster by tucking and folding the foil over the roaster pan.

Turn the roaster oven to 350°F and heat for 1 hour or until the water is boiling vigorously. Reduce the heat to 250°F and allow the head to steam for 12 hours or until the cheek meat pulls away from the bone.

When the barbacoa is done, pull the cheek meat off and remove the jaw bones. You'll find another large piece of meat inside. Remove any other nice chunks of meat you can find.

Cut away excess fat, blackened meat, and cartilage, but don't clean the meat too thoroughly. It is the little bits of fat and mucilage that give barbacoa its distinctive texture. Chop the meat and put it in a bowl. Wet the meat with some of the cooking liquid to keep it moist. You should end up with about 2 pounds of meat.

Serve immediately with the garnishes and sauce.

LENGUA (TONGUE)

Lengua is much easier to make than barbacoa and the flavor is just as good. Just put the tongue in a crockpot on a Saturday night, and you'll have lengua tacos on Sunday morning.

MAKES ABOUT 1 POUND OF MEAT

At 8 P.M., rinse the tongue well and put it in a crockpot with water to cover. Add the garlic and onion. Turn the crockpot on high. At midnight, turn the tongue over and add more water if needed. Turn the crockpot down to low.

In the morning when the tongue is done, the skin will be hard and the meat will be soft. Put it on a cutting board and remove the skin (it should come away easily). Finely chop the meat. Add salt and pepper to taste.

Serve immediately with garnishes and sauce.

1 beef tongue
(about a pound)

3 garlic cloves,
minced

1 onion, cut in half

Salt and pepper

Garnish plate
Fresh tortillas

Lime quarters

Chopped onion

Fresh cilantro

Salsa Verde (page 94),
Smoked Tomato Salsa
(page 223), or Pico de
Gallo (page 170)

CARNE GUISADA

2 tablespoons
vegetable oil

2 pounds sirloin tips,
trimmed of all fat and
gristle and cut into
1/2-inch cubes

1 cup green bell
pepper, chopped

1 cup chopped onions

1 pound small red
potatoes, peeled and
cut into 1/2-inch
cubes

4 garlic cloves,
minced

1 serrano chile,
minced

1/2 cup chopped
tomatoes

1/2 teaspoon salt

1 teaspoon pepper

1/2 teaspoon ground
cumin

1/2 cup tomato sauce

1 tablespoon flour

Beef stew made with sirloin, slow simmered with garlic and a little chile pepper, and served with warm flour tortillas is eaten for breakfast, lunch, and dinner in Texas. Here's a simple version of the classic dish. Serve with warm flour tortillas.

SERVES 6 GENEROUSLY

Heat the oil in a large skillet over high heat. Add the meat and brown for 10 minutes. Do not drain the liquid. Add the bell pepper, onion, potatoes, garlic, chile, and tomatoes and continue cooking for 10 minutes. Add the spices, the tomato sauce, and 2 cups water. Reduce the heat to low, cover, and simmer for 1 hour or until the meat is very tender. Add more water as required. Season to taste.

In a small cup combine 3 tablespoons cooking liquid with the flour. Stir to remove any lumps, then add to the carne guisada, mixing well until evenly thickened.

Tortilla Soup

The quick and easy Tex-Mex version of this Mexican classic is made with Rotel tomatoes and crispy tortilla chips. Made with abundant garlic, it's not only delicious, it's the cure for the common cold.

SERVES 6 TO 8

With poultry shears or a sharp knife, split the chicken in half and rinse well. Place the chicken in a soup pot with 8 cups water, bring to a boil, and reduce to a simmer. Cook for 45 minutes to an hour, until the chicken is completely cooked. Remove the chicken and set aside to cool.

Skim the stock with a slotted spoon and discard any skin or bones. Add the garlic, onion, celery, carrots, potatoes, oregano, and Rotel tomatoes. Return to a boil, then reduce to a simmer and cook for 30 minutes or until all the vegetables are well done. When the soup is nearly ready, cut up some of the chicken meat into bite-size pieces, removing all skin and gristle.

To serve, bring the soup to the table in a tureen and present it with a plate of chicken meat, the garnishes, and the bowl of chips. Each diner should crush some tortilla chips into a soup bowl, add chicken and condiments, and then ladle the soup over the top.

1 whole chicken

3 garlic cloves, minced

1 cup chopped onions

1 cup chopped celery

1 cup sliced carrots

3 small red potatoes, cut into $1/2$-inch dice

1 teaspoon dried Mexican oregano

One 10-ounce can Rotel tomatoes (your choice of heat level)

For the garnish

1 avocado, sliced

$1/2$ cup chopped fresh cilantro

2 limes, quartered

1 fresh serrano chile, minced

Large bowl tortilla chips

DULCES AND DESSERTS

THE PECAN SHELLERS' UPRISING

A Mexican candy seller on West Commerce across from San Antonio's City Hall, late 1800s

O BIDIA RODRIGUEZ LADLES SILVER-DOLLAR-sized dollops of hot candy onto wax paper to cool. Then she dips the ladle back into the syrup simmering in the steel bowl on the hot burner; the recipe calls for sugar, water, pecans, and nothing else. The pecan pieces in each praline amount to little more than one whole pecan, but still they tint the sugar the color of café au lait and give the brittle candies a strong nutty flavor. Rodriguez is a tiny woman who is missing one eye. She tells me in Spanish that she has been making pralines here at Loma Linda Mexican Restaurant for the last eleven years.

With its shabby red vinyl booths and embroidered velvet decorations, the original restaurant of the once popular Loma Linda chain is a Tex-Mex time capsule. It was purchased by Thad and Joyce Gilliam, who have tried to preserve the landmark. The restaurant on Telephone Road in Houston still serves the Anglo coffee-shop version of Tex-Mex that was popular when it opened in 1956. And they still give every customer one of Obidia Rodriguez's pecan pralines.

You will still find pecan pralines at the cash register of almost every Tex-Mex restaurant. But the candies represent more than a cheap dessert. Making candy and selling it on the street was one way that early Mexican immigrants supported themselves.

Gathering pecans, shelling them, drying them, and making them into candies requires a lot of labor, but no more capital than a pot and some sugar. Whole families employed themselves through the fall pecan harvest season with the tasks of collecting wild native pecans, shelling them, drying them, and either selling the cleaned halves or turning them into candies.

"Praline" is a French word, and the patty-shaped pecan-and-brown-sugar candies were introduced into Texas from Louisiana. But the pecan praline is part of Tex-Mex history. And like a lot of Tex-Mex traditions, it has little or nothing to do with Mexico.

CONFECTIONERY, BAKERY AND LUNCH PARLOR

ORIGINATORS OF THE FAMOUS

MEXICAN PECAN CANDIES
MADE BY WHITE PEOPLE ONLY
TYPICAL PACKAGES $1.00 PREPAID AND
INSURED SENT ANYWHERE BY PARCEL POST

ALAMO CHOCOLATES
THE BEST AND MOST POPULAR
CHOCOLATES IN THE CITY

WE MAKE ALL OUR CANDY. ICE CREAM, SUNDAE'S, SODA'S, FRUIT FLAVORS, ETC., ALSO BREAD, PIES CAKES AND COOKIES

BEST COFFEE IN TOWN

Mexican pecan candies "MADE BY WHITE PEOPLE ONLY," circa 1915

Obidia Rodriguez making pralines at Loma Linda Restaurant in Houston

The San Antonio Pecan Shellers' Strike

Thanks to cheap Mexican labor, a pecan-shelling industry developed in San Antonio. In the 1930s, half of the nation's pecans passed through the four hundred pecan-shelling factories scattered around San Antonio. Although mechanized pecan crackers had already been invented, low wages during the Depression made it even cheaper to use Mexican laborers. After cracking the pecans (a job typically done by men because it requires great hand strength) came the meticulous chore of removing the meat from the cracked shells (a job usually done by women). Working conditions were poor, and the fine brown dust from the shells was a suspected cause of San Antonio's high tuberculosis rate.

The shelled pecan market was eventually cornered by one man, San Antonio's "Pecan King" Julius Seligmann. Labor representatives began to look into the low wages and poor working conditions at Seligmann's plants. In 1934, Seligmann cut wages in half, stating, "The Mexican pecan shellers eat a good many pecans, and five cents a day is enough to support them in addition to what they eat while they work." Meanwhile, Seligmann himself made more than half a million dollars over the following three years.

In response, the pecan shellers organized the International Pecan Shellers Union No. 172, part of the newly formed Congress of Industrial Organizations (CIO). On January

Emma Tenayuca shakes her fist on behalf of striking pecan shellers on the steps of San Antonio City Hall.

31, 1938, twelve thousand pecan shellers, almost all of them Hispanic women, walked off their jobs. During the three-month strike they called attention to the exploitation of Mexican laborers in Texas.

The strikers called on a well-known San Antonio labor organizer named Emma Tenayuca Brooks to lead them. Tenayuca Brooks was a member of the Worker's Alliance, which was part of the Communist Party, and her husband, Homer, was a former Communist Party gubernatorial candidate. San Antonio politicians tried to stifle the strike, arresting hundreds of workers. San Antonio's chief of police called the strike a Communist plot to take over the Mexican West Side.

Eventually the strike was settled, and the pecan shellers' wages were raised. But then Congress passed the Fair Labor Standards Act of 1938 establishing a national minimum wage of twenty-five cents an hour. The CIO joined the pecan sheller's union in asking Congress to allow an exemption, knowing that the higher wage would force the pecan industry to remechanize. But the Department of Labor rejected their pleas, and shelling machines soon replaced ten thousand workers.

Wages and working conditions for Mexican laborers remained substandard. But the San Antonio pecan shellers' strike marked the beginning of a new era for Latinos. And the national attention it attracted helped pave the way for Latino labor and political movements that would follow.

STREET SWEETS

The old-time Mexican candy vendors would stand diligently over their wares with a fly whisk, chasing the insects away. Immigrants to San Antonio brought the candy-selling tradition with them. Candies made from cactus, coconut, and caramel were sold on the street, but the most popular Mexican candy in Texas has always been the pecan praline.

LOMA LINDA PRALINES

These are the kind of simple pralines they serve at Loma Linda and other old-fashioned Tex-Mex restaurants.

MAKES 24 PRALINES

Combine the sugars, syrup, butter, and 5 tablespoons water in a saucepan over medium heat. Bring to a boil. Add the pecans and continue cooking until the mixture reaches the soft ball stage (238°F). Remove the pan from the heat and stir vigorously with a wooden spoon until the candy begins to turn opaque. Quickly drop spoonfuls onto aluminum foil and allow to harden. Store the pralines in an airtight tin.

1 cup light brown sugar, firmly packed

1 cup granulated sugar

1 tablespoon light corn syrup

1 tablespoon unsalted butter

1 cup chopped pecans

Aluminum foil, sprayed with nonstick cooking spray

IT'S A FREE COUNTRY

A 1938 WPA interview with a sixty-seven-year-old Mexican woman named Juanita Garcia explains how important pecan pralines were to early Tex-Mex entrepreneurs. Garcia said that her family crossed the river at Del Rio in 1877, when she was six years old.

"This was free country—everything free, pecans, wood, water, wild meat," she told the writer. She married a Mexican ranch hand and got a job cooking on the ranch. "The cowboys all time say they like me to cook, make good tamales and all Mexican food," she said. When her husband hurt his back, Garcia set out to provide for both of them.

"We make a little save on the ranch money, put up a little business, make hot tamales, enchilada and pecan candy," she said. "Pecans all time free, we make wholesale, retail and peddle Mexican foods. Ranchmen all time buy from me, me work hard make good business."

San Antonio, 1939: Santiago Mesa carries a 35-pound "taburete" on his head. His bakery stand contains cookies, pies, and sweet pastries.

PILONCILLO PECAN PATTIES

Piloncillo is old-fashioned, unrefined raw cane sugar. The cones were once sold in the streets by candy vendors. Today you can find it in Mexican markets and in the specialty aisles of grocery stores.

MAKES ABOUT 12 PIECES

Grate or chop the piloncillo into small pieces in a food processor and put them in $1/2$ cup water in a saucepan. Bring the water to a boil. Turn off the heat and allow the piloncillo to sit for 15 minutes or until it melts, using a wooden spoon to break up the pieces.

Add the cinnamon stick and the salt to the piloncillo liquid and bring to a boil. When the temperature reaches the soft ball stage (238°F) remove the pan from the heat and stir in the butter and the vanilla extract. Remove the cinnamon stick.

Beat by hand with a wooden spoon until the candy starts to thicken, about 1 minute, then add the pecans.

Working quickly, drop Ping-Pong-ball-sized spoonfuls of the candy onto an aluminum foil sheet and allow to cool for 30 minutes.

One 8-ounce piloncillo sugar cone (to yield 1 cup grated piloncillo)

2-inch-long cinnamon stick

$1/8$ teaspoon salt

$1/2$ tablespoon unsalted butter

$1/2$ teaspoon vanilla extract

8 ounces pecan halves broken in half (about $1^1/2$ cups)

Aluminum foil, sprayed with nonstick cooking spray

PINEAPPLE SHERBET

"Candy or sherbet?" the waiter in the tuxedo and bowtie at the Tex-Mex restaurant always asked when the meal was over. Orange and pineapple were the usual flavors.

MAKES 1 QUART

Boil the sugar in a quart of water for 5 minutes. Chop the pineapple, cook it briefly in the boiling syrup, then rub it through a sieve. When the fruit is cool, add the lemon juice and follow the directions on your home ice cream maker to begin freezing. When a slush begins to form, add the egg whites and continue freezing.

2 cups sugar

2 cups shredded pineapple, fresh or canned

Juice of 1 lemon

2 egg whites, beaten

Mi Tierra Biscochitos

6 cups well-sifted flour

3 teaspoons baking powder

1 teaspoon salt

1¹/₂ cups sugar, plus ¹/₄ cup mixed with 1 tablespoon cinnamon, on a plate

2 teaspoons anise seed

1 pound lard (see pages 11 and 90)

2 eggs, beaten

¹/₂ cup brandy or sweet wine

Biscochitos are the best thing to get with your coffee when you eat breakfast at a Mexican bakery. Mi Tierra makes my favorite version of these rich Mexican cookies. Sorry, there is no substitute for the lard—it's the secret ingredient!

MAKES 36 TO 48 COOKIES

Put the flour, baking powder, salt, the 1¹/₂ cups sugar, and the anise seed in the bowl of an electric mixer and blend at low speed. Add the lard in small batches, increasing the mixer speed to medium until the lard is well incorporated. Reduce the speed to low and add the beaten eggs and the brandy.

Cover the mixing bowl with plastic wrap and refrigerate for 24 hours.

When ready to bake the cookies, preheat the oven to 350°F. Form the dough into Ping-Pong-ball-sized pieces. Place 12 balls on each of four cookie sheets. Dip a fork in dry flour and press the balls twice to form a crisscross pattern. The resulting cookie should be only about ¹/₄ inch high. Bake for 12 minutes or until the edges and bottoms are golden brown.

Remove from the oven. Using a spatula and spoon, drop the baked cookies one by one into the sugar and cinnamon mixture and roll gently to coat. Set aside to cool.

Mexican Wedding Cookies

Every country has its own variation on these dense nut cookies. In the Tex-Mex version, they are made with pecans (of course) and associated with weddings. They are shaped like crescents instead of the usual balls. Could it be honeymoon symbolism?

MAKES 30 COOKIES

Preheat the oven to 350°F. Grease two baking sheets.

Beat together the butter and the 1/2 cup of confectioners' sugar in the bowl of an electric mixer, at medium speed, until light and fluffy, about 3 minutes. Add the vanilla, salt, and pecans and beat until combined. Remove the mixing bowl from the mixer and mix in the flour, using a wooden spoon. Do not overmix.

Form the dough into crescent shapes and place on the baking sheets. Bake for 12 minutes or until the edges and bottoms are golden brown.

Remove from the oven and allow to cool. Meanwhile, put the 1 cup of confectioners' sugar in a large bowl. When the cookies are cool enough to handle, put a few at a time in the bowl and shake to coat with the sugar. Remove and continue until all the cookies are coated. Then sift confectioners' sugar over each to give them a second sugar coating.

1/2 pound (2 sticks) unsalted butter, at room temperature

1/2 cup confectioners' sugar, plus 1 cup for dusting

1 tablespoon vanilla extract

1/2 teaspoon salt

1 cup coarsely chopped pecan pieces

2 1/2 cups all-purpose flour

FLAN

For the caramel
1 cup sugar

2 tablespoons light
corn syrup

1/4 teaspoon lemon
juice

For the custard
3 large eggs

2 egg yolks

2/3 cup sugar

1 1/2 teaspoons vanilla
extract

1/4 teaspoon
cinnamon

1/8 teaspoon salt

2 cups milk

1 cup light cream

Flan has slowly replaced sherbet and pralines as the most popular Tex-Mex dessert. Here's one that comes out very airy and light in texture.

SERVES 6

Put the caramel ingredients in a saucepan (preferably Teflon-coated) over medium heat with 1/3 cup water and simmer for about 12 minutes, until bubbles on the surface reach a light amber color. If the sugar begins to crystallize on the side of the saucepan, brush it with a wet pastry brush. Swirl the caramel as needed, but do not stir. When the caramel turns light brown, quickly pour it into six 1-cup ramekins, being careful not to get any on your skin.

Preheat the oven to 350°F. Fill an 18 by 12 by 2-inch cake pan with an inch of water and place it in the oven. To make the custard, whisk the eggs, egg yolks, sugar, vanilla extract, cinnamon, and salt in a bowl until well blended, or whisk in an electric mixer at low speed.

Heat the milk and light cream to 160°F in a small saucepan over medium heat. Remove from the heat and slowly pour into the egg mixture, whisking continuously for 1 minute. Pour the whisked mixture into another bowl through a strainer.

Add equal amounts of the strained mixture to each of the six caramel-coated ramekins. Place the ramekins in the water-filled cake pan, cover with a sheet of aluminum foil, and bake for 35 minutes or until a paring knife inserted into the center comes out clean. Remove the ramekins from the oven and allow to cool.

Flan may be served at room temperature or refrigerated. To serve, run a paring knife along the edge of the cup, then place a plate on top of the ramekin and invert.

Homemade Dulce de Leche (Caramel)

Goat's milk cajeta is very popular on both sides of the border and is widely available in Mexican specialty stores (Coronado brand is the most common). If you can't find goat's milk caramel, this easy homemade caramel is a great substitute. Caramel made from cow's milk is usually called dulce de leche *in Latin America.*

Bring water to a boil in a large pot and immerse the can of sweetened condensed milk completely. Reduce the heat to a low boil. Cover and cook the sweetened condensed milk for 3 hours. Remove from the heat and carefully extract the can from the pot with tongs. Allow to completely cool to room temperature before opening with a can opener. Serve as a dessert sauce over vanilla ice cream, crepes, or sundaes.

One 14-ounce can sweetened condensed milk (preferably Eagle brand)

San Antonio Chocolate-Cajeta Flan Cake

This stupendous chocolate caramel flan cake is a favorite dessert in modern San Antonio Tex-Mex restaurants, including Henry's Puffy Tacos. Thanks to Bonnie Walker at the San Antonio Express-News *for the recipe.*

Preheat the oven to 350°F. Place a large baking pan in the oven and add enough water to come 2 inches up the sides of a large Bundt pan. Lightly grease and flour the Bundt pan. Prepare the cake batter according to the directions on the box. Pour the dulce de leche into the Bundt pan, turning the pan to coat as much of the inside as possible. Pour the cake batter into the Bundt pan.

Pour the milks, cream cheese, vanilla, and eggs into a food processor and blend well.

Pour the milk mixture very slowly around the top of the cake. Cover the Bundt pan with foil and set in the water-filled pan in the oven.

Bake the cake for 2 hours. Remove from the oven and let cool for 1 hour. Place a large cake plate on top of the pan and invert. The flan mysteriously migrates while baking and will come out on top of the cake when it is unmolded. Refrigerate before serving.

1 box chocolate cake mix

Homemade Dulce de Leche (see above) or one 10.9-ounce jar Coronado brand goat's milk cajeta

One 14-ounce can sweetened condensed milk

One 14-ounce can evaporated milk

Half 14-ounce can whole milk (use the evaporated milk can to measure)

One 8-ounce package cream cheese, at room temperature

1 teaspoon vanilla extract

8 large eggs

AMERICAN
CHEESE
ENCHILADAS

THE MEXICAN-AMERICAN GENERATION

Second generation Mexican-Americans like the Cuellar brothers created Tex-Mex restaurant empires.

NEON BEER SIGNS GLOW BRIGHTLY IN THE cool darkness of Larry's, a vintage Tex-Mex restaurant in Richmond. It's a blazing hot afternoon, and I sit down at a Formica table to wait for my eyes to adjust. The wooden chairs are painted orange and blue, and there's a bullfight poster hanging on the wall.

I order Larry's Special Dinner, a three-plate extravaganza that includes a cheese enchilada, taco, tamales, rice and beans, chile con queso, and the old-time classic, spaghetti with chili gravy. The taco is made from regular ground beef with a minimum of seasonings and a maximum of chopped iceberg. The tamale and rice and beans are swimming in chili gravy. And the enchilada comes on a separate plate.

The food seems indistinguishable from that of dozens of other vintage Tex-Mex joints—until you dig into the cheese enchilada. As you work away at the rolled tortilla, a miracle takes place on the plate: viscous cheese sauce oozes into the dark chili gravy, creating a delicious masterpiece of brown and yellow swirls.

Like many longtime residents of the Lone Star Republic, I get downright sentimental about the goop that's left on the plate after the enchiladas are gone. Especially at places like Larry's. The cheese here has a certain *je ne sais quoi*, by which I mean that after half an hour of beer drinking, it still has not hardened.

I delicately quiz my waiter about what kind of cheese it is. He answers evasively. Do I really want to know? Then I spot Larry Guerrero, the seventy-five-year-old white-haired patriarch of Larry's Original Mexican Restaurant. He looks very much like the younger, dark-haired version of himself immortalized in the portrait that hangs over the door. I tell him how much I love his cheese enchiladas, and then I start asking questions.

"How does the cheese stay liquid?" I want to know.

ORAL HISTORY
LARRY GUERRERO
*Larry's Original
Mexican Restaurant, Richmond*

"When I opened this place in 1960, I couldn't even spell *enchilada*.

"I went to Felix's and I looked at that restaurant on Westheimer, and I said something like, 'This would do good in Richmond.' So I talked to Felix, he said he'd help me, and he did. I'll tell you who else was in my kitchen when I opened: Mama Ninfa. She had a tortilla factory then. She said, 'I'll help you get started, but when you get going, you buy all your tortillas from me.' And I said, 'You got it.' Felix and Mama Ninfa, they got me off the ground. I have got to give them credit."

Larry Guerrero passed away in the spring of 2003.

RAUL MOLINA JR.

Molina's Restaurant, Houston

"I was born in Houston in 1929. My father was Raul, so I was called Raulito. My family opened our first restaurant on West Gray in 1940. We lived above the restaurant in one room. My brother and I slept on the floor. We didn't need a kitchen; we ate every meal in the restaurant. Restaurants were run by families then. Mom cooked, Dad waited tables, I washed dishes. Things evolved. You grew because your family grew and three families couldn't live off of one restaurant. So you expanded.

"In the old days we served saltines at the table, not chips. We made real meaty chili with coarse ground beef, ancho chile pods, garlic, salt and pepper, and a little comino. We served it by the bowl thickened with cracker meal. You refrigerate it a few days, it didn't taste as good right off the fire.

"People called our food Tex-Mex, but I never paid much attention to all that. Chili con carne is Tex-Mex. But our sauces are Mexican—chicken mole is as Mexican as you can get. I prefer to call it Mexican food.

"When we first opened there were only five or six major Mexican restaurants in Houston. There was us and then there was Leo's, Felix, Mexico City, and the Old Mexico Tavern.

"In 1941, we bought the Mexico City Restaurant on South Main. The Mexico City had originally opened in 1929. They served spaghetti and chili, scrambled eggs and chili, filet mignon with home fries—the old-timers covered all the bases.

"Spaghetti and chili was the original Tex-Mex dish. You made the chili gravy mild for the tastes of the Anglos. My dad told me that most of the Anglos had bad teeth and that's why they liked it."

"It's the type of cheese I buy," he says cryptically.

The top selling cheese for Tex-Mex restaurants is Land O'Lakes Extra Melt, a salesman for a major restaurant supplier tells me. It's what Land O'Lakes calls a performance cheese, a pasteurized, processed American cheese. They don't sell Extra Melt at the grocery store. The closest substitute is that famous processed cheese product called Velveeta.

Sure, that first trip to the checkout counter with the screaming yellow Velveeta box in your shopping cart is going to be embarrassing. But you know it's the only way to summon up the déjà vu flavor of old-fashioned Tex-Mex at home. Just think about the luscious swirls of melted cheese and chili gravy you will soon be eating.

It's easier the second time.

"WE USED KRAFT VELVEETA FOR QUESO, and American cheese for enchiladas," Raul

Dallas Cowboy football players and their wives out to dinner at El Fenix

Molina Jr. tells me over a bowl of chili at the Molina's on Buffalo Speedway in Houston, one of the chain's three locations. "We tried Cheddar, but it was never consistent. During the war, you used whatever cheese you could get," he says with a chuckle.

Molina's chili gravy has more bite and better body than most I've tasted. It's made with ancho peppers and a lard-and-flour roux. Molina's is a family-owned chain that was founded in 1939 when Raul Molina Sr. bought the restaurant where he had worked as a waiter for ten years. Raul Sr. is now in his nineties. His son, Raul Molina Jr., is semi-retired as well. The operation is run by the third generation of Molina family restaurateurs, including Raul the third.

The amazing thing about Molina's is all the kids eating there. I ask a couple named Ken and Martha Johnson, who are seated with their daughters, Caroline, eight, and Annabelle, six, why they chose Molina's for dinner.

"The kids like it. They eat their dinners," Martha Johnson tells me.

I ask her if she doesn't prefer other Mexican restaurants with spicier food and more modern dishes. "Yeah, but if we go somewhere where the food is spicy, the kids won't eat. And then when we get home, they say they're hungry and we have to feed them again," she says. She admits there's a nostalgia factor too. "I grew up eating this kind of classic Tex-Mex. But the truth is, we don't like our food as hot as we used to, either."

One classic Tex-Mex dish that even the kids don't remember anymore is Larry's Spaghetti Mexicano. The fat, overcooked spaghetti strands are drenched in floury chili gravy. I'm astonished to still find this outdated Tex-Mex relic on modern menus.

Spaghetti with chili gravy has been around since the 1920s, when Walker's Austex Chili Company published a recipe for "equal parts spaghettis and chili con carne" under the name "Chili Mac." That Anglo nickname would later come to signify a popular casserole in 1960s western and midwestern suburbia.

It's easy enough to understand why the Anglos who pioneered the Mexican restaurant business in Texas would serve bland fare like spaghetti and chili. But you have to wonder why second generation Mexican-Americans didn't replace the dish with food that was more representative of their culture.

But if you follow the trail of the spaghetti, you can see how the half-Texan, half-Mexican compromise came about. Larry's Original Mexican Restaurant put spaghetti on the menu at the suggestion of Felix Tijerina, who helped Larry Guerrero open his place back in 1960. Tijerina had modeled his own menu after the one at Houston's Original Mexican Restaurant, where he worked for many years.

The rise of the small, inexpensive restaurant in the post–World War II era coincided with the emergence of a new cultural identity for Texas-Mexicans. While the "Immigrant Generation" had sought safety in the anonymity of itinerant farm work, their children, a group that scholars call the "Mexican-American Generation," longed to enter the mainstream and make a name for themselves. For many members of the younger generation, opening a Tex-Mex café was the express route to the American Dream.

No one personifies that rags-to-riches story better than Felix Tijerina. In 1918, the thirteen-year-old took a job as a busboy at the Original. The son of migrant cotton pickers who had moved to Sugar Land from Mexico, he taught himself English while he worked at the restaurant. Tijerina became a friend and trusted associate of the Original's owner, George Caldwell, and rose to the rank of manager.

Caldwell's café was a favorite of Mayor Oscar Holcombe and the downtown Houston business crowd. Selling Mexican culture to Anglos as O. M. Farnsworth had done so successfully at the Original in San Antonio, Caldwell adopted the slogan: "Genuine Mexican Food, Properly Prepared." But the

The menu of Frank Cuellar's Plaza Café in Shreveport, Louisiana

Original's combination plates actually featured spaghetti topped with your choice of chili gravy or Spanish sauce.

Caldwell encouraged Felix Tijerina to open his own Mexican restaurant and the young man took his advice. There were other Mexican-Americans in the restaurant business in Houston, but all of their establishments were located in the barrio. Tijerina was the first Mexican-American to open a Mexican restaurant that catered to Anglos, a daring move at the time.

In his biography of Felix Tijerina, *Mexican American Odyssey,* author Thomas H. Kreneck portrays the attitudes of the time. In 1922, the Houston chapter of the Ku Klux Klan held a barbecue on San Felipe Drive for its more than nine thousand members; the Klan held that Mexican immigrants were in league with the papacy. In that same year, a former superintendent of Houston Public Schools gave a speech vilifying Mexicans in which he declared that "the Rio Grande marks the line between enlightenment and ignorance."

In 1929, twenty-four-year-old Felix Tijerina opened the Mexican Inn a block away from the Original on Main Street. The experience changed the worldview of the young Mexican-American. As a restaurant owner on Main Street, he instantly became a fixture of downtown Houston, famous for his ability to charm Anglos and Mexicans alike. According to scholar Thomas Kreneck, this transformation was part of "the emergence of a bicultural Mexican American identity geared to life in the city."

The price that Mexican-Americans had to pay for the chance to assimilate into the mainstream was a loss of their "mexicanismo," their sense of an exclusively Mexican cultural identity. Instead, they adopted a bicultural existence—living a dual life as both

After his success at El Feniz, founder Mike Martinez (the tall man on the right) returned to the Mexican village of his birth and donated the money to build a water system.

Mexicans and Americans. This bicultural lifestyle gave birth to the hybrids of Tex-Mex. You hear it in the conjunto/rock tempo of Tex-Mex tunes like the Texas Tornado's hit "Hey Baby, Que Paso?" and in the cross-talking bilingual slang of the barrio and the border. And you taste it in Tex-Mex food.

Felix Tijerina followed the formula he had learned from George Caldwell. His advertisements promised "Mexican dishes exclusively" from family recipes handed down for generations. But his menu actually featured the Mexican food that Texas Anglos preferred, including spaghetti with chili.

Early Mexican restaurants like Felix Tijerina's were among the first institutions where urban Anglos and Latinos rubbed elbows with each other. And it was Tijerina's Americanized version of Mexican cooking that brought the races together. Authenticity was sacrificed for the sake of diplomacy.

Unfortunately, the Depression put the Mexican Inn out of business. But in 1937 Tijerina built a second restaurant in the Montrose neighborhood, close to affluent River Oaks. Felix and his wife, Janie, slept in the back of the restaurant and worked virtually around the clock turning the operation into a huge success. He would go on to build six outlets, creating one of the most successful restaurant empires of his day. "For the Finest in Mexican Foods" was Tijerina's slogan.

Felix Tijerina became a role model and a community leader who championed assimilation. A veteran of Mexican-American voter registration drives going back to the 1930s, Tijerina was among Houston's earliest Latino activists. He also rose through the local, regional, and state levels of the League of United Latin American Citizens (LULAC). In 1956 he was elected the organization's na-

Felix Tijerina samples the chili gravy.

tional president and served four consecutive annual terms.

As president of LULAC, Tijerina started the Little Schools of 400. At the time, Mexican-American students suffered an extremely high dropout rate. Tijerina believed that if Spanish-speaking students could learn a little English before entering elementary school, they might stand a better chance.

A pilot program was started in 1957 in Ganado, a small town southwest of Houston and just north of Port Lavaca. Tijerina paid a seventeen-year-old named Isabel Verver twenty-five dollars a week to teach five-year-old Hispanic children four hundred words of English. All the children in the program successfully completed first grade in a school system that had a poor track record: it had failed 50 percent of Spanish-speaking first graders the year before.

Governor Price Daniel asked Tijerina to expand the Little Schools of 400 program to other Texas cities. Speaking on Spanish-language radio stations across the state, he urged Mexican-American parents to get their children involved.

Felix Tijerina went from a thirteen-year-old busboy who didn't speak a word of English to one of the nation's foremost Hispanic leaders. Politicians such as Senator Ralph Yarborough courted his support. He was invited to the LBJ Ranch to consult with Lyndon Johnson about educational programs. His efforts to educate Spanish-speaking kids made quite an impression on the future president.

The Little Schools of 400 became the inspiration for LBJ's Head Start program, one of the most successful federal initiatives in our nation's history.

Felix Tijerina's vision of Tex-Mex biculturalism included a lot more than just spaghetti with chili gravy.

*Felix Tijerina and
Senator Lyndon Johnson
in the rear of a car
at the LULAC National
Convention, Laredo, 1958*

LARRY'S CHEESE ENCHILADAS

1/2 cup vegetable oil

8 corn tortillas
(see page 35)

1 1/2 cups Chili Gravy
(page 74 or 163)

2 cups shredded
American or Velveeta
cheese

1 1/2 cups chopped
onions

1 cup shredded
Cheddar cheese

Larry's Mexican Restaurant is frozen in time, as are many other things about the "Twin Cities" of Richmond and Rosenberg. You can still find Spaghetti Mexicano on the menu at Larry's and the cheese enchiladas are still made with American cheese, just as in the good old days. But the old-fashioned cheese enchiladas taste as good as, or better than, their modern yuppified counterparts. Be sure and have extra tortillas on hand to mop up the puddle of chili gravy and melted cheese left on the plate by these quintessential Tex-Mex enchiladas.

MAKES 8 ENCHILADAS

Preheat the oven to 450°F. Heat the oil in a small skillet over medium-high heat for 3 minutes. Using tongs, place a tortilla in the hot oil for 30 seconds or until soft and lightly browned. Place on absorbent paper and allow to cool before handling.

Ladle 1/4 cup of the chili gravy onto an ovenproof plate. Place 1/4 cup of the American cheese and 1 tablespoon of the chopped onion down the center of a tortilla and roll the tortilla around the filling. Put the tortilla seam side down on the gravy-covered plate. Repeat with another tortilla. Pour another 1/4 cup of the chili gravy over the top and sprinkle with 1/4 cup of the shredded Cheddar. Repeat for all four plates. Bake each plate in the oven for 10 minutes or until the sauce bubbles and the cheese is well melted. Remove from the oven and serve immediately. Garnish with the remaining chopped onions.

Molina's Old-fashioned Chili Gravy

When you make a chili gravy with chile puree instead of chili powder, you get a richer, smoother, and hotter flavor. This is probably what the chile queens' chili gravy tasted like back before chili powder was invented.

MAKES 5 CUPS

Heat the lard in a skillet over medium heat. Stir in the flour and continue stirring for 5 to 6 minutes, until the roux turns a light brown. Add all the dry ingredients and continue to cook for 1 minute, stirring constantly. Add the chile puree and a quart of water, mixing and stirring until the sauce thickens. Turn the heat to low and let the sauce simmer for 15 to 20 minutes. Add water as necessary to adjust the consistency.

1/2 cup lard or vegetable oil

1/2 cup flour

1 teaspoon ground black pepper

2 teaspoons salt

4 teaspoons ground cumin

1 teaspoon dried Mexican oregano

3/4 cup Chile Puree (page 50)

Los Tios Mexican Rice

Here's the spicy way they make "Spanish rice" at Houston's Los Tios Mexican restaurants.

SERVES 4

In a blender, combine the broth, tomato, and garlic. Puree and set aside. Heat the oil in a heavy-lidded skillet over medium heat. Add the onion and sauté until soft, about 5 minutes. Add the raw rice; sauté until it turns opaque without browning. Add the broth puree, chilies, carrots, cumin, and pepper. Salt to taste. Bring the rice to a boil and reduce the heat. Cover tightly and simmer for 25 to 30 minutes. Do not remove the lid during cooking. Allow to stand for 5 minutes after turning off the heat.

2 cups chicken broth

1 tomato, coarsely chopped

1 to 2 garlic cloves

2 tablespoons vegetable oil

1/2 onion, chopped

1 cup raw white rice

2 serrano chiles

1/2 cup minced carrots

Pinch of ground cumin

Pinch of black pepper

Salt

Josie's Plate (Chicken Enchilada with Friday Sauce)

One 15-ounce can tomato sauce

2 tablespoons flour

$1/2$ teaspoon garlic powder

1 tablespoon chili powder

$1/4$ teaspoon ground cumin

Salt

3 tablespoons vegetable oil

4 tortillas

1 cup Stewed Chicken (page 90)

$1/4$ cup chopped onions

$1/2$ cup grated Cheddar cheese

Los Tios Mexican Rice (page 163)

Frijoles Refritos (page 27)

"Catholics can't eat meat on Friday, so we make a meatless enchilada sauce we call 'Friday Sauce,'" says Del Moya Hobbs of Moya's Café in Refugio. *"But Mom used to eat it every day of the week. For her lunch, she would make one chicken enchilada in Friday Sauce with rice and beans. So I told her, 'Mom, I am going to put that plate on the menu and name it after you.'"* Funny to have a dish with Friday sauce that Catholics can't eat on Friday.

SERVES 4

Preheat the oven to 350°F. Heat the tomato sauce in a saucepan over medium heat. Stir the flour into $1/2$ cup warm water until smooth. Add the flour and water slurry to the tomato sauce, stirring to blend evenly. Add the garlic powder, chili powder, and cumin. Salt to taste. Set aside.

Heat the oil in a small skillet over medium-high heat for 3 minutes. Using tongs, place a tortilla in the hot oil for 30 seconds or until soft and lightly browned. Place on absorbent paper and allow to cool before handling.

Warm the tomato sauce and thin with water if it has become too thick. Dip each tortilla in the sauce, then put in a baking dish. Roll $1/4$ cup of the chicken and a tablespoon of the chopped onion into each tortilla, place them seam side down on an ovenproof plate, and ladle more sauce over the top. Sprinkle with cheese. Bake for about 10 minutes or until the sauce bubbles. Transfer each enchilada to an individual plate. Serve with rice and refried beans.

Delia Moya Hobbs
Moya's Café, Refugio

"Moya's Café was founded in 1938. It was my dad's bar. My mom, Josefina Moya, started making tamales to sell to the customers. And then she started making other food. Men would come to sit and drink. Women sat outside in the parking lot and waited for their men to bring food out. Finally, in the 1940s, they got brave and started coming in. We had a jukebox—they taught me to jitterbug.

"In 1960, Dad died and Mom took the bar out. My sister Tony was here in the beginning. She was the waitress. She knew what everyone in the whole town ordered. She's seventy-six now. I am sixty-nine. I was the baby.

"Mom put me in the kitchen when I was in my early twenties. I battled the old cooks. I was supposed to manage them, but they were ornery. Our tamales were famous throughout South Texas—the Mexican taquerias didn't exist back then. Back in the 1930s, a restaurant called Las Palmas was popular. But there was hardly any income around here.

Sharon Coward (left), Delia Moya Hobbs (right), Josefina Moya (pictured)

"Then came the oil boom, and the naval base in Beeville. Lots of sailors came in to eat. They spread the word through the Navy. People from Virginia, Florida, and all started coming in. 'I don't need to advertise. Everybody knows about us,' Mom said.

"We had butter and crackers on the table in the beginning. Nobody had tostadas [tortilla chips]. Houston made tostadas famous. People from Houston came down on their way to Corpus and said, 'We want tostadas.' We didn't have the right tortillas. We use thick tortillas for enchiladas, medium for tacos and nachos. You need thin ones for chips.

"Mom called our food 'Texas-style,' because you can't find it in Mexico. I'm real proud to call our food Tex-Mex. This year [2003] is the restaurant's sixty-fifth anniversary. My daughter Sharon Coward waits tables here now. And her daughter Sarah works here too sometimes, so we're on our fourth generation."

Tortilla autographed by golf great, Lee Trevino

El Fenix Guacamole Salad

Founded in 1918 by Miguel "Mike" Martinez, El Fenix is the oldest Mexican restaurant chain in the Dallas–Fort Worth area. Their guacamole is extremely rich; you can use it as a dip, but it makes a stupendous salad. Several easier variations from other restaurants follow.

MAKES ABOUT 2 1/2 CUPS

Scoop out the avocado flesh and combine in a food processor or molcajete with the other ingredients. Serve in iceberg "cups" with shredded lettuce, chips, and molcajete sauce on the side.

Variations

Los Barrios, San Antonio:
Mash 4 avocados and blend with 1 teaspoon garlic powder, salt, and pepper.

Molina's, Houston:
Mash 3 avocados and combine with 2 chopped tomatoes, 1 chopped onion, and salt.

El Chico, Dallas:
Chop 2 avocados and mix with 1/2 cup Spanish Sauce (page 78), juice of 1/4 lemon, and salt.

4 ripe avocados

2 tomatoes, parboiled, peeled, and minced

1/2 teaspoon salt

3/4 teaspoon garlic powder

1 jalapeño chile, seeded and minced

1/2 teaspoon hot pepper sauce

1 tablespoon fresh lemon juice

1/4 onion, minced

1 tablespoon olive oil

Molcajete Sauce (page 24)

The five Cuellar brothers parlayed their mother's tamale and chili recipe into a family restaurant dynasty.

EL CHICO'S SALSA FRIA (PICO DE GALLO)

3 tablespoons
Key lime juice
(see page 13)

1/2 cup chopped Texas
1015, Vidalia, Maui, or
other sweet onions

2 cups very ripe
homegrown or
heirloom tomatoes,
chopped

2 tablespoons fresh
jalapeño, serrano, or
chile pequins, minced

1/2 teaspoon sea salt

1/2 teaspoon freshly
milled black pepper

2 tablespoons
chopped fresh
cilantro

El Chico in Dallas was one of the first Texas restaurants to serve the chunky un-cooked picante sauce that now goes by the name pico de gallo (the name means "rooster's beak" and refers to the rapid-fire chopping sound the cook's knife makes while preparing it). This is an adaptation of El Chico's original Salsa Fria (cold sauce) that takes advantage of modern "designer" produce.

MAKES 2 1/2 CUPS

Pour the lime juice in a measuring cup with the onions and allow to marinate for 20 minutes or more. Combine all the ingredients in a bowl just before serving and mix well. Adjust the seasonings to taste. Serve fresh.

*Frank Cuellar Sr. with his wife Julia (both on far right, behind the counter)
and son Frank Jr. (seated on the stool) at the family's first restaurant in Terrell, 1935*

The Cuellar Family

Adelaidas and Macario Cuellar were Mexican immigrants who ran a small farm in Kaufman. In 1926, Adelaidas set up a food stall at the Kaufman County fair. Fair-goers raved about her tamales and chili con carne. Her sons were inspired to turn Mama's recipes into a restaurant business. The family's first cafés in Kaufman and Terrel failed during the Depression, but subsequent ventures in Shreveport, Oklahoma City, Dallas, and Fort Worth were extremely successful. The chain expanded across the South and Southwest during the 1960s and 1970s. Today there are close to one hundred El Chico franchises.

MOLINA'S HOT RELISH (ESCABECHE)

2 tablespoons vegetable oil

1 small onion, sliced thick

5 garlic cloves, quartered

15 jalapeño chiles, rinsed

1 pound carrots, peeled and sliced 1/2 inch thick (approximately 2 cups)

1 tablespoon salt, plus more as needed

1 teaspoon dried Mexican oregano, or more, if stronger oregano flavor is desired

4 bay leaves

1 1/2 cups white vinegar, plus more as needed

"My dad [Raul Sr.] really liked the hot relish [escabeche] when he visited Mexico," says Raul Molina Jr. "So he started experimenting and came up with his own recipe. That was one of Molina's innovations. We have had hot relish on every table since 1955."

MAKES 3 PINTS

Heat the oil in a large soup pot over medium-high heat. Add the onion and sauté for 3 minutes, then add the garlic. Continue cooking for another minute or two until the onion is soft. Add 2 quarts water and bring to a boil. Add the chiles and carrots and cook for 5 minutes or until slightly softened.

Add the salt, oregano, and bay leaves and simmer for another minute. Divide the chiles, carrots, and onion among three 1-pint Mason jars. When the cooking liquid has cooled, add 1/2 cup vinegar to each jar and top off with the cooking liquid until three-quarters full. Keep in the refrigerator.

CHILI MAC

"Take spaghetti and chili con carne, mix together in equal portions and you will have one of Mexico's most popular dishes," according to an old Mexene chili powder recipe for "Chili Mac."

  This combination became popular in Cincinatti, where spaghetti topped with chili and Parmesan is known as "two way" chili (if you add onions it's three ways, etc.). Chili mac also went on to become a popular ground meat and macaroni "hot dish" in the western and midwestern United States. There are countless variations—here's an easy version from the Texas Beef Council.

SERVES 4

Brown the ground beef with the bell pepper, onion, and garlic in a large saucepan over medium heat for 8 to 10 minutes, until the beef is no longer pink. Break the beef into crumbles and pour off the drippings.

  Stir in the tomatoes, tomato sauce, macaroni, and taco seasoning, and add 3/4 cup water; bring to a boil. Reduce the heat, cover tightly, and simmer for 15 minutes or until the macaroni is done to taste.

  Remove the pan from the heat and season to taste. Top with the grated cheese if desired and let stand for 5 minutes before serving to allow the cheese to melt.

1 pound ground beef

1/2 cup chopped green bell pepper

1/2 cup chopped onion

1 garlic clove, minced

One 14.5-ounce can Rotel tomatoes, undrained

One 8-ounce can tomato sauce

3/4 cup uncooked elbow macaroni

1 packet taco seasoning mix, or homemade recipe (see below)

1 cup grated Colby Jack cheese, optional

You can make your own taco seasoning mix by combining the following ingredients:

1 tablespoon chili powder

1/4 teaspoon garlic powder

1/4 teaspoon onion powder

1/4 teaspoon crushed red pepper flakes

1/4 teaspoon dried oregano

1/2 teaspoon paprika

1 1/2 teaspoons ground cumin

1 teaspoon sea salt

RECIPES *Different* WITH . . .

Magic MEXENE *All-Purpose* SEASONING

PUFFY, CRISPY, AND CRAZY

THE LOST ART OF THE TACO

Tacos, cervezas, and mariachis

THE CHIPS AT CARO'S RESTAURANT IN RIO Grande City aren't like any I've ever seen before. They are hot out of the fryer and puffed up like little triangular pillows. Caro's calls them "tostadas" and serves them with salsa and guacamole. I surmise that the chips must be made of fresh masa, just like Caro's "puffed tacos."

These tacos are made by frying raw tortillas made of moist fresh masa. The steam trapped inside the tortillas makes them bubble up as they fry. The result is a taco shell that puffs up into a delicious thin and crispy shape. They are very fragile and must be served hot out of the fryer.

"How long has Caro's made puffy tacos?" I ask Juan Caro, the owner.

"Ever since I've been here," he says.

"How long have you been here?" I ask, looking around the tiny restaurant. It's located in a simple house on a side street. It's not easy to find; the sign outside is tiny. From where I am seated, I can see about a dozen tables.

"I am seventy-one," he says. "And I have worked here ever since I could walk. My mother, Modesta Caro, opened this restaurant in 1937. She served tacos, envueltos, and enchiladas. There was a high school about a half a mile down that street, and there were no school lunches in those days. So the kids ran over here and ate. Two tacos and a drink were twenty-five cents. Fort Ringgold was still open then, and there were a lot of military people in town."

Fort Ringgold was established during the Mexican War to guard the border. It was once home to Robert E. Lee. But the historic fort was deactivated in 1944, one of a series of setbacks that has kept this quaint river town sparsely populated and seldom visited.

Rio Grande City has been the scene of several racial battles, including a major riot in

Frank Caro and a portrait of his mother, Modesta Caro

1888. The conflicts pitted the Mexican population against Anglo law enforcement agencies. The Texas Rangers, an organization notorious among Tejanos for shooting first and asking questions later, has always had a significant presence in Rio Grande City. "There was a lot of prejudice toward Hispanics, and there still is," says Juan Caro. "But things started changing when Kennedy became president."

But Rio Grande City also remembers an era of grandeur. La Borde House, a two-story brick inn was designed by Parisian architects in 1899. With its wrought-iron railings and shaded verandas, the building would look right at home in New Orleans. The architecture reminds you that at one time Rio Grande City was a cosmopolitan port.

In the mid-1800s, riverboats came up the river from the Gulf of Mexico to dock here and pick up cotton and hides. Rio Grande City was the only American community in the Lower Rio Grande Valley besides Brownsville, and its shipping docks served the farmers and ranchers for many miles on both sides of the river.

The riverboat era ended on the Rio Grande when the Texas-Mexican Railway connected Corpus Christi and Laredo in the 1880s. The Army closed Fort Ringgold in 1944, and Rio Grande City stopped growing. Today, its lovely buildings and once lavish homes pleasantly surprise visitors. A sprinkling of antique shops, cafés, and other tourist-oriented businesses struggle to make the town attractive to outsiders. But many of the biggest buildings stand shuttered and empty.

Caro's Restaurant stays open in part because so many people are willing to drive so many miles to eat here. Caro's is among the most legendary Tex-Mex restaurants in the state. The tiny eatery has never compromised its cooking.

There are actually three Caro's restaurants in Texas. In 1954, Juan's sister opened her restaurant in Fort Worth on Bluebonnet Circle. Several other Caro family members opened one in McAllen a few years ago.

"I had a restaurant in Fort Worth once too," says Juan Caro. "I opened it after I got out of the service. But when my mom died, I came back here to keep this one open." Juan Caro's wife comes in every day at 5 A.M. to start cooking. "We still make our own masa from corn," Juan Caro says. "We make our own pralines, just like my mom did." Everything is made from scratch, every day.

"We had a billboard once," Juan Caro says with a chuckle. "The slogan said, 'No Can Openers.' "

The puffed tacos are outstanding. They are thicker than the usual San Antonio version, and the masa is still a little chewy in the middle. Yet the outside of the tortilla is puffy and crisp. Mine was topped with beef picadillo, lettuce, tomato, and salsa.

I ask Juan Caro about the term "Tex-Mex."

He shakes his head. "Tex-Mex? It means nothing to me."

"But the puffed tacos, you don't find those

HENRY'S PUFFY TACOS

"My uncle Ray Lopez opened Ray's Drive-In in the early 1950s. It was Uncle Ray who trademarked the 'puffy tacos' name,"

Rick Lopez, Henry's Puffy Tacos

says Rick Lopez at Henry's Puffy Tacos in San Antonio. "My dad worked for Uncle Ray, and then he opened his own place called El Taco. They closed the street for construction and El Taco went out of business. Then we moved out to California for a while. We moved back in 1978, and my dad opened the first Henry's Puffy Tacos at Bandera and Woodlawn. Now every place says they make puffy tacos. But we sell the most. People eat between seven hundred and fourteen hundred puffy tacos a day here. We make a hundred pounds of fresh masa every morning."

in Mexico," I argue. "Your food isn't like the food over in Mexico."

"But why should I call it Tex-Mex?" he shrugs. "I just call it food. It's the same with the tacos. We just called them tacos in the beginning. But my son, Cary, he started calling them 'puffed tacos.' He wants us to say 'puffed tacos' on the menu because up in San Antonio they are making a big deal about puffy tacos. I say: 'What's the difference?' We have always made them this way."

HOT, FRESHLY FRIED TACOS WERE ONCE the best thing about Tex-Mex. When you asked for tacos at a Tex-Mex restaurant in the 1940s, the tortillas were fried to order. There were several methods. Some restaurants and taco stands simply fried regular corn tortillas into a U shape and then filled the hot shells with a picadillo and toppings.

Others filled the tortillas with a pre-made picadillo first, then fastened them closed with a toothpick and fried them with the filling inside. The hot taco was then carefully pried apart and the cold tomatoes, lettuce, and salsa were shoved inside. The combination of hot and cold fillings is absolutely delicious.

But the most exciting treats were called "crispy tacos" or "puffy tacos." These were made with fresh masa. When you ordered the taco, a tortilla was formed in a tortilla press, but instead of cooking the tortilla on a comal as usual, the cook dropped the raw tortilla into hot oil or lard. Depending on how it was handled, the tortilla would balloon into various shapes. Some cooks made puffy tacos U shaped like regular tacos, but more often, a puffy taco would simply be pressed in the middle so it formed a shallow V.

Today, Tex-Mex lovers comb the state for old-fashioned made-to-order tacos. A few old-time Tex-Mex restaurants still make them the way they used to—as do some modern restaurants, particularly in San Antonio, where popular demand is driving their revival.

The Old Mexico in Corpus Christi is one of

*Lyndon Johnson toasts Lady Bird
at El Matamoros restaurant in Austin
on their 25th wedding anniversary*

those old-fashioned restaurants that never stopped making crispy tacos. In fact, the Lopez family is responsible for some of the best crispy tacos in the state. Josephine Falcon Lopez joins me at my table as the waitress sets my taco before me. I ordered a "Crazy Taco," which is a crispy tortilla topped with ground beef, chopped tomato, and lettuce, with a generous helping of chile con queso poured over the top. The cheesy topping oozes down into the lettuce and tomato. The taco is messy to eat and outrageously rich.

Josephine Falcon Lopez
and her "Crazy Tacos"

"It's halfway between a taco and chalupa," says Mrs. Lopez of the crispy taco's unique shape. She and her husband, Joe, opened the Old Mexico Restaurant in Corpus Christi in 1945, and the menu has never changed. She

smiles, pointing to a portrait of her and Joe on the wall behind us: "I was twenty-nine when we first opened, Joe was thirty. From the beginning, we always made our own tortillas."

Josephine Falcon Lopez is eighty-one. As we talk, I realize that the gracious white-haired lady has long lived at the center of the Tex-Mex universe. Her cousin Sonny Falcon is known as the Fajita King in Laredo, where she grew up; he is widely credited with being the first person to sell fajita tacos in Texas. Her husband's brother Munroe Lopez once owned the El Matamoros restaurant on East Side Drive in Austin, affectionately known as "El Mat" to Austinites. It was the restaurant that introduced crispy tacos to Austin, and

ORAL HISTORY
LUCILLE QUIÑONES HOOKER
Jacala Restaurant, San Antonio

"My family's restaurant, El Rancho, made the first puffy tacos in San Antonio in 1953. We never wanted to call our food Tex-Mex, though. Tex-Mex was slang. I associate Tex-Mex with *pachucos*, or 'chucs,' as we called them—Mexican hoods, border people.

"We grew up on the North Side. My sister and I both went to Incarnate Word [High School]. She ran around with the cotillion girls, but she never got invited to their parties because our name was Quiñones. In the 1950s and 1960s,

you weren't proud to be Mexican. My friends never came to our restaurant. I was one of the twelve finalists for Miss Fiesta 1964. It was supposed to be an audience vote. I was the only Mexican girl.

"The newspaper said, 'Although Miss Quiñones received two-thirds of the votes, she was second runner-up.' That hurt. Sure, it's a little better now than it was back then, but things have never really changed. The color of your skin will always make a difference."

was a favorite of LBJ's. In fact, LBJ and Lady Bird celebrated their twenty-fifth wedding anniversary there.

Josephine's daughter, Linda Tanguma, was very concerned when she heard I was writing a book about Tex-Mex history. "We have never served Tex-Mex at the Old Mexico restaurant," she said indignantly. "We only serve authentic Mexican food here." I promised her I would mention that fact in the book.

Why have the fresh-fried crispy tacos that were once so much a part of Tex-Mex become so rare? The low-fat dietary consciousness played a big part. No matter how much you blot them or drain them, crispy tacos and puffy tacos are greasier than pre-formed taco shells.

And though such made-to-order tacos are fun to eat, they are also expensive to make. The food costs are higher, and because it takes longer to make each taco, labor costs are higher too. And then there's waste. The thin skin of the outermost part of a puffy taco often becomes brittle. When the tacos crumble, customers send them back.

"I had crispy tacos at El Matamoros in Austin around 1949," remembers Raul Molina Jr. of Molina's in Houston. He was a student at the University of Texas at the time. "I loved them. They were great.

"We tried puffy tacos at Molina's for a while, but you get busy and they get all busted up. It costs too much," Molina said. "We started making pre-formed taco shells in the late 1940s. We made the forms out of empty tin cans crushed into that taco shape."

When Taco Bell and other fast food chains started selling cheap tacos in pre-formed shells in the 1960s, most Tex-Mex restaurants followed their lead. By 2000 there wasn't a single restaurant selling made-to-order fried tacos in Houston.

With luck, the puffy taco renaissance in San Antonio will lead to a revival across the state. One thing's for sure: once you've tasted fresh-fried tacos, you won't bother eating tacos in pre-formed taco shells anymore.

LEB-MEX

El Patio, which opened in 1952, has always been Lady Bird Johnson's favorite Tex-Mex restaurant. Owner Mary Ann Joseph tells me that Lady Bird always orders the chalupa.

The Joseph family is Lebanese. So is the Karam family in San Antonio, a Tex-Mex family dynasty that owns Karam's and Mexican Manhattan in that city. Many people are surprised to find Lebanese-Americans cooking Tex-Mex, but it's actually an old tradition.

Paul and Mary Ann Joseph, El Patio

Mexico's Lebanese immigrants have been responsible for lots of Mexican food traditions. The most popular tacos in Mexico City, tacos al pastor, for instance, are made on the vertical roasters that the Lebanese brought to Mexico to make shawarma.

I asked Mrs. Joseph about her own family history. "My family was headed for New York," she said. "But when they got to Ellis Island, one of the children had pinkeye. They wouldn't let them into the country, so they stayed on the boat and got off in Mexico." Her family lived in Mexico for a while, then moved to the Lower Rio Grande Valley, she told me. She met her husband, Paul Joseph, at a church function. Cooking Mexican food was always second nature to these Lebanese-Texans.

Baseball's Goofiest Mascot: The Puffy Taco

Voted baseball's "goofiest mascot" by *USA Today's Baseball Weekly,* The Puffy Taco, sponsored by Henry's Puffy Tacos, comes out on the field and runs the bases at every San Antonio Missions (AA Texas League) game. And in a now familiar spectacle, children pour from the stands and tackle the taco before he can reach home plate.

The mascot never even gets close—a good thing, because The Puffy Taco doesn't slide well. Once Wesley Ratliff, the man inside the Puffy Taco, gets his six-foot-tall costume on straight, a puffy brown tortilla shell encases his back, while fabric tomato tufts, lettuce flaps, and grated cheese fringe stick out from under his lapels.

A Homemade Taco Dinner

The best way to eat homemade tacos is to put all the fillings and condiments on the table and let everybody make their own tacos. The taco shells stay hotter that way, and your family or guests can make their tacos just the way they like them.

Ground beef is the most common filling for Tex-Mex tacos (see Ground Beef Tacos, page 188) but Stewed Chicken (page 90) is also very popular. Fried shrimp or catfish fingers are also popular modern taco fillings. Vegetarians might want to substitute textured vegetable protein (TVP) for beef in the recipe for beef picadillo.

It's okay to take shortcuts. If you're in a hurry, there's nothing wrong with using packaged taco seasoning in your ground meat or bottled salsa instead of homemade.

Just don't substitute pre-formed taco shells! If you've never fried your own taco shells before, try it. It's easy and the difference in flavor is enormous!

To assemble a taco, you begin by spooning a couple of tablespoons of the meat filling into the bottom of the shell. Then you might add grated cheese or guacamole, or maybe some salsa. On top of that, chopped tomatoes and chopped iceberg lettuce are common. But it's fun to mix it up.

Tostadas are customarily topped first with a layer of refried beans, then cheese and chopped tomato or sometimes guacamole, with a pile of lettuce on the very top.

Here's a list of taco ingredients to have ready on the table.

For each taco
1/4 cup meat filling

1 tablespoon grated Cheddar or Monterey Jack cheese

1 tablespoon chopped tomato

1 tablespoon chopped iceberg lettuce

1 tablespoon Salsa Picante (page 205)

1 tablespoon Guacamole (page 167)

Optional toppings
Black olive slices

Pickled jalapeño slices

Chopped fresh cilantro

Sour cream

Refried beans

Homemade Taco Shells

12 yellow corn tortillas

Vegetable oil for frying (preferably peanut)

Frying your own taco shells with store-bought tortillas is really easy. The darker, denser, yellow corn tortillas work better than the fluffy white corn tortillas. If the tortillas are very fresh, they will puff up with air bubbles, creating semi-puffy taco shells. Stale ones will stay flat. The perfect taco shell will be a little bit flexible and chewy. Don't fry it too crisp, or it will shatter when you bite it.

MAKES ONE DOZEN

Pour the oil into a small skillet or sauté pan. How much oil you use depends on the size of the pan. If you pour the oil 1/2 inch deep, it's easy to make the U shape. With practice, you can use less oil by gently basting it where you need it.

Place the pan over high heat. It will take 5 to 7 minutes for the oil to reach the optimum frying temperature of 350°F. A tortilla slipped into the oil at the proper temperature should bubble immediately. If the tortilla spits and bubbles violently, the oil is too hot. Control the heat to keep the oil at the right temperature.

To fry the taco shells
Preheat the oven to warm. Line a baking sheet with several paper towels. Slip a tortilla into the hot oil. Flip it after 5 seconds. After another 5 seconds, as the tortilla starts to harden a little, use a pair of tongs to flip one side up, forming a U shape. Hold it there for 10 seconds until it sets in that position. Flip the U over, and for 10 seconds fry the side that had been elevated. If the taco shell starts closing, spread the tongs on the inside of the U to keep it open. The taco shell should be golden brown. The whole process should take about 1 minute if the oil is at 350°F. If the taco shells are getting brown, turn down the heat. As you finish each taco shell, put it on the baking sheet and blot gently with paper towels, then put the sheet in the oven to keep the tacos shells warm. Rush the shells to the table as soon you have enough for everybody to make a taco. Then start another batch of taco shells. Allow at least two tacos per person, three for big eaters.

To fry a tostada or tortilla chips
A tostada (chalupa) is a corn tortilla fried flat. Slip the tortilla into the hot oil and when it starts to harden, turn it several times with tongs until done. This should take about 1 minute. Drain on paper towels.

For tortilla chips you can use hotter oil, since you want the chips crisp. Cut the tortillas into quarters or smaller. Fry in 375°F oil for about 45 seconds or until lightly browned, stirring constantly to prevent sticking. Drain on paper towels. Salt while warm.

PUFFY TACO SHELLS

These are a little more complicated: first you have to make the tortillas! But it's worth the bother. The biggest danger with puffy tacos is that once your friends and family taste them, they will beg you to make them all the time. If you already have a tortilla press, you'll find that the whole thing is really pretty simple.

2 cups masa harina

1 teaspoon salt

Peanut oil for frying

MAKES 8 SHELLS

Combine the masa, salt, and 1 1/4 cups warm water in a large bowl and mix until a smooth dough forms. Knead for a few minutes or until flexible. Pull off pieces of dough and roll them into eight golf ball–sized pieces.

Place a ball between two round pieces of plastic wrap (see page 15), and with a rolling pin or tortilla press, flatten the ball into a tortilla between 4 1/2 and 5 inches in diameter and 1/8 inch thick.

Fill a deep skillet with 1 inch of oil and heat to 375°F. Maintain this heat by adjusting the flame.

Slip a tortilla into the hot oil and, with a spatula, baste hot oil over the top until the tortilla puffs up. After 1 minute, flip it over and use the spatula to crimp the tortilla in the middle to form a U shape or boat shape while it continues frying for another minute. After 2 or 3 minutes, it should hold its shape and look golden brown. Drain on paper towels. Serve each taco immediately!

VARIATIONS

Caro's Tostadas:
To make puffy chips like the ones Caro's in Rio Grande City serves, cut a raw tortilla into eight wedges and fry the wedges until golden brown. These should puff into pillow shapes. Serve with guacamole and salsa.

El Patio's Chalupas:
Fry raw masa tortillas flat until golden brown and crisp, then top each with 1/2 cup refried beans, 1 tablespoon chopped tomato, 1 tablespoon sliced iceberg lettuce, and 1 tablespoon guacamole.

Taco Village's Crispy Tacos:
After forming the tortillas, cook each one for 2 minutes on each side on a hot comal to reduce the moisture. Fry into a U shape in 350°F oil until well browned. These shouldn't be puffy.

Rick Lopez and his sister Imelda are two of the four siblings that run Henry's Puffy Tacos, the famous San Antonio restaurant founded by their dad, Henry Lopez.

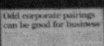

PUFFY TACO

Odd corporate pairings
can be good for business

GROUND BEEF TACOS

For the filling

1 tablespoon
vegetable oil

1/2 onion, chopped

1/2 pound ground beef

1 garlic clove, minced

1 serrano chile,
stemmed and chopped

1/2 teaspoon salt

1 teaspoon chili
powder

1/4 teaspoon ground
black pepper

1/4 teaspoon ground
cumin

For the tacos

1 1/2 cups grated
Cheddar or Monterey
Jack cheese

1 1/2 cups chopped
tomato

1 1/2 cups chopped
iceberg lettuce

6 fresh-fried taco
shells (see page 184)

1 cup Salsa Picante
(page 205) or favorite
salsa, optional

Making a ground beef taco filling ain't rocket science. You just cook ground meat with Tex-Mex seasonings. This recipe is a little spicy, but feel free to skip the serranos and substitute a packaged taco seasoning mixture for the spices, especially if you're cooking for kids. Many taco seasoning mixes, such as Old El Paso and Ortega, come in your choice of spicy or mild.

MAKES 6 TACOS

Heat the oil in a skillet over medium-high heat and cook the onion until it begins to wilt, about 2 minutes. Add the meat and sear, chopping with a spatula into small pieces until the pink color is gone. Add the garlic and chile and cook for 2 minutes or until the garlic is soft. Add the salt, chili powder, black pepper, cumin, and a tablespoon of water, mix well, and cook for 2 to 3 minutes or until well blended.

To assemble the tacos, put 1/4 cup meat mixture, then 1/4 cup each cheese, chopped tomato, and lettuce on each taco shell. Drizzle with salsa if desired.

VARIATION

Old Mexico Crazy Tacos:
Fill a puffy taco shell with beef, tomato, and lettuce, then ladle 1/4 cup Chile con Queso (page 202) over the top.

EL FENIX ORIGINAL TACOS

The earliest Tex-Mex crispy tacos were filled first and then fried. Some taco stands sealed the taco with a toothpick, but in this recipe, the filling is sticky enough to hold the tortilla together. The trick here is to stuff the tortillas and then drop them immediately into the hot oil. If you hesitate for even a few seconds, the tortilla will begin to crack along the bottom.

MAKES 2 DOZEN

Heat 2 tablespoons oil in a large skillet over high heat. Cook the ground meat, chopping it with a spatula to brown it evenly. Add the onions, salt, and bell pepper and continue cooking until the onions and pepper are soft. Pulse the potato, tomato, and spices in a food processor or mash in a bowl until smooth. Add the tomato and potato mixture to the meat and cook for a minute to combine. Add the flour and stir until thickened.

Heat the oil in a skillet over high heat to 350°F. Put a heaping tablespoon of filling in the middle of a tortilla, press it together gently, and lower it into the hot oil, being careful not to splash yourself. If it doesn't bubble right away, the oil isn't hot enough. When the taco is well browned, flip it over and cook the other side. When it is nicely browned on both sides, remove the taco from the oil with tongs, rotating it over the skillet to drain both sides. Then place it on a paper towel and blot it gently to absorb the excess oil. Open the hot taco gently and stuff with tomato, chopped lettuce, and salsa to taste. Press lightly to reseal and serve immediately.

For the taco filling
2 tablespoons oil

1 pound ground beef

1/2 cup chopped onions

1 tablespoon salt

1/2 cup chopped green bell pepper

1 potato, baked and peeled

1 tomato, cored

1 teaspoon ground black pepper

1/2 teaspoon garlic powder

1/2 teaspoon ground cumin

1 tablespoon paprika

1 tablespoon chili powder

3 tablespoons flour

For the tacos
24 yellow corn tortillas

3 cups peanut oil (or enough to fill the skillet to a depth of 1 inch)

2 cups chopped tomatoes

2 cups chopped lettuce

1 cup favorite salsa

CHAPTER 11

The Junk Food Era

NACHOS, BEAN DIP, AND FRITO PIE

Authentic Frito™ Pie is properly served in a torn-apart bag of chips.

MOST OF THE YEAR, DOWNTOWN PLAZA in Piedras Negras, Mexico, is a quiet, shady park, inhabited primarily by shoeshine men who ply their trade on benches under the trees. But on this sultry Saturday afternoon in early October, the plaza is mobbed. There is a huge stage set up for this evening's concert and beauty pageant. In booths around the park, people are cooking nachos.

Today Piedras Negras, birthplace of the nacho, is celebrating the 2002 Festival Internacional del Nacho. I'm here as one of the judges of the nacho-cooking competition. The contest will take place in a couple of hours after the judges are served a ceremonial lunch. Meanwhile, I wander the plaza to see what's going on.

Up near the stage, the world's largest nacho is taking shape on an enormous triangular griddle heated by propane burners. A crowd gathers to watch as men in red polo shirts pour Wesson oil on the griddle and fire it up. Adalberto Peña is the head nacho chef. After the oil is hot, he gives the order and the men begin spreading masa. "It takes fifty kilos [110 pounds] of masa and forty pounds of cheese," Peña tells me. When the masa and cheese are in place, four gallons of pickled jalapeños are applied. When the big nacho is done cooking, it's cut into pieces and distributed to the crowd. The dough is so thick, it ends up tasting like a masa pizza. It's a little charred on the edges, but it's still pretty good.

All around the park, competitors work furtively in their booths, concocting the perfect nacho according to their own secret recipes, as the judges sit down to a steak lunch. The judges include representatives from the Mexican Department of Tourism, commercial impresarios, and officials from a major bank headquartered across the border in Eagle Pass. Many of the men are in suits and ties; their wives wear lovely dresses. I am the lone gringo judge, and, in a Hawaiian shirt and shorts, I'm dressed for the part.

There are two categories: traditional nachos and specialty nachos. When all the entries have been tasted, and all the judges' votes have been tallied, the winner of the 2002 International Nacho Festival nacho-cooking competition turns out to be the Moderno Restaurant, the place where nachos were invented. Their specialty entry, shrimp nachos, was heaped with fresh shrimp. The traditional

The inventor of the nacho, Ignacio "Nacho" Anaya, 1969

Preparing the world's largest nacho

entry was pretty close to the original nacho that a waiter invented back in 1941.

In 1969, Bill Salter, a staff writer for the San Antonio *Express-News* tracked down Ignacio "Nacho" Anaya to get the real story of the nacho's invention. His nickname, it turns out, didn't come from his creation; it's just the usual Mexican nickname for Ignacio.

"These four ladies were sitting at a table drinking chicos," Anaya told Salter. Chicos were a popular cocktail of the era made with tequila and blackberry liqueur (see page 236). The women, who were American tourists, wanted some fried tortillas, but there was nobody in the kitchen. So, explained Anaya, "I sliced a tortilla in four pieces, put some cheese and slices of jalapeño on top, and stuck it in the oven for a few minutes." The women loved the cheesy crisps and wanted to know what they were called so they could order them again. "Just call them Nacho's *Especial*," Anaya told them.

"Nacho's Special," eventually shortened to "nachos," became the most popular appetizer at the Moderno. Eventually, the original Moderno where the nacho was invented was torn down and replaced by a new building. Ignacio Anaya moved across the border and opened Nacho's Restaurant in Eagle Pass. He never made any money on his invention. "The only man making money on nachos is the man selling the cheese and jalapeños," he told the reporter.

To say that Anaya "invented" a piece of tortilla with cheese and chile on it is a little ridiculous. No doubt the snack had been prepared countless times before. It's more accurate to say that Nacho Anaya gave his name to the nacho, and the name stuck.

Nevertheless, the town of Piedras Negras is very proud of the nacho. An official plaque in the plaza reminds visitors that this is the birthplace of the snack. The town hopes that its International Nacho Festival will encourage more tourists to visit. Like all Mexican border towns, Piedras Negras depends on American visitors for much of its income.

BARTOLO "MR. CHIPS" MARTINEZ

The first corn chips sold in San Antonio were the triangular Tostada brand corn chips of B. Martinez Sons Company, according to Ray Martinez, grandson of company founder Bartolo Martinez.

The chips were sold in San Antonio and South Texas beginning about 1912. An eight-ounce bag sold for five cents. Bartolo Martinez also marketed Tostada corn chips in bulk to San Antonio restaurants, including the Original Mexican Restaurant, where the chips were served to customers while they waited for their food. Thus began the custom of serving tortilla chips with guacamole, salsa, and bean dip as an appetizer, Ray Martinez says.

The Martinez Sons Company grew and eventually concentrated on their Tamalina-brand dehydrated masa product. Though the company still exists, it no longer makes the corn chips.

That dependence dates back to the late 1920s and 1930s when Prohibition transformed Piedras Negras and other sleepy Mexican villages along the Texas border into bustling centers of commerce. Huge bars, restaurants, and nightclubs were built to accommodate the crowds of thirsty Americans who poured across the bridge for an evening of cocktails and entertainment. The audience of Americans encouraged importers of Mexican handicrafts to build huge gift shops in the border towns. Business also picked up for the prostitutes of the Zona Rosa, as well for bootleggers and smugglers.

Today, the tradition of crossing over into Mexico for a few cocktails endures, thanks in large part to the fabulous bars and restaurants that were built there during Prohibition—and to the Tex-Mex food and cocktail traditions they started.

Nacho Anaya didn't make any money on the nacho, but from the 1940s through the 1960s, a lot of people hit it big in the Tex-Mex food business. As the automobile began to dominate American culture, people went out to eat in astonishing numbers. Drive-ins, hamburger stands, and roadhouses replaced the stuffy hotel restaurants that once defined American dining. And Tex-Mex restaurants were perfectly positioned to take advantage of the postwar demand for casual, inexpensive food.

Chef and food historian Larry Forgione has called the 1950s and 1960s the "Dark Ages of American Cuisine." During this era, American consumers began to consider canned, frozen, and packaged foods as labor-saving miracles. And there was little consumer resistance when restaurants began cutting the same corners. The fast food era had begun, and Tex-Mex lent itself perfectly to the drive-through mentality.

In 1952, in the Southern California town of San Bernadino, the McDonald brothers opened their first drive-in restaurant. In the same town, in the same year, Glen Bell, the founder of Taco Bell, began to work on a new vision for Mexican food.

There were taco stands in Southern California at the time, but the tacos were filled and fried to order. "They were delicious," remembers Glen Bell, "but if you wanted a dozen, you were in for a wait." Bell started experimenting with pre-fried taco shells to speed the process. He started Taco Bell in 1962 with forty shares of stock, each worth a hundred dollars. The stock split 30,000 to 1 when the company was sold. In 1978, Pepsico bought Taco Bell's 868 drive-in restaurants in a deal worth many millions.

"Mexican restaurants were really good back in the 1950s. But then things got commercialized," laments Raul Molina Jr. of

David E. Pace with his picante sauce, 1966

Molina's in Houston. "Taco Bell messed it all up. Taco Bell doesn't sell to Mexicans. When Taco Bell calls a pita sandwich a gordita, Mexicans laugh. But I guess the Anglos don't know any better."

Mariano Martinez of Mariano's Mexican Cuisine has even less patience for the Los Angeles–based chains and their Cal-Mex creations. "An enchirito, what is that? Did an enchilada mate with a burrito?"

Just as the automobile changed the way Americans ate out, television changed the way they ate at home. Was it the Frito Bandito who made us buy all those chips and dips? Or were we just looking for things to eat in front of the TV set?

The Fritos-and-bean-dip craze is one of many Tex-Mex snack-food success stories. According to Duane Rutherford, his father, E. S. "Rocky" Rutherford, and a partner named William Chambers invented Texas Tavern Jalapeño Bean Dip in 1955. The dip originally came in a tiny 3.5-ounce can that was sold primarily in bars.

"I think a little can sold for like twentynine cents when it first came out," remembers Duane Rutherford. "Everybody ate it on Fritos corn chips. So my dad went to visit Elmer Doolin, the founder of the Fritos company, and they got to be good friends. They made a deal and in 1958, Frito bought fifty-one percent of Texas Tavern and starting selling Dad's bean dip. They put it on wire racks with the chips. It was a big hit."

The original recipe for Texas Tavern Jalapeño Bean Dip was more complicated than you might imagine. Rocky Rutherford was a demanding cook. His dip recipe required a special pepper mash that he fermented in an oak barrel. Tabasco sauce is also made by fermenting pepper mash in oak barrels, but unlike the Avery Island pepper sauce, Rocky's mash contained primarily green bell peppers.

At first Rocky Rutherford used whole pinto beans, but then he found out he could buy imperfect split pintos for half the price. "The

The Frito Bandito Flap

In his book *Shot in America: Television, the State, and the Rise of Chicano Cinema* (University of Minnesota Press, 2000), Chon Noriega explains the role of the Frito Bandito in the Chicano rights movement:

In 1967, Frito-Lay Corporation launched a national advertising campaign featuring an "unshaven, unfriendly, and leering" Frito Bandito who stole Anglos' corn chips at gunpoint. Initially, Frito Bandito commercials appeared during children's television shows, where they were an "unqualified success," leading Frito-Lay to use the character in all its television and print advertising. Despite growing protests from Mexican-American groups, the Frito Bandito, developed by Foote, Cone & Belding Communications, sold a lot of corn chips during its four-year run. Frito-Lay was not alone in using a "bandito" to sell products. In the late 1960s and early 1970s, several companies used advertisements featuring Mexican revolutionaries. But most other corporations dropped the offending advertisements after protests from Chicano groups formed to confront racist stereotypes.

In response to these protests, and in concert with their expansion of the national advertising campaign, Frito-Lay "sanitized" the Frito Bandito. According to Owen J. Burns, who supervised the Frito-Lay account at Foote, Cone & Belding, this meant: "One. Less grimacing. Two. No beard or gold tooth. Three. Change in facial features to guile rather than leer. Four. Friendly face and voice. These changes acknowledged the "negative" stereotype and social impact of the Frito Bandito, while maintaining the basic premise of a Mexican "bandito" who steals corn chips.

Since Frito-Lay would not respond meaningfully to their complaints, Chicano groups turned to broadcasters. By December 1969, KNBC-TV in Los Angeles and KRON-TV and KPIX-TV in San Francisco had agreed to boycott Frito Bandito ads. A year later, however, the ads were still running. In January 1971, a $610 million suit was filed against Frito-Lay in federal court "for the malicious defamation of the character of the 6.1 million Mexican Americans in the United States."

In 1971, under increasing pressure as members of Congress, local television stations, and the press joined the cause, Frito-Lay reluctantly dropped the Frito Bandito campaign.

biggest problem with making bean dip is what to do about the brown spot," Duane Rutherford chuckles. It seems that when bean dip is canned, oxidation creates an unsightly dark brown spot on top that consumers find unappetizing. Rocky Rutherford's solution to the problem was to turn the bean dip cans upside down. "If you want to see the brown spot, just open a can of bean dip from the bottom," Duane says with a chuckle.

In the 1950s, the market for bean dip was mostly Anglo. In fact, Rutherford's Texas Tavern company marketed a different line of canned goods targeted to Mexican *braceros*. *Braceros,* which means "strong arms" in Spanish, was the name given to documented farm workers from Mexico who were allowed to work in Texas on temporary visas. "The *bracero* program required you to provide food

The Moderno's classic nachos

for the workers," Duane Rutherford explained. "My dad made canned menudo and canned beans for *braceros* under the Panchito brand."

In the 1960s, when Johnny Carson featured Fritos corn chips and bean dip on his television show, the product gained a national following. "Carson played word games with 'jalapeño' like he couldn't pronounce it," Rutherford remembers. "He'd say, 'hal-a-PEENY-yo' and 'hal-a-PAINY-yo.'" The route drivers in San Antonio were furious about Carson's clowning with the Spanish language—until the demand for bean dip suddenly took off and they started making a lot more money.

The Fritos and bean dip craze brought the basic flavors of beans, chiles, and corn to a mainstream audience all over the country. According to Duane Rutherford, "Once you got an appetite for Fritos and bean dip, you were hooked on the Tex-Mex taste."

FRITOS CORN CHIPS

Legend has it that the Frito-Lay company got its start in 1938 when Elmer Doolin, a young ice cream salesman, bought a five-cent package of corn chips at a San Antonio café. Doolin hunted down the maker of the corn chips and bought the company for a hundred dollars. He made the first chips in his mother's kitchen. In the late 1930s, Doolin and his mom turned out about ten pounds an hour, and he sold about ten dollars' worth a day from his Model T Ford. Doolin wasn't the only guy selling corn chips in San Antonio at that time, but his decision to give his corn chips a brand name would make him very wealthy. He later teamed up with a Georgia potato chip salesman named Herman W. Lay to found Frito-Lay.

BROWN'S NACHOS

Brown's Mexican Food on Hackberry Street in San Antonio opened in 1945. The current owners, James and Nora Hammon, have run it for over fifty years. At Brown's, nachos come eight to an order. There are three varieties: plain cheese, bean and cheese, and bean, cheese, and avocado. They put the jalapeño slices on the side of the plate so you can make each nacho as hot or mild as you like.

MAKES 8 NACHOS

Place the cheese in the center of the chip. Place the assembled nachos on a broiler pan and broil for 3 minutes or until the cheese bubbles. Serve on a plate with the jalapeño slices on the side.

8 heaping teaspoons shredded Cheddar cheese

8 large Tostitos "Restaurant Style" tortilla chips or equivalent

8 jalapeño slices

VARIATIONS

Bean and Cheese:
Spread a tablespoon of refried beans on each chip, then proceed as directed.

Bean and Cheese and Avocado:
Spread a tablespoon of refried beans on each chip, then proceed as directed. Serve with a scoop of guacamole on the side of the plate.

Gooey Nachos:
Substitute half a slice of Kraft Singles for the Cheddar.

Homemade Nacho Chips:
Stack 3 corn tortillas on a cutting board and cut into quarters, for a total of twelve pieces. Deep-fry in hot oil until crispy and drain. Substitute for store-bought tortilla chips.

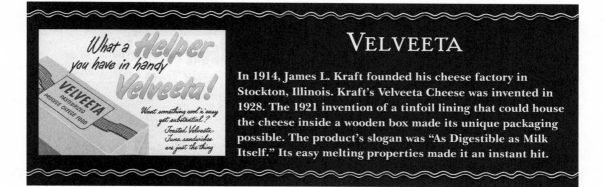

VELVEETA

In 1914, James L. Kraft founded his cheese factory in Stockton, Illinois. Kraft's Velveeta Cheese was invented in 1928. The 1921 invention of a tinfoil lining that could house the cheese inside a wooden box made its unique packaging possible. The product's slogan was "As Digestible as Milk Itself." Its easy melting properties made it an instant hit.

Rudy Cruz, founder of the El Popo Mexican food company, checks on the tortillas at El Popo tortilla factory.

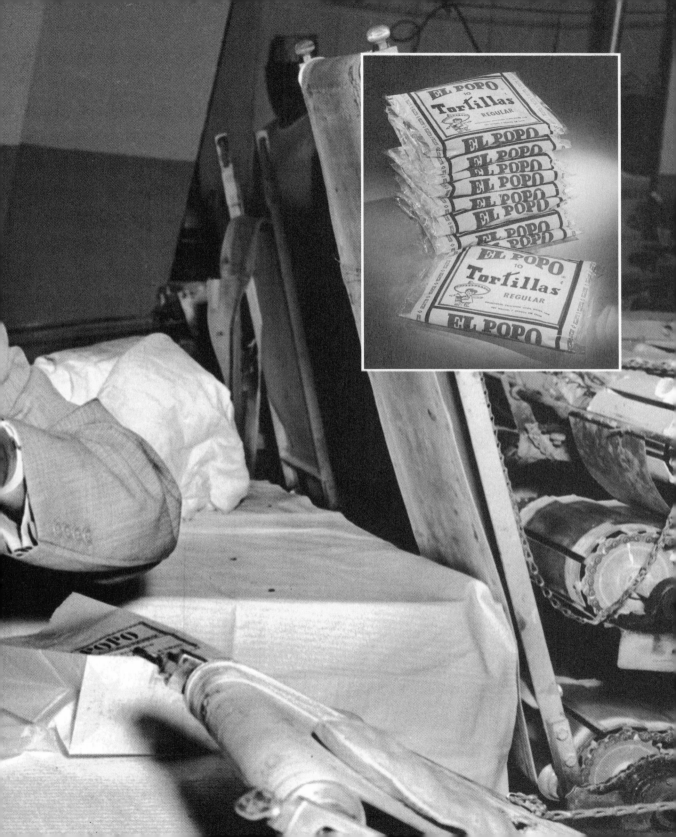

MI TIERRA'S CHILE CON QUESO

1 cup Velveeta cheese,
cut into pieces

1 cup grated sharp
Cheddar cheese

1/2 cup heavy cream

1 tablespoon minced
jalapeño

1/4 cup minced tomato

1/4 cup minced onion

You can make this in the microwave or a double boiler on the stovetop, but be fore-warned that the cheese quickly gets cold and unappetizing. That's why many people prefer to make chile con queso in a crockpot. You ladle small amounts into the serving bowl as needed while the rest stays warm. Serve warm with tortilla chips or Fritos corn chips for dipping.

MAKES ABOUT 2 CUPS

Combine the cheeses in a double boiler, microwave, or crockpot heat gently until the cheese melts. Add the cream and stir until smooth. Add the other ingredients and stir well.

Keep leftover dip covered in the refrigerator and reheat as needed.

VARIATIONS

Rotel Chile con Queso:
Melt 1 pound chopped Velveeta chunks in a crockpot or double boiler and stir in a can of Rotel tomatoes with green chiles.

Salsa con Queso:
Melt 1 pound chopped Velveeta chunks in a crockpot or double boiler and stir in 2 cups Salsa Picante (page 205) or one 16-ounce jar Pace Picante Sauce.

ROTEL AND THE HOT TOMATOES

The Texas party band Rotel and the Hot Tomatoes is named after the popular Tex-Mex canned tomato product first concocted by Carl Roettele at his family canning plant in Elsa, Texas, in the early 1940s. He called the brand Rotel because nobody could spell his name. Roettele's most popular product was a combination of tomatoes and green chiles that made it possible to cook with chiles without messy roasting and peeling. According to the company's website,

Rotel Tomatoes and Green Chilies were little known beyond Texas until 1963, when the wife of a popular politician in Washington bragged to a national magazine that they were the secret to her chili con carne recipe. Rotel is now owned by grocery giant ConAgra Foods Inc., and their customer service reps in Omaha have no idea who that politician might have been. Today, Rotel's various blends of spicy tomatoes are a popular shortcut in chili con queso, tortilla soup, chili mac, and many other recipes.

Bean Dip

Home-cooked frijoles refritos taste much better than the canned kind as a side dish. They taste great in bean dip too. But if you want to summon up childhood memories of the bean dip you ate from the can, start with canned refried beans.

MAKES ABOUT 2 1/2 CUPS

Put the red bell pepper, onion, vinegar, garlic powder, Tabasco sauce, and chili powder in a food processor and pulse a few times until the peppers and onions are minced. Add the beans and puree until well combined. Serve with Fritos.

1/4 cup chopped red bell pepper

1/4 cup chopped onion

1 teaspoon red wine vinegar

1 teaspoon garlic powder

1 teaspoon Tabasco sauce

1/2 teaspoon chili powder

2 cups (or one 16-ounce can) cold refried beans (page 27)

Fritos corn chips for dipping

Seven-layer Dip

This strange concoction is a favorite at cocktail parties and anywhere Texans gather in front of a television to watch football. Use extra thick tortilla chips or large size Fritos corn chips for dipping.

MAKES 9 CUPS

In a 9 by 13-inch baking dish, layer the bean dip, then guacamole, then chopped green onions and sour cream. Sprinkle chili powder evenly over the sour cream. Add a layer of chopped tomato and sliced olives. Finish with a layer of grated cheese. Refrigerate for 15 to 20 minutes before serving with chips.

Variation

Seven-layer Parfait Dip:
Make individual servings by layering ingredients in a margarita or martini glass.

2 1/2 cups Bean Dip (see above)

1 1/2 cups Guacamole (page 167)

1 cup chopped green onions

1 1/2 cups sour cream

1 tablespoon chili powder

1 large, chopped, very ripe tomato (approximately 2 cups)

1 cup sliced black olives

1 1/2 cups grated Monterey Jack or Cheddar cheese

Tortilla chips for dipping

Frito™ Pie

4 cups Fritos corn chips

2¹/₂ cups chili con carne

¹/₂ cup chopped onion

2 cups shredded Cheddar cheese

¹/₄ cup jalapeño slices, optional

Elmer Doolin's mom, Mrs. Daisy Dean Doolin, invented Frito Pie. (This fact is often disputed by New Mexicans, who think it was invented at the Woolworth's in Santa Fe, where a famous version of Frito Pie was served until the store closed in 1997.) New Mexicans champion elaborate gourmet recipes made with New Mexican red chiles.

SERVES 4

Put the Fritos corn chips in the bottom of a small baking pan and spread the chili evenly over the top. Sprinkle with onions, cheddar, and jalapeños if desired. Bake at 350°F for 5 minutes or until the cheese is melted. Use a spatula to transfer servings to a plate or bowl.

Variations

Original Frito™ Pie:
Open a 1.75-ounce bag of Fritos corn chips. Into the bag, pour ¹/₂ cup chili, ¹/₄ cup shredded Cheddar, 1 tablespoon chopped onion, and a couple of jalapeño slices. Eat it out of the bag.

Taco Style:
Top each serving with ¹/₂ cup shredded iceberg lettuce and a ¹/₄ cup chopped tomatoes.

New Mexican Frito™ Pie:
Substitute Chile Colorado con Puerco (page 113) for the chili con carne and top each serving with a dollop of sour cream and some chopped green onions.

SALSA PICANTE

Fresh jalapeños were the secret ingredient of David Pace's popular hot sauce. But when he started selling his pepper sauce in Texas in 1947, there were still a few problems. "My sauce bottles exploded all over the grocery shelves because I couldn't get the darned formula right," the founder of Pace Picante Sauce reportedly remarked. Here's a homemade version of the famous sauce.

MAKES 2 CUPS

Combine all the ingredients with 1^1/$_3$ cups water in a pan over medium heat. Bring to a boil, then reduce the heat and simmer for 30 minutes or until thick. When cool, place in a covered container and refrigerate overnight. Serve as a chip dip, taco sauce, or table sauce, or heat in a saucepan and use as a substitute for Spanish sauce or ranchero sauce.

One 10.75-ounce can tomato puree

^{1}/$_3$ cup chopped onion

^{1}/$_4$ cup chopped fresh jalapeño peppers with seeds

2 tablespoons white vinegar

^{1}/$_4$ teaspoon salt

^{1}/$_4$ teaspoon dried minced onion

^{1}/$_4$ teaspoon dried minced garlic

SIZZLING FAJITAS

TEJANO TASTES FROM THE VALLEY

*Cattlehands eating lunch,
Refugio County, circa 1950*

M ARIA LAGUNAS IS SLAPPING DOUGH balls into tortillas. I stand watching her near the front door of the original Ninfa's on Navigation Street, in Houston. After a short wait, we are seated in the old dining room near a huge enlargement of Mama Ninfa's wedding picture.

"She was skinny then," says our waitress, with a laugh. "I think she was eighteen or nineteen in that picture." In photos of the latter-day Mama Ninfa, she appears well fed. I order her specialty—fajitas.

The green and red hot sauces served with the chips at Ninfa's have radically different heat levels. The red is hot, while the green is mild and creamy. Ninfa's was the first place to make a big deal of serving red and green hot sauces, Houston food lovers remember. The original Ninfa's here on Navigation Street is also largely responsible for the fajita craze that swept the country late in the last century.

A press release distributed to the media a few years ago read: "It is a fact that a true legend of the food business, Mama Ninfa Laurenzo of Houston, Texas, originated the first fajita in the United States in 1973."

The year 1973 was a remarkable one in the Mexican restaurant business; it could be called the year that the paradigm shifted. It was the year the term "Tex-Mex," as a food description, first appeared in print, according to the *Oxford English Dictionary*.

The Cuisines of Mexico, by Diana Kennedy, was published in 1972; by 1973 it was a national sensation. For the first time ever, an author clearly spelled out the difference between real Mexican food and Americanized Mexican cuisine to stateside diners. It was no coincidence that Kennedy's cookbook, Mama Ninfa's restaurant, and the term "Tex-Mex" all entered the American food scene at the same time.

MAMA NINFA LAURENZO
(1924–2001)

Mama Ninfa Laurenzo was born Maria Ninfa Rodriguez in 1924. She lived on a small farm in the Lower Rio Grande Valley  near Harlingen with her eleven brothers and sisters. She married Domenic Thomas Laurenzo, an Italian-American from Rhode Island, and together they moved to Houston.

In 1949, the couple opened the Rio Grande Tortilla Co. on Navigation Street. In 1969, her husband died. In 1973, Mama Ninfa decided to turn the tortilla factory into a restaurant with ten tables and forty chairs in front and a tortilla factory in back. She sold 250 tacos al carbon, made with inexpensive fajita meat, on the first day of business. She went on to become the most famous Tex-Mex restaurateur of her generation. Mama Ninfa died in 2001 at the age of seventy-seven.

Tex-Mex legend Mama Ninfa

Thanks in part to the influence of Kennedy's friend Craig Claiborne at *The New York Times*, *The Cuisines of Mexico* became the definitive book on Mexican cooking. Its sermons on the inferiority of this country's Mexican food were accepted as gospel by food-savvy Americans who soon started using the derogatory term Tex-Mex to describe it. (Savvy is a Tex-Mex word, by the way, from the Spanish *saber.*)

In the introduction of his recent cookbook, *Matt Martinez's Culinary Frontier,* third-generation Mexican restaurant owner Matt Martinez Jr. of Matt's Rancho Martinez in Dallas and son of Matt Martinez of Matt's El Rancho in Austin remembers his first encounter with Kennedy at a cooking class.

Cesar Chavez in Austin, 1990

"She said she only did authentic Mexican food, not Tex-Mex," Martinez fumes. His family had been serving Mexican food in Texas for three generations and this was the first time he had heard it called Tex-Mex. "I was so insulted." Mexican restaurant owners across the state fought against the term. But Martinez took the opposite tack: he decided to call everything he cooked Tex-Mex and do what he could to make the style famous.

The sizzling metal platter comes to the table with the traditional warning "Very hot plate!" The strips of beef are black on the outside and extremely tender with a charred flavor and a pleasant hint of garlic and pepper. The fajitas are served on a nest of caramelized onions with green pepper slices on top. A fried tortilla shell in the shape of a cup holds lettuce and tomatoes, guacamole, and sour cream. I roll up a huge taco of salty beef, soft sweet onions, and smooth guacamole in a warm flour tortilla and bite in. The familiar flavor of the fajita taco is like an old friend.

But in truth, fajitas came along late in the history of Tex-Mex.

In the mid-1970s, while Diana Kennedy was teaching classes across the country, demonstrating the flavors of real Mexican cooking, radical changes were taking place in the Mexican-American community. Fiery leaders like Cesar Chavez challenged the status quo. Hispanic leaders who were seen as too cozy with the establishment, like Felix Tijerina in Houston and Rudy Cisneros in Austin, were denounced by the young radicals.

Minority groups of all kinds began to demand a multicultural model of American society that allowed them to retain their ethnic identities.

When Kennedy pointed out that Tex-Mex was a bastardized version of Mexican food, America fell into step behind her. First of all, because she was right. And second, because authentic or not, the Texas-Mexican food of Felix Tijerina's generation didn't reflect the spirit of the times. Tex-Mex had become "Uncle Tomás" food. It was Mexican food for white people. Baby boomers were ready to graduate to something more exciting—they wanted to eat the kind of food that Mexicans ate.

Enter the fajita.

Mama Ninfa is one of several restaurateurs who claimed to have invented Tex-Mex fajitas. So what's the story?

In 1984, a Texas A&M animal science professor named Homero Recio was so fascinated by the fajita craze and its effect on the beef industry (fajita meat went from $.49 a pound in 1976 to $2.79 a pound in 1985) that he obtained a fellowship to trace the origins of the fajita. While the word "fajita" didn't appear in print until 1975, Recio discovered that the word was in use among butchers of the Lower

Butchers at La Gloria Food Market's meat counter, San Antonio, circa 1950

Rio Grande Valley in the 1940s. Fajita is the diminutive form of *faja*, which means belt or girdle in Spanish. Fajita refers to the diaphragm muscle of a steer, which looks something like a short belt. It's the piece of meat called a "skirt steak" in English.

According to Recio, the actual originators of what we call fajita tacos were the Hispanic ranch hands who were given the head, intestines, and other unwanted beef cuts such as the diaphragm as part of their pay. They pounded the diaphragm, marinated it with lime juice, and grilled it. Then they cut it up and ate the meat with salsa and condiments on flour tortillas. Although the name "fajita" and the serving style is unique to Texas, a similar grilled diaphragm "steak" is also common in the Mexican state of Nuevo Leon, where it is called *arrachera al carbon*.

The first commercial fajitas may have been sold by Sonny Falcon, the man who the *Laredo Times* called the Fajita King. Falcon introduced grilled fajita tacos at a stall in an outdoor fes-

tival in Kyle, Texas, in 1969. He used only the thick, tender inner skirt flap meat. It was trimmed, butterflied (cut in half lengthwise), and grilled, just as in the northern Mexican recipe for arracheras, but instead of serving the meat as a steak, as in northern Mexico, Falcon chopped the meat against the grain into bite-sized pieces and served it on flour tortillas as "fajita tacos."

A short time later, the Round-Up Restaurant, which opened in Pharr, Texas, in 1969 became the first restaurant to serve fajita meat. According to an article by John Morthland in *Texas Monthly* in March 1993, the concept of serving the meat on a sizzling platter with guacamole, salsa, and flour tortillas was originated by the Round-Up's owner, Otilia Garza. The Round-Up closed under mysterious circumstances in the mid-1980s.

But the restaurant that is most closely associated with fajitas is Ninfa's. In 1973, Ninfa's began serving "tacos al carbon" made from fajita meat, which they later trademarked as "tacos al Ninfa." Sometime later, they began to use the name "fajitas." The restaurant caught the spirit of the times and Houstonians flocked to the tiny dining room. Ninfa's fajitas became a sensation that was imitated across the country.

Without any knowledge of the history or definition of the term, Mexican restaurants and their customers soon blurred the definition of "fajita" to mean any grilled meat served with flour tortillas and condiments. Soon chicken fajitas and shimp fajitas (which might be translated as chicken belts and

1979: Pantaleon Cortes and his family lead the Texas Farm Workers in a march from Muleshoe to the capital building in Austin to demand farmworkers' rights.

shrimp skirts) began appearing on Mexican restaurant menus.

The fajita craze caught on for a number of reasons. First, old-fashioned Tex-Mex had given Americans a craving for Mexican flavors, but the low-fat movement made many diners wary of lard-laden beans and cheesy enchiladas. Grilled meats and vegetables were a better fit with the new diet. Second, the emphasis on fresh salsas coincided with the skyrocketing popularity of chile pepper–based ethnic cuisines. And third, fajitas seemed more authentically Mexican than "señorita platters" and the rest of the Tex-Mex dishes that seemed to be making their way toward the bustray of history.

The fact is, of course, fajitas eaten with spicy salsas and fresh flour tortillas didn't come from Diana Kennedy's cookbook or interior Mexico. They came from the Lower Rio Grande Valley. It was more authentic all right, but it wasn't authentic Mexican, it was authentic Tejano.

"I grew up in the Lower Rio Grande Valley," Mama Ninfa told me on the phone about a year before she died. "I was just serving the same kind of good honest food at my restaurant that we used to eat at home. Fajitas were an old family recipe." Grilling steaks or fajita meat on a backyard grill and serving the meat chopped up with condiments and flour tortillas was a typical backyard barbecue for Tejanos in the Lower Rio Grande Valley.

Grilled meats are a tradition in northern Mexico as well. But the difference between Tejano cooking in the valley and northern Mexican cooking is the ingredients. Modern American beef, for example, is much more tender than the tougher range-fed beef across the border, so it lends itself better to grilling. In Mexico, the old cowboy tenderizing techniques of pounding and marinating had to be used on the diaphragm muscle. Tejano butchers, on the other hand, were getting thick, tender skirt steaks from midwestern meat packers that required no preparation at all. In reality, it was the national distribution of feedlot-fattened American beef that started the fajita craze.

" 'Botanas' used to mean bar snacks, chicken livers, chips and hot sauce, little stuff.

The L.R.G.V. (Lower Rio Grande Valley)

Railroads and irrigation turned the barren delta of the Lower Rio Grande into a major agricultural center at the turn of the twentieth century. Land that sold for twenty-five cents an acre in 1903, the year before the railroad arrived, sold for three hundred dollars an acre by 1910.

Winter garden crops like cabbage and onions thrive there in the semitropical climate. But the most important crop in the region is grapefruit. Beginning in the 1940s, the L.R.G.V. also became known as a resort area for migrating "snowbirds."

Deep-sea fishing, the white beaches of South Padre Island, and easy access to Mexican border cities are all important tourist lures.

Meanwhile, *colonias*, makeshift housing developments with no running water or sanitation, house thousands of legal and illegal immigrants from Mexico and Central America. The L.R.G.V is the most overwhelmingly Hispanic area of the United States. Even according to census figures, which underreport illegal aliens, the area is 85 to 90 percent Hispanic.

It was the free food they gave away at happy hour in the bars," remembers Joe Alonso, who owns several Tex-Mex restaurants in the Lower Rio Grande Valley. Literally, botanas means "plugs," like sink stoppers, because it's what you use to stop your hunger. It's the same thing as the tapas of Spain or the bocaditos in Mexico.

"But when I got back from Vietnam in the early 1970s, the Round-Up restaurant in Pharr had changed the meaning of botanas." The Round-Up was a drive-in where people would drink beer in their cars, Alonso remembers. The owner, Tila Garza, put grilled fajita meat on top of a plate of nachos and chalupas with some guacamole and lettuce around it and served it as a free botanas platter. It was so popular, she started selling it instead of giving it away. And then she put the fajita meat she served on the botanas platter on a sizzling comal and added it to the menu.

"I had a restaurant called Senorial in Alamo at the time," Alonso says. "Everybody came in and asked for a botanas platter." Alsono thinks Senorial was the second restaurant to serve the fajitas-covered botanas. Instead of serving a communal platter, Alonso served his botanas on individual plates with rice and beans on the side. Now the botanas in the Valley are usually chips, refried beans, and cheese with some grilled meat on top. It used to be just fajitas, but now you can get sausage, carnitas, tripas, seafood, anything you want on top of a botanas platter.

One thing's for sure, nobody in the Valley calls chicken livers "botanas" anymore.

"Things evolve in the restaurant business," says Joe Alonso. "That's what happened to Tex-Mex—nobody serves tamales anymore—nobody serves chili anymore either. Now everybody wants fajitas. I used to have a whole fajita section on my menu."

There are still lots of fajita choices at Alonso's Tres Rios restaurant in McAllen. Fajitas Monterrey are covered with cheese. Fajitas toreadas are fajitas marinated in

ORAL HISTORY
JOE ALONSO
Alonso's Tres Rios, McAllen

"Tex-Mex is the best of theirs combined with the best of ours. I call my food 'True Tex-Mex.' Who can dispute that?

Tex-Mex food is the best of Mexican food blended with American practicality. We use American ingredients, because that's what we have. We use Land O'Lakes American cheese because it melts—and people love it. Mexicans love American ingredients too. My dad used to come across the border from Mexico to shop for food when he lived in Reynosa. Hamburger is cheaper over here than it is in Mexico. When you say Tex-Mex in Mexico, they think of the music, not the food. They don't know what a 'Mexican plate' is over there!"

chipotle and grilled with serranos and onions. The sombrero platter features fajitas grilled with bacon and topped with tomato, onion, bell pepper, and mozzarella. And then there's the chicken fajitas.

"It was stupid people in Austin who started serving chicken fajitas," says Alonso with disgust. "There is no such thing." But like many other Hispanic Tex-Mex restaurant owners, Alonso got tired of arguing about the Spanish translation and started serving them himself. "Ladies wanted a low-fat version of fajitas, they didn't want to eat all that red meat," he says with a shrug. "And you can't argue with demand."

THE LIVING LEGEND

The legendary waiter Manuel De Leon, nicknamed "Meme," is pictured here with Muhammad Ali at the Round-Up Restaurant in Pharr. The Round-Up was a favorite of celebrities and Mexican politicians, and with wealthy drug smugglers until it closed in the mid-1980s.

De Leon is currently a waiter at La Casa Del Tacos in McAllen, where his manager describes him as "Meme, the Living Legend, the man of the gold, waiter to the famous." De Leon is weighed down with pounds of gold jewelry that hang from his neck, his lapels, and all over his jacket. His manager tells me, "All the gold he wears was given to him as tips."

Sonny Falcon's Fajitas

The original fajita tacos bear little resemblance to what you find in a restaurant today. Falcon never marinated the meat; it was simply trimmed, butterflied (cut in half horizontally), grilled, and then chopped against the grain into bite-sized pieces. Here's Sonny's recipe as explained by his son Danny Falcon. Sonny used to serve his fajita tacos with a little picante sauce and a whole lot of meat.

MAKES 6 FAJITA TACOS

Heat a charcoal or gas grill. Using a sharp knife, remove any membrane or silver skin from the meat and butterfly each flap by slicing it in half horizontally with a sharp knife so that the two halves are barely joined. Grill over a hot fire for 12 to 15 minutes, until well done. Add salt and pepper to taste.

Transfer to a cutting board and chop against the grain into small pieces. Divide the meat among the tortillas and top with the salsa.

1 pound fajita flap meat

Salt

Ground black pepper

6 warm flour tortillas

Salsa Picante (page 205)

Favorite Fajita Fixin's

When the sizzling fajita platter comes to the table, here a few things you might want to have ready:

- Warm flour tortillas (see page 34)
- Guacamole (page 167)
- Refried beans (page 27)
- Grilled onions
- Grilled pepper strips (rajas) (see page 10)
- Salsa fria (see page 170)
- Smoked Tomato Salsa (page 223)
- Ninfa's Red Sauce (page 219)
- Ninfa's Green Sauce (page 219)
- Grated cheese
- Shredded lettuce
- Chopped tomatoes
- Chopped fresh cilantro
- Pickled jalapeños
- Lime quarters
- Pitcher of margaritas (see Chapter 13)

NINFA'S SHOWCASE FAJITAS

Zest of 1 large orange
(about 1 tablespoon)

Juice of 2 lemons
(about $1/4$ cup) plus 2
teaspoons zest

$1/4$ cup pineapple
juice

$1/4$ cup sherry or
Zinfandel

$1/4$ cup Kikkoman soy
sauce

1 garlic clove, minced

1 tablespoon ground
black pepper

3 dried whole chiles
de arbol, crushed

3 tablespoons clarified
butter

2 skirt steaks, no
more than $3/4$ inch
thick, from the
outside cut

12 warm flour tortillas

Condiments of choice

This is the recipe Mama Ninfa gave out to the many publications that asked for her fajita recipe in the late 1980s. It tastes great, but it's a lot more complicated than the recipe they actually use at the restaurant. The fruit and fruit juices were probably an embellishment added for home cooks.

SERVES 6 TO 8

Grate the orange and lemon zests. Combine the zest with $1/4$ cup water, the pineapple juice, lemon juice, sherry, soy sauce, garlic, black pepper, chiles, and butter in a large baking dish.

Using a sharp knife, remove any membrane or silver skin from the meat. If the meat is thicker than $3/4$ inch at the thickest part, cut it in half horizontally (butterfly) so that it will cook evenly. Place the skirt steaks in the marinade and turn to coat. Cover the dish with plastic wrap and marinate at room temperature for 2 hours.

Light a charcoal grill or gas grill. Grill the fajitas over high heat for 5 to 7 minutes on each side, until done. Remove the meat from the grill.

Cut the meat crosswise into finger-length strips and place on a platter. Serve with tortillas and an array of your favorite condiments.

NINFA'S RED SAUCE

Chiles de arbol, the very hot, skinny dried chiles used in this recipe, make a very hot but very flavorful table sauce with a bright red color.

MAKES 2 CUPS

Bring water to a boil in a medium saucepan over medium heat and add the tomatoes and garlic. Reduce the heat and simmer for 5 minutes or until the tomatoes are soft. Remove from the heat and drain.

In a blender, combine the tomatoes, garlic, chiles, cilantro, and salt. Blend until smooth. Turn into a bowl; cover with plastic wrap and chill.

4 medium-sized (about 1 1/4 pounds) very ripe tomatoes, coarsely chopped

3 garlic cloves

1 fresh jalapeño chile, stem removed

2 dried chiles de arbol, diced

4 cilantro sprigs, chopped

1 teaspoon salt

NINFA'S GREEN SAUCE

Ninfa's creamy green table sauce tastes like a cross between salsa verde and guacamole. It's easy to make and goes great with fajitas.

MAKES 6 CUPS

Bring water to a boil in a large saucepan over high heat and add the tomatillos and chiles. Reduce the heat and simmer for 10 minutes or until the vegetables are soft. Remove from the heat and drain.

Peel, pit, and slice the avocados.

Combine the tomatillos, chiles, and avocados in a food processor or blender and process until smooth.

Pour into large bowl and add the salt and cilantro. Stir in the sour cream to achieve desired thickness. Cover and refrigerate until ready to serve.

12 tomatillos, peeled

3 serrano chiles

4 avocados

1 1/2 teaspoons salt

1/4 cup chopped fresh cilantro

2 cups sour cream

"Steak Fajitas" (Tacos al Carbon)

1 1/2 pounds sirloin

2 garlic cloves, slivered

1/4 cup olive oil

2 tablespoons chili powder

Salt

Lemon wedges

12 warm flour tortillas

Condiments of choice

One of the first establishments to cash in on the fajita craze was the restaurant in Austin's Hyatt Hotel. But since fajita meat required so much preparation, they substituted sirloin. The Hyatt served the grilled steak with a pile of soft flour tortillas and other taco fillings such as guacamole, sour cream, and salsa, so that patrons could roll their own tacos at the table. Here's a recipe for grilled sirloin tacos, fajita-style.

MAKES 12 FAJITA TACOS

Heat a gas or charcoal grill. Pierce the steaks with a knife and insert the garlic slivers. In a bowl, combine the olive oil and chili powder and turn the steaks in the mixture until well coated. Salt the steaks to taste and put them in a shallow dish while the coals are heating. Grill the steaks over a fairly hot fire, turning once, for 4 to 6 minutes on each side, until at desired doneness.

Transfer the steaks to a cutting board, slice them against the grain into strips, and squeeze the lemon over the strips. Serve with tortillas and condiments of choice.

"Chicken Fajitas"

For years, Tejanos argued that shrimp fajitas and chicken fajitas, which might be translated as "shrimp skirts" and "chicken girdles," were completely meaningless terms. But no one paid much attention to the finer points of Spanish translation. Eventually, even Sonny Falcon gave up. In his short-lived restaurant in Austin, the Fajita King started serving chicken fajitas too. "It killed me to do it, but I got tired of trying to explain it to everybody," Falcon conceded.

MAKES 8 FAJITA TACOS

Combine the onion, oregano, lemon juice, and olive oil in a blender. Puree until smooth. Transfer the puree to a bowl and turn the chicken breasts in the mixture until well coated. Cover and marinate for about 4 hours in the refrigerator.

Heat a gas or charcoal grill. Remove the chicken from the marinade and grill over a hot fire, turning once, for 2 minutes on each side. Move the chicken to a cooler part of the grill and cook, turning as needed, for 6 to 8 minutes or until cooked through.

Transfer the chicken breasts to a cutting board and slice them into long strips against the grain. Salt to taste. Divide the chicken strips among the tortillas on a serving platter and bring to the table with condiments of choice.

1 onion, quartered

2 tablespoons dried Mexican oregano

2 tablespoons fresh lemon juice

$1/2$ cup olive oil

Four 7-ounce boneless, skinless whole chicken breasts

Salt

8 warm flour tortillas

Condiments of choice

McAllen Fajitas

1 pound fajita flap meat

1 tablespoon Tex-Mex Dry Rub (page 132)

1 cup Kikkoman soy sauce

1 cup fresh lime juice

4 garlic cloves

6 warm flour tortillas

Condiments of choice

Here's a typical Tex-Mex restaurant fajita recipe. It's not quite as simple as Sonny Falcon's plain grilled meat and not quite as complicated as Mama Ninfa's fancy recipe for magazines.

MAKES 6 FAJITA TACOS

Using a sharp knife, remove any membrane or silver skin from the meat. If the meat is thicker than $3/4$ inch at the thickest part, cut it in half horizontally (butterfly) so that it will cook more quickly. Sprinkle the meat with dry rub and press it in with your hands. Combine the soy sauce, lime juice, and garlic in a shallow pan. Place the meat in the pan, cover, and marinate overnight.

Light a charcoal or gas grill. Grill the meat over a hot fire for 5 to 7 minutes on each side, until well done. Transfer to a cutting board and chop against the grain into pencil-thin pieces. Serve with tortillas and an array of condiments.

Variations

Fajitas Toreadas:
Add one pureed chipotle chile to the marinade and grill thinly sliced onions and green bell peppers with the meat.

Fajitas Monterrey:
Grill thinly sliced onions and green bell peppers with the meat and top with grated Cheddar or American cheese.

Sombrero Platter:
Grill bacon strips and thinly sliced onion and green bell peppers with the meat and top with mozzarella.

Wheat-flour tortillas have long been the daily bread of South Texas thanks in large part to Carl Hilmar Guenther (1826–1902), a German master millwright who built San Antonio's first flour mill in 1859. The company he founded, C.H. Guenther & Son, Inc., still produces the most popular flours in Texas.

Botanas Platter

The Round-Up Restaurant in Pharr deserves much of the credit for making fajitas famous. The chopped grilled meat was originally served there on top of the botanas platters. Fajitas-topped botanas platters are still among the most popular Tex-Mex dishes in the Lower Rio Grande Valley.

SERVES 4 OR MORE

Preheat the oven to 350°F. Distribute the tostada shells and the tortilla chips around a large decorative ovenproof platter. Drizzle all over with the refried beans. Add the jalapeño slices and sprinkle with cheese. Place the platter in the warm oven until the cheese melts. Top with the fajita meat. Tuck guacamole, lettuce, and tomato along one side of the platter. Serve with a pie server and a large spoon and let your guests dish it up themselves.

Variation

Joe Alonso's Botanas Plates:
Divide the same ingredients among ovenproof plates if you don't want to serve from a communal platter.

8 tostada shells

32 tortilla chips

3 cups warm refried beans (thinned with water or bean broth)

$1/2$ cup pickled jalapeño slices (or more or less to taste)

2 cups shredded Cheddar cheese

4 cups fajita meat, grilled

1 cup Guacamole (page 167)

1 cup chopped lettuce

$1/2$ cup chopped tomato

Smoked Tomato Salsa

By the time the fajitas are done, the coals are perfect but there's nothing left to cook. Well, here's a recipe that's designed to take advantage of those leftover coals. Smoking tomatoes is a great alternative to roasting them in a comal or in the oven. And smoked tomatoes are really outstanding in salsa. I put the tomatoes and peppers on the grill while I'm eating dinner, and then make salsa while I'm cleaning up. It tastes great with the leftovers the next day.

MAKES 2 TO 3 CUPS

Place the tomatoes, onion, and jalapeños on a hot grill, a good distance from the direct fire, and let them smoke for at least 15 minutes, turning several times. Remove the skin from the tomatoes and transfer the tomatoes, onions, and jalapeños to a food processor. Add the lemon juice and puree until chunky, about 30 seconds. Transfer to a bowl and add cilantro. Salt to taste. This will keep in the refrigerator for up to a week.

3 tomatoes, quartered

$1/2$ onion, sliced in rings

2 jalapeño chiles, halved lengthwise

1 tablespoon fresh lemon juice

$1/2$ cup chopped fresh cilantro

Salt

chapter 13

FROZEN OR ON THE ROCKS?

THE MARGARITA REVIVAL

*Shaking cocktails
at the Cadillac bar*

THE COARSE SALT ON THE RIM OF THE COCK-tail glass primes my tongue for an avalanche of tequila snowcone. I am drinking frozen margaritas at Mariano's Mexican Cuisine in Dallas. And on a brutally hot summer afternoon, a big mouthful of this adult Slurpee cools down the cranium like nothing else.

The frozen margaritas here are served in chunky, thick-stemmed glasses that remind me of beer schooners. The menu offers lots of top-shelf margarita alternatives, but I have ordered one of Mariano's original frozen margaritas. The tequila is really little more than a background flavor. The salt of the rim and the sweet and sour of the drink mix are far more pronounced than the liquor—which makes the drink very popular with college kids and other imbibers on training wheels.

Mariano Martinez, the restaurant's owner and the man who made frozen margaritas famous, joins me in the corner booth. Over several of the icy cocktails, he repeats a saga he has told many times before: the story of how he revolutionized the frozen margarita.

"When my father [Mariano Martinez Sr.] opened his restaurant, El Charro, in the 1950s, you couldn't sell liquor by the drink in Texas restaurants. But he made frozen margaritas for people who brought their own tequila. So when I opened this restaurant in 1971, people came to me for margaritas too," says Martinez. "Dad gave me his recipe—it was tequila, lime juice, and orange liqueur. His secret ingredient was a splash of simple syrup. You put it in the blender with ice until it got slushy."

The Texas legislature passed the "liquor by the drink" amendment in 1970. Beer and wine were already available in restaurants in "wet" counties, but local option elections were to determine whether restaurants could serve cocktails. In 1971, Dallas voted yes.

Selling cocktails was enormously profitable, and Martinez struggled to make Mariano's Mexican Restaurant *the* place for frozen margaritas. "I taught my bartender how to make the drink, but people complained about it. They said it tasted different every time. I tried to talk to the bartender about it one night, but he was sick of squeezing all those limes and threatened to quit," remembers Martinez.

"The next morning I was getting coffee at the 7-Eleven and saw some kids getting Slurpees out of the machine," he says. "That's when it hit me." Southland Corporation, the parent of 7-Eleven, wasn't eager to help Martinez purchase frozen drink machines, so he ended up buying a soft-serve ice cream machine. "We tinkered with the machine and the recipe for a long time," he says with a laugh. "We had a lot of tasting parties. We only had one machine, and it would run out every night."

When you make a frozen margarita in a blender, you dilute the drink with added ice, he explains. But if you put the same ingredients in an ice cream machine they won't freeze because the alcohol content is too high. First he experimented with diluting the solution with enough water to allow it to freeze. But the resulting cocktail tasted too weak. The solution, Martinez tells me triumphantly, was to increase the sugar. With a high enough brix level (the scientific measurement of sugar content), you can freeze quite a bit of alcohol.

The frozen margaritas at Mariano's Mexican Cuisine became an instant sensation. The

Frozen margarita machine inventor, Mariano Martinez

Dallas Cowboys started coming by at happy hour; Trini Lopez and Lee Trevino hung out there. But it was students from nearby Southern Methodist University who really spread the drink's fame. Within a decade, frozen margarita machines were blanketing the state in new-fallen slush.

Texas "Mexican" restaurants were struggling with the authenticity problem in the 1970s. Those deemed to serve old-fashioned "Tex-Mex" began to lose ground to those that claimed to have "interior Mexican" menus. A reputation for good, cheap frozen margaritas saved many old Tex-Mex institutions. And the unbeatable combination of fajitas and frozen margaritas launched a Tex-Mex comeback in the late 1970s and early 1980s.

Mariano Martinez never received a patent or trademark for his idea. He doesn't think it would have been possible anyway. "I just started making margaritas in a machine that already existed," he says with a shrug. Luckily, his margarita bucket was a financial success. The invention is still found in liquor and grocery stores. Pouches contain all the ingredients you need to make a margarita, except the tequila. You mix them up in the plastic bucket and put it in your freezer, then you scoop out frozen margaritas with an ice cream scoop.

"Every coed at SMU had a margarita bucket in the freezer," giggles a friend who attended the college in the early 1980s.

"I go places now and I tell people I invented the frozen margarita, and they say, 'Yeah, right,' " says Martinez.

As for the debate about who invented the original margarita, Martinez doesn't much care. The original drink was never all that popular anyway, he points out. The popularity of the frozen cocktail sparked the revival of its predecessor. The original shaken margarita owes it popularity to . . . the Slurpee machine.

Regardless of who invented it, there's no argument that the margarita changed the Tex-Mex restaurant business. Restaurants built from the 1940s through the 1960s didn't even have bars. From the 1970s on, the bar became the center of every Tex-Mex restaurant. In a state where temperatures can exceed ninety degrees six months out of the year, the frozen margarita became an enormous draw. Tex-Mex restaurants have lured customers with bigger, better, and stronger margaritas ever since.

Along with the new focus on the bar came a different attitude about dining. Whereas customers had once come to eat and quickly departed, now the Tex-Mex restaurant became a hangout. Cocktail-friendly foods, like chips and salsa, with accompaniments such as chile con queso and guacamole, soared in popularity as happy hour appetizers turned into a drinking man's dinner.

Eventually, postmodern cantinas like Xalapeño Charlie's and La Zona Rosa in Austin combined Tex-Mex food and Tex-Mex cocktails with live music. After all, where else would you want to listen to Tex-Mex tunes?

Frozen Margaritas

3 shots (6 ounces)
silver tequila
(preferably
Herradura "Silver")

1 shot triple sec or
Cointreau

3 heaping tablespoons
frozen limeade
concentrate

2 cups crushed ice

Coarse salt

Lime wedge

Here's the easy way to make frozen margaritas at home. The frozen limeade concentrate makes the drinks extra slushy without the addition of too much ice. Don't get the limeade concentrate out of the freezer until you need it!

MAKES 1 LARGE OR 2 SMALL FROZEN MARGARITAS

Combine the tequila, triple sec, limeade concentrate, and crushed ice in a blender and puree until slushy. Put the salt in a saucer. Wet the rim of the glass with the lime wedge. Invert the glass in the saucer and coat the rim with salt. Pour the slushy mixture into the salted glass.

Variations

Orange Margarita:
Pour a "floater shot" of Grand Marnier over the top of the drink and garnish with an orange slice.

Two-tone Swirled Raspberry Margarita:
Pour 1 shot (2 ounces) Chambord (raspberry liqueur) into a clear margarita glass, then pour the slush over the top.

Two-tone Swirled Strawberry Margarita:
Put 3 tablespoons pureed strawberries in a clear glass and pour the margarita over the top.

Astroturf Green Margarita:
Pour a shot of Midori (melon liqueur) into a clear glass and pour the margarita over the top.

Who Invented the Margarita?

The margarita is a success with a thousand fathers (and a few mothers). Among those claiming credit for the original drink's invention are a San Antonio society dame, Mrs. William (Margarita) Sames (pictured left), who first served her Margarita's cocktail at a party in Acapulco in 1948; a Juarez bartender named Francisco "Pancho" Morales, who says he accidentally invented the drink on July 4, 1942, while trying to make something else; and bartenders in Pueblo, Tijuana, and a host of other places. But until the frozen margarita came along, the original shaken version was seldom encountered.

CHUY'S MANGO MARGARITAS

You can use mango nectar if fresh mangos are too expensive, but this drink tastes much better with the fruit. If the drink tastes too sweet, add more lime juice.

MAKES 2 MARGARITAS

Combine all the ingredients except the lime slices in a blender and blend until slushy. Serve in large martini glasses. Garnish each glass with a lime slice.

2 shots (4 ounces) silver tequila

1 shot Cointreau

1/4 fresh mango, peeled and chopped

1/2 cup fresh orange juice

Juice of 1/2 lime

1 cup crushed ice

Lime slices

TWO-TONE SANGRIA

Here's a Tex-Mex twist on the fruity wine cocktail. This version tastes like a margarita with a wine floater.

MAKES 4 COCKTAILS

Prepare the limeade according to the instructions on the can. Fill 4 tall glasses with ice. Fill halfway with limeade. Add a shot of tequila and stir. Carefully pour red wine into each glass so that the red wine layer floats on top of the limeade layer. Garnish with a slice of lime floating on top.

1 container frozen limeade

4 shots (2 ounces each) silver tequila

1 bottle red wine of your choice

4 lime slices

TEX-MEX MUSIC

"Uno, dos, one, two, tres, cuatro . . ."

That count-off to "Wooly Bully" holds the key to understanding Tex-Mex music and its place in the cosmos of rock and roll. The bilingual enumeration isn't just an exotic, unconventional beginning to a giddy rhythm ride. For Sam Samudio, better known as "Sam the Sham," the turbaned hepcat who led the Pharoahs, screaming "uno, dos, one, two, tres, cuatro" was just what came naturally to a kid who grew up in the East Dallas barrio—where the First World meets the Third World, and the Tex meets the Mex.

*Tex-Mex music's history of mixing and meshing, borrowing and reinventing, has been going on since the 1870s, when Germans and Bohemians arrived in the Texas-Mexico borderlands bearing accordions, the instrument that would become the cornerstone of the conjunto sound. (*Conjunto *means "group or band" in Spanish.)*

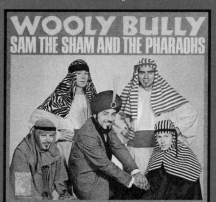

The emergence of conjunto artists like Narcisco Martinez and Lydia Mendoza coincided with Texas gringo performers, like Bob Wills & His Texas Playboys, soaking up Mexican sounds and repackaging them for their audiences. But it took rock and roll to give Tex-Mex real currency. From the Tex perspective, Buddy Holly's distinctive vaquero lilt blazed the trail. The Mex half of the proposition was articulated by Richie Valens, the pride and joy of East Los Angeles, who took a Mexican classic called "La Bamba," and revved it up into something new.

Before Valens stormed the charts, though, Baldemar Huerta, performing under the name of Freddy Fender, was already honing a reputation in

the Rio Grande Valley as the Tex-Mex Elvis. Fender, who played to his audience by singing rock and roll and blues in both Spanish and English, broke into the mainstream with his 1956 hit, "Wasted Days, Wasted Nights."

In fact, Mexican-Americans all over Texas were doing their own interpretation of rock and roll, filtering it through an ethnic gauze that rendered the music slower and more rhythm-heavy, swaying and braying with backbeats. Like all variations of early rock, black music provided the strongest influences—blues, rhythm 'n' blues, doo wop, soul— but Tex-Mex simmered those sounds in spice and salsa.

San Antonio's Sunny and the Sunliners became the first Mexican-American group from Texas to appear on American Bandstand with their 1962 hit "Talk to Me." 1965's Tex-Mex hit "Wooly Bully" was quickly followed by "96 Tears" by ? and the Mysterians (a.k.a. Question Mark and the Mysterians), a band of Michigan Mexican-American teens with family roots in Texas. Both songs shared dynamic similarities with the music of English bands like Manfred Mann and the Zombies.

The British Invasion, which put a damper on many regional styles of music, launched Tex-Mex into international prominence, "She's About a Mover," the 1965 hit by Doug Sahm's band the Sir Douglas Quintet, bore a striking beat-on-top-of-the-beat resemblance to Rubber Soul–vintage Beatles— and not by accident. Houston indie producer Huey Meaux, who had also overseen "Talk To Me," dressed up the Quintet in Carnaby Street fashions and tried to pass them off as English, rather than

KING OF TEX-MEX

DOUG SAHM
(SIR DOUGLAS)

TEXAS TORNADOS

Texan. "Just don't open your mouths," Meaux advised his clients.

"She's About a Mover" may have sounded British, but Texas music aficionados could hear Augie Meyers's trademark roller rink Vox organ for what it was: a chili-bowl synthesis of bajo sexto guitar backbeat, and accordion riffing on a modified polka.

No single performer grasped the atmospherics of Tex-Mex quite like Doug Sahm, a white boy from San Antonio who was a child prodigy on the steel guitar and whose life changed when he saw Freddy Fender perform at a San Antonio drive-in in 1958.

His album, **Doug Sahm and Band**, was hyped for its superstar lineup of supporting musicians, including Bob Dylan. But the recording was really noteworthy for introducing accordionist Flaco Jimenez, also from San Antonio. Sahm's next album, **Texas Tornado**, included an original, "Soy Chicano," that was embraced by Mexican-Americans as an anthem of brown pride.

In 1974, Sahm found Freddy Fender, who was working as a mechanic, and talked him into coming out of retirement. Fender soon topped the Billboard pop charts with "Before the Next Teardrop Falls" and a reworked version of "Wasted Days, Wasted Nights."

Meanwhile, Mexican-Texans were lifting elements of rock for their own regional style. Little Joe Hernandez of Little Joe y La Familia added salsa, rock, and a raised consciousness to the Tejano mix, ultimately setting the stage for the crossover stardom of Selena in the early '90s.

On the Tex side, the '80s saw the rise of Joe King Carrasco's punked-up Nuevo Wavo, Brave Combo's nuclear polka, and Sahm's own Border Wave sound. Then Sahm hooked up with Meyers, Fender, and Jimenez to form the Texas Tornados, the Tex-Mex supergroup that racked up a couple of Grammys and the biggest chart action for Tex-Mex since the mid-'60s.

The process of border hybridization has continued unabated—from Randy Garibay's chicano blues to the Tex-Mex ska of Mexico's Plastina Mosh and Houston's Los Skarnales, from the South Park Mexican's version of rap to Flaco Jimenez's collaborations with the Rolling Stones, Linda Ronstadt, and Dwight Yoakum.

As Sam Samudio would tell you, taking it Tex-Mex is as easy as "uno, dos, one, two, tres, cuatro."
—Joe Nick Patoski, *The Journal of Texas Music History*, vol. 1, no. 1, spring 2001, pp. 12–14.

TEX-MEX IN MEXICO

Some of the greatest institutions of Tex-Mex were built on the Mexican side of the border in the 1920s and 1930s during America's experiment with Prohibition. Ma Crosby's in Acuña is still beloved for its potent margaritas and its patio. The elegant Moderno in Piedras Negras is famous for inventing the nacho. It was also *the* place to drink a tequila cocktail called a "Chico." The Drive-In in Matamoros is known for outlandish appetizers like smoked eel on avocado halves, served in an opulent velvet-curtained cocktail lounge. La Fogata in Reynosa is an elegant Spanish colonial mansion where the melted cheese appetizer called *queso flameado* is the thing to order. The Kentucky Club in Juarez, across the border from El Paso, serves a definitive

shaker version of the margarita they call a "Mexican Margarita."

But the most famous of them all, the Cadillac Bar in Nuevo Laredo, is gone. It's hard to say whether the Cadillac was most famous for the food, its cocktails, or its music, but it was always a wild scene. Its former site is now occupied by the El Dorado Bar. The Cadillac name was sold to the Landry's restaurant corporation, which now operates Tex-Mex restaurants under that name. The original Cadillac was opened on July 4, 1929. The founder, a New Orleans bartender, had once worked for the legendary saloon owner Henry C. Ramos. The Cadillac Bar's cocktail specialty was the "Ramos Gin Fizz," which was invented by Ramos in New Orleans.

CADILLAC GIN FIZZ

Both the New Orleans and the Nuevo Laredo version of the gin fizz were hand shaken for five minutes or more. The action of the ice cubes agitates the cream and egg white into a delicious frothy consistency. Don't despair if it isn't perfect the first time; this is a difficult drink to get just right.

MAKES 1 COCKTAIL

Put everything except the club soda, orange, and cherry in a cocktail shaker with cracked ice and shake vigorously for 5 minutes or until very frothy. Strain the mixture into a tall glass, filling it three-fourths of the way up, then top off with club soda and stir. Garnish with an orange slice and a cherry.

1 shot (2 ounces) gin

1 shot (2 ounces) heavy cream

1/4 shot (1/2 ounce) fresh lemon juice

Dash orange blossom water

1 teaspoon powdered sugar

1 egg white

Club soda

Orange slice

Maraschino cherry

BREWERY WORKERS, SAN ANTONIO, 1895

Cerveza was the original Tex-Mex beverage. Shiner Bock, Lone Star, and Pearl are a few of the Texas beers created by Czech and German brewers around San Antonio at the end of the nineteenth century. All three brands are still popular today. South of the border, German immigrants introduced such excellent brews as Bohemia, Negra Modelo, and Dos Equis. While margaritas have become identified with Tex-Mex restaurants, beer is the most popular alcoholic beverage in the state. Texans consume more beer per capita than residents of every state except Wisconsin.

MODERNO'S CHICO

1 shot (2 ounces)
silver tequila or gin

1 shot (2 ounces)
blackberry liqueur

Fresh lemon juice

Simple syrup (see
Note)

Soda water

When Ignacio Anaya first whipped up his nachos at the Moderno in Piedras Negras, it was for a group of American women who were sitting in the restaurant drinking "Chicos," a popular cocktail of the World War II era. Moderno's current bartender Martin Zamarripa, reports that hardly anyone drinks Chicos anymore. They can be made with either tequila or gin, he says, but always with blackberry (zarzamora) liqueur.

MAKES 1 COCKTAIL

Fill a tall glass half full of ice. Add the tequila and the blackberry liquer. Fill a shot glass with one-third lemon juice and two-thirds simple syrup; pour over ice. Top off the glass with soda water. Stir.

NOTE

To make simple syrup, combine 1 cup sugar with $1/2$ cup boiling water.

KENTUCKY CLUB'S "MEXICAN MARGARITA"

Crushed ice

Juice of 2 Mexican or
Key limes

Coarse salt

2 shots (4 ounces)
silver tequila

2 shots (4 ounces)
Cointreau

Mexican and Key limes are the little ones. If you substitute Persian limes (the big ones), you'll need only one. This is a very strong cocktail. It should be treated like a martini.

MAKES 2 COCKTAILS

Fill a shaker glass with crushed ice and squeeze the lime juice into it. Wet the rims of two 4-ounce cocktail glasses with what's left of the lime. Dump a little salt on a dish towel and spin the moistened glass rims in it. Shake off the excess salt. Add the tequila and Cointreau to the shaker glass. Shake the cocktails with the ice and strain into the glasses, pouring carefully to avoid messing up the salted rims.

Sangrita

Sangrita, a concoction made of orange juice and chiles, is a popular chaser for those who like their tequila straight up. La Viuda Sanchez is a brand found in most Texas liquor stores, but it's easy enough to make. The tequila and the sangrita are traditionally served in two identical tall shot glasses.

MAKES 8 TO 10 COCKTAILS

Combine all the ingredients in a bottle or jar, mix well, cover tightly, and chill. Store in the refrigerator for up to 4 days.

Variation

Mix the tequila and the sangrita in the same glass over ice to make the cocktail called a petrolero.

> $3/4$ cup fresh Seville orange juice or $1/2$ cup fresh orange juice mixed with $1/4$ cup fresh lime juice
>
> 1 tablespoon Valencia or other cayenne pepper sauce
>
> $1/2$ teaspoon salt

Michelada

Michelada, roughly translated, means "my cold beer." At many Houston ostioneras (Mexican oyster bars), they add a tablespoon or more of hot sauce to your beer glass when you ask for a michelada. Here's a milder variation popping up in Tex-Mex restaurants.

MAKES 1 COCKTAIL

Salt the rim of a chilled beer mug by rubbing it with the lime and dipping it in the coarse salt. Squeeze the lime into the mug. Add the Worcestershire and Tabasco. Pour in the beer and serve.

Variation

Serve in tall glass over ice.

> $1/2$ Key lime
>
> Coarse salt
>
> 2 dashes Worcestershire sauce
>
> 1 teaspoon Tabasco or other hot pepper sauce
>
> 12 ounces light Mexican beer (such as Corona)

CHAPTER 14.

From Paris, Texas, to Paris, France

TWENTY-FIRST-CENTURY TEX-MEX

The Indiana Café, a Tex-Mex restaurant on the Left Bank in Paris

TEX-MEX

TABAT

CAFÉ

RESTAURANT
BAR

HOURS
à moitié prix
h30 à 20h

ON THE COVER OF CHUY'S MENU, A MATA-dor swishes his cape in front of a Cadillac sporting a longhorn hood ornament. "Fine Tex-Mex," the menu proclaims. I get the Comida Deluxe Dinner. The guacamole retains the shape of a mini ice cream scoop, the refried beans are crusty, and the queso is pure Velveeta. The Tex-Mex sauce on the very cheesy enchiladas is made of ground beef and whole chiles; it's much richer than your average flour-thickened chile gravy. The margarita is *fuerte,* the hot sauce is *picante,* and the chips are served slightly *caliente.*

From my two-tone vinyl booth, I look out over a dining room furnished with 1950s-style chrome dinettes. The silverware comes in a white paper bag that says "Sanitized for Your Protection" on one side and offers a Catholic, Protestant, and Jewish grace on the back. With its painted fish mobiles, broken-tile mosaics, and shrine to Elvis Presley, Chuy's is not your typical Tex-Mex restaurant. Or is it?

The Texas Chuy's chain (not be confused with Chuy's of Southern California) was founded on Austin's Barton Springs Boulevard in the early '80s by two Anglos, Mike Young and John Zapp. From the beginning, the decor—including black-velvet paintings of Elvis, and a retro "Air-Conditioned" sign on the door featuring a penguin with a scarf and earmuffs—made it clear that Chuy's was a tongue-in-cheek send-up of old-fashioned Tex-Mex restaurants.

In the early 1980s, lots of other wacky Mexican restaurants also opened in Austin.

Many seemed to draw their inspiration from the Beer Garden of Armadillo World Headquarters, the legendary music hall on Barton Springs Boulevard. When I was nineteen (legal drinking age at the time), I used to eat nachos and drink Lone Star at the Armadillo Beer Garden. It was among the grungiest restaurants I have ever seen—the disposable carpet tiles were always soaked with beer—but no one who ate there will ever forget it.

The kitchen staff included such larger-than-life characters as Big Rikki the Guacamole Queen, a sometime groupie and occasional cook. Big Rikki was known for her nachos, which were actually whole tostadas spread with refried beans, piled high with jalapeños, and loaded with melted cheese; they were three for a dollar.

Eventually Rikki turned over the kitchen to a more accomplished cook, Jan Beeman, an earth mother who came from a commune in San Angelo. A couple of music fans from Corpus Christi brought Jan a cooler of Gulf shrimp fresh from the coast whenever they came to see a show. Jan took advantage of the awesome heads-on, never-been-frozen crustaceans by putting them in her famous shrimp enchiladas. Traveling musicians made those enchiladas famous.

AWHQ prided itself on serving musicians real food instead of the usual deli snacks supplied by other concert venues, and the word got around. "Van Morrison's agent called from Arlington one night and told me Van wanted to come back and play a fourth night," remembers AWHQ founder Eddie Wilson. Morrison had already played his scheduled three nights, but Jerry Garcia told him that he shouldn't have missed Jan Beeman's shrimp enchiladas. So Morrison turned around and drove back to Austin to play an unscheduled set on a Monday night—just for the enchiladas.

"They were just big fresh Gulf shrimp in a typical Tex-Mex tomato and chile sauce," says Wilson. But back then, nobody had ever seen fresh shrimp enchiladas. Beeman's Armadillo kitchen became so famous among musicians that when the Beach Boys played a concert at Austin's Palmer Auditorium, they wrote a clause into their contract demanding that Armadillo's kitchen provide the backstage catering.

Tragically, the Armadillo World Headquarters went out of business on New Year's Day, 1980. But several new bars and cafés opened in the same Barton Springs neighborhood, and they kept the spirit alive. Xalapeño Charlie's was a Tex-Mex restaurant that featured a happy hour with live music. "Charlie Dugan was a wildman," remembers Eddie Wilson, "and I think Xalapeño Charlie's was the first of the 'hippy Tex-Mex' restaurants."

In 1981, another restaurant debuted on downtown Austin's Congress Avenue. The restaurant was named Las Manitas (Spanish for "little hands"), but its owners, sisters Cynthia and Lidia Pérez, couldn't afford a new sign. Instead, they used the old one that had belonged to the last occupant, the Avenue Café, and called their restaurant Las Manitas Avenue Café.

The humble Las Manitas, with its long counter and narrow front dining room, was an instant hit. The same year they opened the restaurant, the Pérez sisters founded La Peña, an organization that provides wider exposure

Big Rikki, the Guacamole Queen, prepares her avocado salad onstage at Armadillo World Headquarters before a concert. The tortilla chip hat with guacamole and hot sauce trim was designed by AWHQ artist-in-residence, Jim Franklin.

La Peña

Cynthia Pérez (left), Lidia Pérez (right), and María Elena Martínez founded Austin's La Peña in 1982, inspired by a restaurant-based art organization in Berkeley, California, also called La Peña. The first "peña," an evening of poetry, art, and music, celebrated International Workers' Day on May 1, 1982.

Since its inception, La Peña has mounted a new show each month at the Las Manitas gallery. Besides organizing solo exhibitions for established artists and new talents, La Peña presents thematic group exhibitions such as the annual show devoted to the Virgin of Guadalupe, originally organized in conjunction with a local chapter of the Sociedades Guadalupanas. La Peña also hosts dances, poetry readings, theatrical and musical performances, and an annual film series.

to Latino visual artists, poets, and musicians. The walls of the restaurant were La Peña's first gallery space. By 1985, La Peña had grown into a Latino-arts umbrella organization serving all of Central Texas. Today it is one of the foremost organizations of its kind in the country and draws funding from the National Endowment for the Arts.

Las Manitas has became an Austin landmark, the favorite Mexican breakfast hangout for everyone from the gay and lesbian community to the city's lawyers and politicos. Over the years, the menu has expanded from simple tacos and enchiladas, and now includes such exotica as Central American breakfasts and elaborate Mexican soups. To satisfy the hip crowd in the capital city, the menu includes Aus-Mex favorites such as migas with mushrooms and shrimp enchiladas, as well as only-in-Austin dishes like vegetarian tamales and scrambled eggs with soy-gluten chorizo.

Though their style of cooking is unique to Austin, Cynthia and Lidia Pérez don't call their food Tex-Mex. Like Gloria Reyna, the current owner of Matt's El Rancho, and the daughter of its founder, Matt Martinez Sr., the Pérez sisters consider their cooking pure-bred Latino. For them, the term "Tex-Mex" carries the taint of something bastardized.

Zapp and Young, the two Anglos who founded the wacky Chuy's chain, have no such reservations. I stopped by Chuy's offices near the original restaurant in Austin one afternoon to look through their archives. As far as I could tell, Chuy's was the first self-proclaimed Tex-Mex restaurant in Texas.

In 1982, their first menu said, "Chuy's, Comida Deluxe." In 1986, the words "Tex-Mex Deluxe" appeared. "We embraced the term 'Tex-Mex' pretty early," says Mike Young. By 1986, he remembers seeing the term in the national press all the time, but he believes that people in the rest of the country were mistaken about what Tex-Mex really meant.

To Mike Young, who grew up eating Tejano food in the Lower Rio Grande Valley, Tex-Mex was the style he'd first encountered in San Antonio, a style whose signature dish was a cheese enchilada in chili gravy, topped with raw onions. But Young also recognized that to the general public, 'Tex-Mex' had become a broader category. Rather than fight the broader notion, Young embraced it.

Chuy's may have been the first restaurant in Texas to call itself Tex-Mex, but it wasn't the first in the world. That distinction, like so many other culinary honors, belongs to the French. To the vast amusement of Texans, Tex-Mex became the hottest food trend in Paris in the 1980s. By the early '90s, Tex-Mex restaurants were springing up all over the world.

CAFÉ PACIFICO'S CHEESE ENCHILADAS came cloaked in a rich red chile colorado sauce. But it was the cheese itself that captured my attention—sharp, tangy, and perfectly melted, with the aroma of a Swiss fondue. This cheese enchilada was the best I'd ever had. Which was quite a surprise, in the Montparnasse section of Paris.

"What kind of cheese do you put in these enchiladas?" I asked the waitress.

"It's an aged Gruyère," she said in an English accent.

I asked her if she thought Tex-Mex was a just a passing fad here. "No, Tex-Mex has outlived fad status in Paris," she said. "It's here to stay."

The year was 1993, and I had spent the better part of a Sunday afternoon sampling Parisian Tex-Mex restaurants. I tried a burrito at Indiana Café on Boulevard St-Germain; some huevos and chorizo at Del Rio Café, in the Beaux-Arts district; and a few tamales at

Claude Benayoun

"The French love it because it's an identifiably American cuisine," she told me in her living room over a glass of champagne. "It's everywhere you look now. My winemaker in Provence, a real Frenchman's Frenchman, clears his palate with tortilla chips at wine tastings."

How did Tex-Mex first catch on in Paris? I asked Austin restaurateur Claude Benayoun. A co-owner of the Vespaio Italian restaurant on South Congress Avenue, Benayoun is a wiry, energetic man in his late thirties with a shaved head and an easy smile. I met him one morning at the Texas French Bread bakery, a few doors down from his restaurant, and he gave me his account over an espresso.

Benayoun earned his MBA in hotel and restaurant management at the University of Paris in 1980. After graduation, he came to the United States to continue his studies in California. While passing through Texas, he sampled Tex-Mex food and was intrigued by both the strong flavors and the name.

"Tex-Mex"—he pronounced it dramatically in his French accent. "To a Frenchman, it sounds like cowboys and Indians, like the Wild West. And the food was all so crunchy and spicy, it fit the image."

After Benayoun returned to Paris, he was offered the opportunity to open a restaurant in the newly hip Le Marais district of the fourth arrondissement. The restaurant would be housed in a twelfth-century building with a dance-studio complex. Benayoun decided to serve Tex-Mex. "We had cowboy and Indian pictures on the wall. I even put the cowboy boots I bought in Texas up on a shelf. The Studio, as the place was called, opened in March 1983.

Mexi&Co., on rue Dante across the river from Notre Dame. Much of the food was mediocre, but some of it, like the cheese enchilada, was astonishingly good.

Everywhere I went, I asked people why the French found Tex-Mex so intriguing. The manager of the Del Rio Café, Yseult Naudé Plassard, summed up the appeal: *"La cuisine Tex-Mex garde le parfum de temps des pionniers"* (Tex-Mex cuisine recaptures the essence of the pioneer times).

After my restaurant tour, I visited Paris food writer Patricia Wells to get her take.

"Was it the first Tex-Mex restaurant in Paris?" I asked Benayoun.

"That's what they tell me," he said.

"But why Tex-Mex? Why not authentic Mexican food?"

"We had a Mexican chef for a while. He made mole for a Day of the Dead celebration one year. Everybody hated it. Mexican food is too elaborate, too old-fashioned for Paris. But Tex-Mex! Tex-Mex is simple. It's honest. And you know, the French are crazy about Texas."

"Even now?" I wonder.

"Yes, even now, despite George Bush, and the death penalty, deep down inside, French people have a special fondness for Texas," he assures me.

Still, Benayoun's Tex-Mex concept was not an instant success. "Parisians don't like to eat with their hands," Benayoun says with a laugh. "They were trying to eat nachos and crispy tacos with a knife and fork."

"Business was pretty slow for a couple of years," he says. "We got lots of American ex-pats, but not so many French people. I started wondering if I had made a mistake. But then the movie *Betty Blue* came out, and things went completely crazy."

An Academy Award nominee for Best Foreign Film of 1986, *Betty Blue* starred Beatrice Dalle as a mentally unbalanced beauty named Betty and Jean-Hughes Anglade as a struggling novelist named Zorg. In the movie's first scene, Zorg leaves Betty after lovemaking and races across town on his motorcycle. He flies in his front door just in time to save a pot of chili con carne from burning.

Zorg, whose writing is dismissed as modernistic garbage by pompous Paris publishers, is a rebel without a beret. His and Betty's alienation from the mainstream of French culture is the movie's central theme. It is expressed in strikingly uncharacteristic views of the French landscape, including desert-like panoramas reminiscent of the American West—and also by Zorg's taste in food and drink. When a Paris bartender asks him what he wants, Zorg orders tequila. The bar doesn't have any. But somewhere Zorg finds a bottle.

In several drinking bouts, including a wild party sequence, Zorg introduces his friends to a drink he calls a "tequila rapido." Known as a tequila slammer in the United States, it consists of a shot of tequila and a splash of soda poured together into a glass, covered with a cloth, slammed hard on the bar, and consumed while the bubbles are still over-flowing. The movie ends tragically with the self-destructive Betty drugged beyond con-ciousness in a mental ward, where Zorg nobly smothers her to end her suffering. In the final scene, the griev-ing Zorg sits in his kitchen eating chili con carne.

"*Betty Blue* was our *Easy Rider*," remembers Benayoun. "It was un-believably popular in France. And after the movie came out, every-body in Paris wanted a shot of tequila and a bowl of chili." As Tex-Mex came to symbolize the alienation of free-spirited youth, business at the Studio soared. "Within a few years, a dozen Tex-Mex restau-rants had opened in Paris," Benayoun remem-bers. "I think I heard there are something like sixty of them there now. There are even a cou-ple of tortilla factories."

The trend soon spread to the rest of France and beyond. Since my visit to Paris in 1993, I have eaten Tex-Mex enchiladas in Bangkok, visited a Tex-Mex restaurant in Buenos Aires, and heard reports of Tex-Mex restaurants in Amsterdam, Oman, and Tokyo.

Surely the most intriguing cross-cultural trend is the emerging popularity of Tex-Mex in Mexico. Margaritas are still considered a gringo cocktail, but they can be found at almost any Mexican hotel these days. And in resort areas, Tex-Mex chains such as Señor Frog's and Carlos and Charlie's are popular not only with American tourists, but with Mexican nationals as well.

"CHUY'S, FINE TEX-MEX," READS THE sign on Barton Springs Boulevard. A crowd of college students from the nearby University of Texas are waiting in line for tables, so I sit at the bar and order what the menu calls "Classic Tex-Mex Cheese Enchiladas." The bartender (who has an earring, a long pony-tail, and a name tag that reads "Uly") sets my enchiladas in front of me. They are coated with an unctuous red chile sauce that looks more like the one I ate in Paris than the light brown chili gravy you get at Matt's El Rancho, just a few miles down South Lamar Boulevard.

Though Chuy's proclaims itself a Tex-Mex restaurant, it has become famous for its green chile festivals. The restaurant imports the peppers from Hatch, New Mexico. "Our classic Tex-Mex enchiladas aren't really classic Tex-Mex, either," Mike Young says with a laugh. "They are made with whole chiles, not with chili powder." But strict definitions have never been the point. It is the crazy border spirit of Tex-Mex that Chuy's adopted.

Mike Young got it before anybody else in Texas. He realized that the Europeans were seeing something we weren't. They liked Tex-Mex for the same reason they liked blue jeans. Both were inexpensive, informal, and part of the American West. And if Tex-Mex could be hip in Europe, there was no reason why it couldn't be hip in Texas too.

So Mike Young set out on a defiant yet play-ful campaign to champion the underdog. At a time when old-fashioned Mexican restaurants like Monterrey House and Loma Linda were losing business because customers considered them "too Tex-Mex," Chuy's went against the grain.

The menus proclaimed "Fine Tex-Mex"—an apparent oxymoron. The restaurants' T-shirts bore slogans like "Don't Mess With Tex-Mex." "Fine Tex-Mex" migrated to the high-visibility outdoors, to the restaurants' signs. And the strategy worked. The mini-chain now has nine restaurants in Houston, Austin, Dallas, and San Antonio. Chuy's brought the international love of Tex-Mex back home to the United States.

"Rock and roll is like Mexican food," critic Dave Hickey wrote in the *Village Voice* in 1975. "As it improves in quality, it stops being what it is." I called Hickey and asked him to clarify his famous comment.

"When I said 'Mexican food,' I meant Tex-Mex," the University of Nevada professor of art theory explained over the phone. He said he didn't like authentic Mexican food, which he had never even heard of in 1975.

Hickey's analogy explains something that many food writers have never understood. Tex-Mex is simpler than classical Mexican cooking, and it's also more exciting. Tex-Mex is a joyously primitive American cuisine, just like rock and roll is a joyously primitive American music.

And like rock and roll, Tex-Mex is both nostalgia-provoking and forever young. It reminds some of a bygone era, while it keeps evolving with the borderland culture it springs from.

"Tex-Mex has become a name for the peas-ant cooking of the Southwest," says Mike Young of Chuy's. "And the beauty of peasant cooking, whether it's French country cooking or Tex-Mex, is that it is simple, honest, and affordable. I don't know what will happen to Southwestern cuisine or interior Mexican restaurants years from now, but Tex-Mex will always be here."

Jan Beeman's AWHQ
Shrimp Enchiladas

**2 pounds heads-on
shrimp plus 8 large
shrimp for garnish**

2 tablespoons butter

**1 cup chopped Roma
tomatoes**

**2 cups chopped
onions**

**1 cup chopped green
bell pepper**

**1 serrano chile,
minced**

**1 tablespoon all-
purpose flour**

**1 tablespoon chili
powder**

**1 teaspoon ground
cumin**

1 teaspoon salt

1/4 cup vegetable oil

8 corn tortillas

1 cup sour cream

**1 cup chopped roasted
green chiles
(see page 107)**

**1 cup grated Oaxacan
string cheese or other
easy melting cheese**

**1/2 cup chopped green
onions**

The Grateful Dead played a free concert at Armadillo World Headquarters on Thanksgiving Day, 1972. The band requested Mexican food, but some of them didn't eat meat. So AWHQ kitchen whiz Jan Beeman invented her now famous shrimp enchiladas for the occasion. Here's a home adaptation of her recipe.

MAKES 8 PLUMP ENCHILADAS

Shell the shrimp and place the cleaned meat in the refrigerator. Place the shrimp heads and shells in a pot with 3 cups water, bring to a boil, and reduce to a simmer. Cook the stock for 15 minutes, then strain. Return the stock to the pot and discard the shells. Heat the stock to boiling, then turn it off. Poach the shrimp in the hot liquid for 2 to 3 minutes or until just cooked. Strain and reserve the shrimp and stock.

Heat the butter in a skillet and sauté the tomatoes, 1 cup of the onions, the bell pepper, and green chiles for 3 to 5 minutes, until soft.

Toast the flour, chili powder, and cumin in a small dry pan until lightly toasted and fragrant. Sprinkle the flour and spices and the salt over the onion mixture, stirring until all the lumps dissolve. Add 1 cup or more of shrimp stock, stirring well until the mixture forms a thick sauce. Ladle enough of the mixture into a Pyrex baking dish to cover the bottom.

Preheat the oven to 350°F. In a small skillet, heat the oil over medium-high heat for 3 minutes. Using tongs, place a tortilla in the hot oil for 30 seconds or until soft and lightly browned. Place on absorbent paper and allow to cool before handling. Put 1/4 cup of the cooked shrimp, a tablespoonful of sour cream, and a sprinkling of the remaining cup of chopped onions, the green pepper, and green chiles in the center of the tortilla. Roll the tortilla around the fillings and place seam side down in a baking dish that will fit 8 enchiladas. Repeat until all the tortillas have been filled and arranged in the baking dish. Pour a little extra sauce across the top of the assembled enchiladas. Top with the cheese and green onions and put a shrimp on top of each enchilada. Bake until the sauce bubbles. Serve immediately.

ELVIS GREEN CHILE~FRIED CHICKEN

As the story goes, Chuy's owner Mike Young set out with twenty dollars in his pocket to buy decorations for his original restaurant. He came upon a guy selling black velvet paintings by the side of a road and bought one of Elvis. Over the years, customers donated their own souvenirs until the walls were covered with Elvis memorabilia.

This dish is popular at Chuy's annual celebration of Elvis's birthday. Dredged in potato chips and topped with hot green chile sauce, this is chicken the way Elvis would have liked it.

SERVES 4

Flatten the chicken with a tenderizing mallet into a thin cutlet. Put the flour, beaten eggs, and potato chip crumbs into three separate, large shallow dishes. Add the black pepper to the potato chips and stir.

Fill a deep frying pan with oil to the depth of $1/2$ inch and heat over high heat until very hot (390°F). Dip a chicken cutlet in the flour and rub to coat well. Dip the flour-coated chicken in the egg and then the potato chips, turning and pressing to cover with a thick layer. Gently lower the chicken into the hot oil and fry for 2 to 3 minutes on each side, until the batter is golden brown and the chicken is cooked through.

Drain the chicken briefly on absorbent paper, then transfer to a plate and top with $1/2$ cup of the heated sauce. Repeat with the remaining chicken cutlets.

4 boneless, skinless chicken breast halves

$1/2$ cup all-purpose flour

2 eggs, beaten

$1^1/2$ cups crushed Lay's Potato Chips

1 teaspoon ground black pepper

Oil for frying (preferably peanut)

2 cups heated Chile Macho (page 110) or Salsa Verde (page 94)

CHUY'S GREEN CHILE STEW

1 whole chicken, cut into 8 pieces

1 to 2 tablespoons vegetable oil

6 cups onions cut into 1/2-inch-thick slices

4 cups carrots cut into 1-inch dice

6 garlic cloves, minced

4 cups tomatillos, husked, rinsed, and quartered

4 cups quartered Roma tomatoes

1 tablespoon salt

1 tablespoon ground black pepper

2 quarts plus 2 cups chicken broth

6 cups small red potatoes cut into 1-inch dice

2 cups chopped roasted green chiles (see page 107)

1/2 cup chopped fresh cilantro

1 cup diced green onions

Flour tortillas

This chicken–green chile stew is a favorite during the early autumn chile harvest season. For the annual Green Chile Festival, each Chuy's restaurant sets up a chile roaster in the parking lot. The roasters use a rotating wire mesh drum and heavy-duty propane burners to roast several bushels of green chiles at a time.

SERVES 6 TO 8

Cook the chicken pieces in a heavy-bottomed pot over medium heat in vegetable oil, about 15 minutes, until nicely browned. Drain all but 1 tablespoon of the drippings. Add the onions, carrots, and garlic and sauté until the onions begin to brown, about 10 minutes. Add the tomatillos, tomatoes, salt, and pepper and cook for another 5 to 10 minutes. Add the chicken broth and red potatoes. Bring to a boil, turn the heat down to a simmer, and cook for about 30 minutes or until the chicken is thoroughly cooked and the vegetables are tender.

Remove the chicken from the pot and when cool enough, pull the meat from the bones. Discard the bones and skin. Chop the meat into bite-sized pieces and return it to the pan. Add the green chiles, cilantro, and green onions. Simmer for another 5 minutes. Serve hot with fresh flour tortillas.

Montparnasse Gruyère Enchildas

Life is too short to eat cheap cheese. French Beaufort or a well-aged Swiss Gruyère are perfect for these French cheese enchiladas. No wonder Tex-Mex caught on in Paris!

MAKES 6 ENCHILADAS

Preheat the oven to 350°F. In a small skillet, heat the oil over medium-high heat for 3 minutes. Using tongs, place a tortilla in the hot oil for 30 seconds or until soft and lightly browned. Place on absorbent paper and allow to cool before handling. Repeat until all the tortillas have been dipped. Pour the chile sauce in the hot oil remaining in the pan and heat for 3 minutes. Put 1/3 cup of the cheese and a few chile strips on each tortilla. Roll the tortilla around the filling and place seam side down in a baking dish that will fit 6 enchiladas. Repeat until all the tortillas have been filled and arranged in the baking dish. Pour the sauce over the top of the tortillas, sprinkle with the remaining cheese, and bake until the sauce bubbles. Garnish with chile strips.

1/4 cup vegetable oil

6 corn tortillas

2 cups Red Chile Sauce (page 106)

3 cups grated Gruyère cheese

2 roasted poblano chiles, cut into strips

FRIED OYSTER NACHOS

Peanut oil for frying

Buttermilk for
dredging

Flour for dredging

12 fresh raw oysters

12 large tortilla chips
(preferably round)

1/2 cup Mango Salsa
(see below)

In 1995, Austin chef David Garrido and I co-authored the cookbook Nuevo
Tex-Mex, *based on the cooking style Garrido pioneered at his restaurants.
Garrido serves a more elegant version of these oyster nachos at Jeffrey's
Restaurants in Austin and Washington, D.C., where they have long been a fa-
vorite of the Bush family.*

MAKES 12 NACHOS

Fill a small skillet to a depth of 1 inch with oil and heat to 375°F. Put
the buttermilk and flour into two shallow bowls. Soak the oysters in
buttermilk, then dip them in flour. Fry each oyster for 45 seconds to 1
minute, or until lightly browned. Transfer the oysters to absorbent
paper to drain.

To serve, put a teaspoonful of salsa on each chip, then a fried oyster.

MANGO SALSA

1 cup skinned and
diced mango

1 poblano chile,
rinsed, skinned, and
seeded

1 red bell pepper,
stemmed, seeded, and
diced

1/4 cup diced red
onion

1 cup diced pineapple

1 jalapeño chile,
minced

2 tablespoons fresh
lemon juice

1/4 cup chopped fresh
cilantro

Salt

Garrido invented this tropical pico de gallo *with seafood in mind. Try it with
grilled salmon. If you can't find a very ripe mango, try another fleshy summer
fruit such as a peach or nectarine.*

MAKES ABOUT 3 CUPS

Combine all the ingredients in a bowl and refrigerate for 15 minutes
to allow the flavors to blend.

BLUE CRAB SALSA

This salsa from David Garrido's and my cookbook, Nuevo Tex-Mex, *makes an instant salad or a great garnish. A dab turns a grilled fish fillet into a wonderfully complex entree. Check out the salad variations that follow.*

SERVES 4

Combine all the ingredients in a bowl and chill for 20 minutes.

VARIATIONS

Crab-stuffed Tomatoes:
Hollow out 4 medium tomatoes. Use the flesh for the recipe, then stuff the tomatoes with the crab mixture and serve as a salad on a bed of lettuce.

Crab-stuffed Chile Salad:
Roast 4 Anaheim chiles. Remove the skin, then chill them thoroughly. Slit lengthwise, remove the seeds, and stuff each chile half with crab salsa. Serve cold on a bed of lettuce.

$1/2$ pound fresh lump blue crabmeat, picked over

$1^1/2$ tablespoons minced serrano chile

$1/2$ cup chopped fresh cilantro

$1/2$ cup diced tomato

$1/4$ cup celery cut into small dice

$1/4$ cup chopped fresh basil

2 tablespoons extra virgin olive oil

2 tablespoons fresh lemon juice

Salt

Nuevo Tex-Mex chef David Garrido

Red Snapper Ceviche

12 ounces Gulf red
snapper fillet, skinned
and cut into 1/2-inch
dice

1/2 cup fresh lime juice

Salt

1 large tomato, seeded
and chopped

1 Texas red
grapefruit, peeled and
segmented

1 tablespoon very
finely sliced ancho
chile shreds

2 tablespoons minced
fresh cilantro

3 tablespoons finely
chopped green onion

Tortilla chips

Perfect with limey margaritas or icy Pilsners, this Gulf Coast ceviche makes a great summer appetizer. If you're nervous about serving raw fish, you can steam the snapper for ten minutes first. You need plenty of lime juice to marinate the ceviche, but you don't want to serve it all, so drain off what you don't need.

SERVES 6

Combine the snapper, lime juice, and salt in a nonreactive bowl. Cover and refrigerate for at least 5 hours (preferably overnight) to "cook" the fish. Strain the lime juice and reserve.

Combine the snapper with the tomato, grapefruit, chile, cilantro, and green onion and about half of the reserved lime juice, or enough to give the ceviche a salsa-like consistency. Serve on a platter surrounded by tortilla chips.

Migas Especiales con Hongos

2 tablespoons
vegetable oil, plus
more if needed

2 tortillas, cut into
1/2-inch strips

2 cups sliced
mushrooms

1 garlic clove, minced

4 eggs, beaten

1/2 cup grated
Monterey Jack cheese

1/2 cup ranchero
sauce (page 30)

Warm tortillas

This is one of the most popular breakfasts at Las Manitas in Austin. The Pérez sisters don't like it when I call their food Tex-Mex, but then again, neither does Gloria Reyna at Austin's premier Tex-Mex institution, Matt's El Rancho. Serve with refried black beans and tortillas.

SERVES 2

Heat the oil in a small skillet over medium-high heat. Fry the tortilla strips, stirring until crisp. Remove the strips and reserve. Add the mushrooms and garlic to the hot oil and cook for 5 minutes or until the mushrooms are done and any moisture released has evaporated. Turn the heat to medium and add a little more oil if necessary to keep the eggs from sticking. Pour the eggs over the mushrooms and cook, scraping from the bottom. When nearly set, add the tortillas strips and the cheese. Cook until the cheese melts. Divide the eggs between two plates and top each with 1/4 cup ranchero sauce.

HUEVOS WITH VEGETARIAN CHORIZO

Here's another favorite Las Manitas breakfast—scrambled eggs with vegetarian chorizo. In other parts of the state, this kind of modernized Mexican fare is often called "Aus-Mex." With all due apologies to the Pérez sisters, I call it twenty-first-century Tex-Mex.

SERVES 6

Combine the textured vegetable protein with 2 cups hot water, then squeeze out the excess moisture (or follow the directions on the package). Combine the vegetable protein, chili powder, paprika, salt, garlic powder, cumin, and vinegar in a food processor. Process until well blended, about 20 seconds. Chorizo may be kept in an airtight container in the refrigerator for up to a week.

For each serving of chorizo and scrambled eggs, scramble 2 eggs in a teaspoon of oil in a skillet over medium-high heat, and add a teaspoon of the onions and half a teaspoon of the chiles. Cook for 3 minutes or until the onion is wilted. Add 1/4 cup of the vegetable protein mixture and cook for 3 minutes or until browned. Cook, scraping the bottom, until the eggs are done as desired.

1 1/2 cups dry textured vegetable protein (TVP)

1 teaspoon chili powder

2 teaspoons paprika

1 teaspoon salt

1/4 teaspoon garlic powder

1/4 teaspoon ground cumin

2 tablespoons red wine vinegar

6 teaspoons vegetable oil for frying

1/4 cup chopped onion

2 tablespoons chopped serrano chile, or to taste

12 eggs

BIBLIOGRAPHY

Andrews, Jean. Peppers: *The Domesticated Capsicums*. Austin: University of Texas Press, 1984.

Atkinson, Leland. *Cocina!* Berkeley: Ten Speed Press, 1996.

Barrios, Virginia B. *A Guide to Tequila, Mezcal and Pulque*. Mexico D.F.: Minutiae Mexicana, S. S., 1988.

Bayless, Rick. *Authentic Mexican*. New York: Morrow, 1987.

Bayless, Rick. *Mexico One Plate at a Time*. New York: Scribner, 2000.

Blakely, Elizabeth. *The San Antonio Tex-Mex Cookbook*. San Antonio: Caxton House Publishing, 2000.

Bridges, Bill. *The Great American Chili Book*. New York: Rawson, Wade Publishers, Inc., 1981.

Butel, Jane. *Jane Butel's Tex-Mex Cookbook*. New York: Harmony Books, 1980.

Creechan, Mary Lou and Jim. *Beginning With Chiles*. Edmonton: Tiengui Del Norte Publishing, 1999.

De León, Arnoldo. *Ethnicity in the Sunbelt: Mexican Americans in Houston*. College Station: Texas A&M University Press, 2001.

Denker, Joel. *The World on a Plate: A Tour through the History of America's Ethnic Cuisine*. Boulder: Westview Press, 2003.

Dobie, J. Frank. *A Vaquero of the Brush Country* (Reissue). Austin: University of Texas Press, 1998.

Eckhardt, Linda West. *The Only Texas Cookbook*. New York: Gramercy Publishing Company, 1981.

Fehrenbach, T. R. *Lone Star: A History of Texas and the Texans*. New York: American Legacy Press, 1983.

Fernández-Armesto, Felipe. *Near A Thousand Tables: A History Of Food*. New York: The Free Press, 2002.

Fergusson, Erna. *Mexican Cookbook*. Albuquerque: University of New Mexico Press, 1934.

Flemmons, Jerry. More *Texas Siftings: Another Bold and Uncommon Celebration of the Lone Star State*. Fort Worth: Texas Christian University Press, 1997.

Foley, Neil. *The White Scourge: Mexicans, Blacks, and Poor Whites in Texas Cotton Culture*. Berkeley: University of California Press, 1997.

Gabaccia, Donna. *We Are What We Eat: Ethnic Food and the Making of Americans*. Cambridge, MA: Harvard University Press, 1998.

Howard, Josefina. *Rosa Mexicano: A Culinary Autobiography with 60 Recipes*. New York: Penguin Putnam, 1998.

Hurley, Elizabeth. "Come Buy, Come Buy." *Folk Travellers: Ballads, Tales and Talk*. Dallas, Texas. SMU Press, 1953.

Jesús F. de la Teja, ed. *A Revolution Remembered: The Memoirs and Selected Correspondence of Juan N. Seguín*. Austin: State House Press, 1991.

Kennedy, Diana. *The Art of Mexican Cooking*. New York: Bantam Books, 1989.

———. *The Cuisines of Mexico*. New York: Harper & Row, 1972.

Kittler, Pamela Goyan and Sucher, Kathryn P. *Food and Culture*. Belmont: Wadsworth/Thomson Learning, 2001.

Kreneck, Thomas H. *Mexican American Odyssey: Felix Tijerina, Entrepreneur and Civic Leader, 1905–1965*. College Station: Texas A&M University Press, 2001.

Linck, Ernestine Sewell and Roach, Joyce Gibson. *Eats: A Folk History of Texas Foods*. Fort Worth: Texas Christian University Press, 1989.

Lucero, Al. *The Great Margarita Book: A Handbook With Recipes*. Berkeley: Ten Speed Press, 1999.

Luchetti, Cathy. *Home on the Range: A Culinary History of the American West*. New York: Villard, 1993.

Mariani, John. *Virtual Gourmet Newsletter*, http://pages.prodigy.net/johnmariano

Martinez, Matt. *Martinez's Culinary Frontier*. New York: Broadway Books, 1997.

Martinez, Zarela. *The Food and Life of Oaxaca*. New York: MacMillan, 1997.

Noriega, Chon A. *Shot in America: Television, the State, and the Rise of Chicano Cinema*. Minneapolis: University of Minnesota Press, 2000.

Patoski, Joe Nick. "Uno, Dos, One, Two, Tres, Quatro." *Journal of Texas Music History*, 1:1 (Spring 2001): 12-14.

Peyton, James W. *El Norte: The Cuisine of Northern Mexico*. Santa Fe: Red Crane Books, 1995.

———. *La Cocina de la Frontera: Mexican-American Cooking from the Southwest*. Santa Fe: Red Crane Books, 1994.

———. *New Cooking from Old Mexico*. Santa Fe: Red Crane Books, 1999.

Pilcher, Jeffrey Michael. "Recipes for *Patria*: Cuisine, Gender, and Nation in Nineteenth-Century Mexico." *Recipes for Reading*. Edited by Ann Bower. Amherst: University of Massachusetts Press, 1997.

———. *Vivian Tamales: The Creation of a Mexican National Cuisine*. Fort Worth: Texas Christian University Press, 1993.

Price, Byron B. *National Cowboy Hall of Fame Chuck Wagon Cookbook*. New York: Hearst Books, 1995.

Quintana, Patricia. *The Best of Quintana*. New York: Stewart, Tabori, and Chang, 1995.

Root, Waverley and De Rochmont, Richard. *Eating in America: A History*. Hopewell: The Ecco Press, 1976.

Scheer, Cynthia. *Mexican Cooking*. San Francisco: Owlswood Productions, 1978.

Stephenson, Patricia and Young, Alice. *Discovering Mexican Cooking*. San Antonio: The Naylor Company, 1958.

Tannahill, Reay. *Food in History*. New York: Three Rivers Press, 1988.

Thompson, Celia. *History of Marfa and Presidio County, Texas, 1535–1946*. Austin: Nortex Press, 1985.

Thorne, John. *Serious Pig*. New York: North Point Press, 1996.

Tijerina, Andrés. *Tejanos and Texas Under the Mexican Flag, 1821–1836*. College Station: Texas A&M University Press, 1994.

Tolbert, Frank X. *A Bowl of Red*. New York: Doubleday, 1967.

Trevino, Diana Barrios. *Los Barrios Family Cookbook*. New York: Villard, 2002.

Weatherford, Jack. *Indian Givers: How the Indians of the Americas Transformed the World*. New York: Fawcett Columbine, 1988.

Works Progress Administration (WPA). "America Eats" (unpublished manuscript). Library of Congress.

Zamora, Emilio, Cynthia Orozco, and Rodolfo Rocha. *Mexican Americans in Texas History*. Austin: Texas State Historical Association, 2000.

INDEX

PHOTO CREDITS

Collections of the Institute of Texan Cultures, The University of Texas at San Antonio: pages ii–iii, viii–ix, xx–1, 8–9, 12, 22, 23, 25, 26, 32–33, 38–39, 41, 42, 43, 44, 47, 52–53, 58, 64, 67, 80–81, 83, 84, 92–93, 102, 104, 112, 116, 117, 128–29, 138–39, 140, 142, 144, 146, 182, 195, 200–201, 205, 206–7, 211, and 222.

Marc Burkhardt: illustration, pages iv–v.

Robb Walsh: pages xii, 18, 20, 29, 49, 61, 69, 96, 100, 125, 155, 165, 176, 177, 180, 186–87, 193, 198, 215, 227, 238–39, 245, 246, and 249.

Will van Overbeek: pages xiv–xv, 62–63, 124, 174–75, 209, 224–25, 228, 232, and 244.

Journal of Texas Shortline Railroads: pages xviii–xix and xix.

Erin Mayes: pages xix, 7, 10, 11, and 190–191.

Drue Wagner: illustration, page 15.

Texas State Library and Archives Commission: pages 16–17, 87, and 114–15.

Ethan Houser: page 19.

Collections of the Library of Congress: pages 21, 56–57, 82, and 120.

Courtesy Cisco's Bakery: page 30.

Courtesy Casa Rio Restaurant: page 51.

Harry Ransom Humanities Research Center, The University of Texas at Austin: pages 76–77, 122–23, 234–35.

Collections of St. Mary's University: page 85.

Marfa Public Library Archives (Junior Historian Files): pages 98–99, 101, and 108–109.

Courtesy Stephanie Spitzer: page 105.

The Center for American History, The University of Texas at Austin, Russell Lee Collection: pages 118 and 133; Robert Runyon Collection: page 119.

Houston Press photo by Troy Fields: page 141.

Frank Cuellar Collection, University of North Texas Archives: pages 152–53, 157, 168–69, and 171.

Courtesy Larry's Original Mexican Restaurant: page 154.

Courtesy El Fenix: pages 156, 158–159, and 166.

Courtesy Felix Mexican Restaurant: page 160.

LBJ Library, photo by (gift of) Alfredo G. Garza: page 161; photo by Frank Moto: page 179.

Courtesy El Patio: page 181.

Courtesy San Antonio Missions Baseball Club: page 182.

San Antonio Express-News: page 192.

Courtesy Rotel and the Hot Tomatoes: page 202.

Courtesy Ninfa's: page 208.

Alan Pogue: pages 210 and 212–13.

Courtesy Manuel De Leon: page 216.

Courtesy Chuy's: page 240 and back cover.

Courtesy Eddie Wilson: page 241.

Nancy E. Goldfarb, Black/Gold Photography: pages 242–43.

Courtesy Jeffrey's Restaurant: page 257.

SACVB, photo by Al Rendon: back cover.

VELVEETA is a registered trademark; used with the permission of Kraft Foods: page 199.

Frito, Fritos and the Frito Bandito, are registered trademarks of the Frito-Lay corporation: pages 196–97 and 204.

Mail-Order Sources

All of the ingredients in this book are common throughout the Southwest and most of the rest of the country. If you have a Mexican market in your town, you should have no trouble finding everything you need. If you can't find some of the fresh produce we use, the item you're looking for may just be out of season. If you live in an area where Mexican ingredients are unavailable, try these mail-order sources.

www.texmex.net
Molcajetes, tortilla presses, ancho chiles, spice mixes, and a full line of Rotel products are available here. Also a great online source for hard-to-find items such as San Antonio–style red tortillas. There's also lots of free manufacturers' recipes.

TEXAS SPICE COMPANY
P. O. Box 3769
Austin, Texas 78764
512–444–2223
Catalog available
A good source for dried chiles and freshly ground chile powders, ground cumin, and dried Mexican oregano.

KITCHEN/MARKET
218 Eighth Avenue
New York, New York 10011
888–468–4433
www.kitchenmarket.com
A good New York source for Mexican spices, tortilla presses, chiles, herbs, and seeds.

PENDRY'S
1221 Manufacturing
Dallas, Texas 75207
800–533–1870
Catalog $2
Molcajetes, chiles, cumin, chili powders, and dried Mexican oregano are all in the catalog.

SUPERBLY SOUTHWESTERN
3816 Edith Blvd.
Albuquerque, New Mexico 87107
800–467–4HOT; 505–766–9598
www.hotchile.com
A source for whole or chopped frozen roasted green chiles, New Mexican chile powders, and dried chiles.

www.richters.com
www.linglesherbs.com
Seeds and nursery plants for Tex-Mex herbs.

About the Author

Robb Walsh is the author of *Legends of Texas Barbecue Cookbook* and the co-author of *A Cowboy in the Kitchen* and *Nuevo Tex-Mex*. He is also the restaurant critic of the *Houston Press* and an occasional commentator for NPR's *Weekend Edition*, and has served as the food columnist for *Natural History*. He has been nominated for nine James Beard awards, and has won twice.